Interlacing

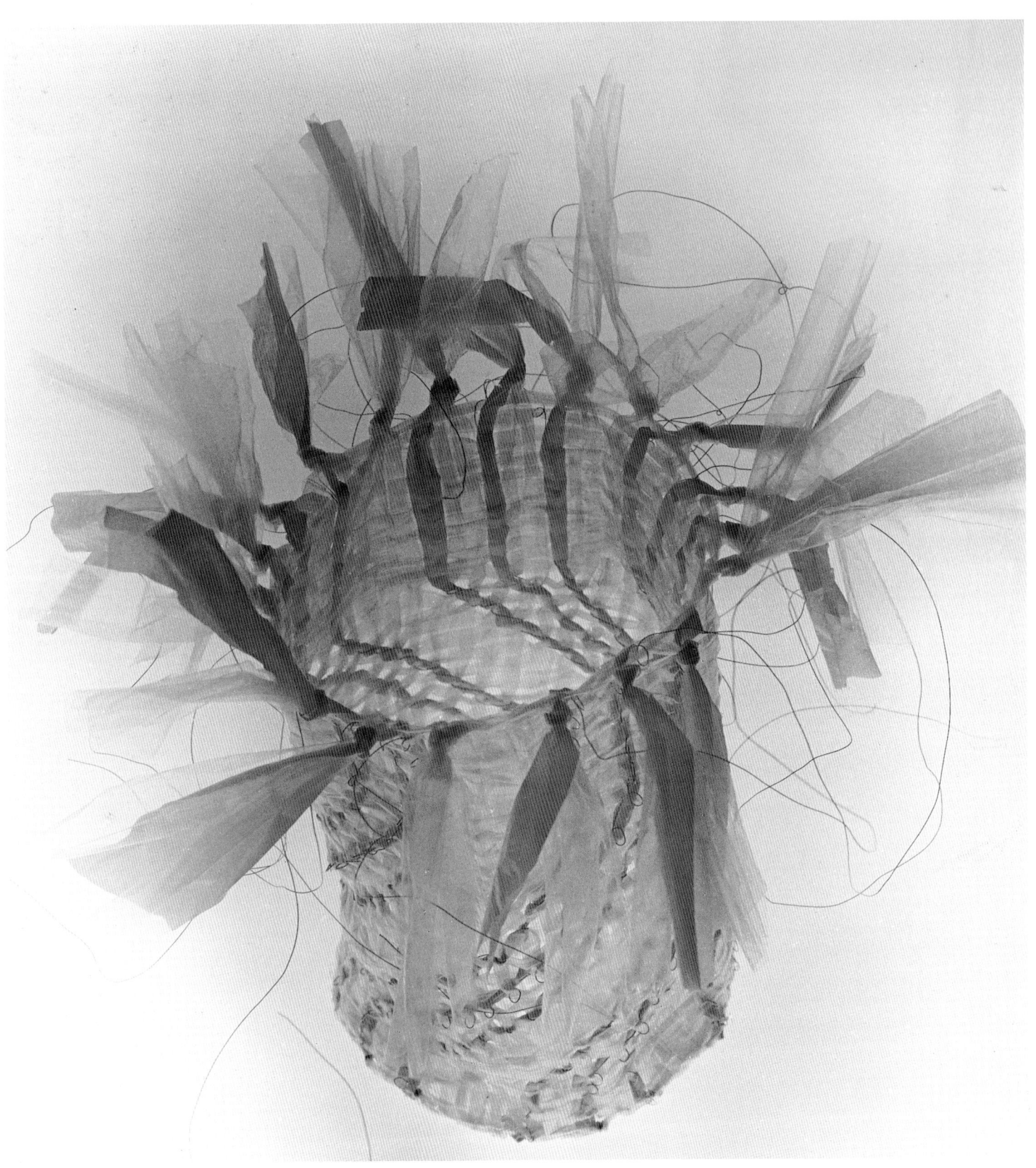

Interlacing
the Elemental Fabric

Jack Lenor Larsen
with Betty Freudenheim

KODANSHA INTERNATIONAL
Tokyo, New York, and San Francisco

A Dedication—to Ladies

This, my seventh book, is the first to bear a dedication. It seems time to acknowledge a mother who taught organization, a fairy godmother who gave me the world, Professor Hope Foote, who taught taste, Margaret Hosmer who bequeathed vision and reality, Win Anderson and Dawn McNutt who bestow life, Virginia Harvey whose knowledge and caring is unfathomable, Wendy Mogey, Norma Sams and Betty Freudenheim who made this book possible, and so many more.

---

title page photograph
The translucent basket form is given pattern and structural support by diagonal elements wrapped with fine wire. A most casual edge finish adds to the fantasy.

untitled, 1979
Lois Bryant, U.S.A.
1/1 plaiting
plastic film, stainless steel wire
7" × 8" × 8"

Photographs are by David Arky unless otherwise credited.
Objects are from the collection of Jack Lenor Larsen or the artists unless otherwise credited.

Drawings and structural models are by Betty Freudenheim.

Note: All objects reproduced here are plaited unless other techniques are specified.

Distributed in the United States by Kodansha International/USA Ltd., through Harper & Row, Publishers Inc., 10 East 53rd Street, New York, New York 10022.

Published by Kodansha International Ltd., 2-2 Otowa 1-chome, Bunkyo-ku, Tokyo 112 and Kodansha International/USA Ltd., with offices at 10 East 53rd Street, New York, New York 10022 and The Hearst Building, 5 Third Street, Suite 400, San Francisco, California 94103.

Copyright in Japan, 1986, by Kodansha International Ltd.
All rights reserved.
Printed in Japan
First edition, 1986

Library of Congress Cataloging-in-Publication Data

Larsen, Jack Lenor.
    Interlacing: the elemental fabric.

    Bibliography: p.
    Includes index.
    1. Hand weaving. 2. Braid. 3. Textile crafts.
I. Freudenheim, Betty. II. Title.
TT848.L375 1986 746 86-45065
ISBN 0-87011-778-5 (U.S.)
ISBN 4-7700-1278-0 (in Japan)

Contents

The premise	10
Origins	17
The precursors	30
Meanings, modifiers, methods: the intangible tools	38
Classification	65
Braiding	114
Beginnings and endings	156
Materials and color effects: the reality and the appearance	182
Applications	216
Motif and symbol: the philosophical resonance	248
The implications: a postlogue	267
Bibliography	269
Glossary-index	275

1 |
Working with fine strips of grass, the weaver birds of India interlace more skillfully than their African counterparts. These nests are so light they can hang on slender rushes; the long tunnel entrance deters predators.

2 |
basket for *ikebana*
random plaiting
bamboo
18″ × 10″
Japan, early 20th century
collection: Florence Duhl, New York

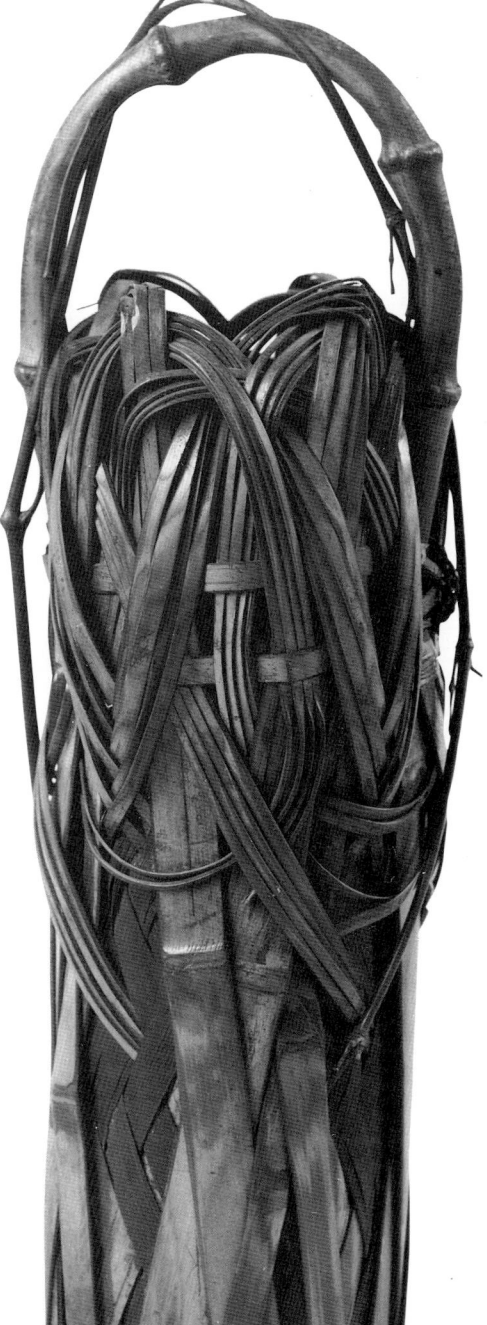

2–4. Although it seems doubtful that specimens of weaver birds' nests reached Japan, there are marked affinities between such nests and some Japanese baskets for flower arrangement. The two examples in Plates 2 and 4 are but modest instances of this highly developed art form in which asymmetrical, random plaiting is prized. The contemporary basket by Hisako Sekijima is of vines plaited so intriguingly that it appears complete without flowers.

3 |
basket, 1979
Hisako Sekijima, Japan
random plaiting
Akebia quinata
20″ × 20″ × 20″

4 |
basket for *ikebana*
random plaiting
bamboo
Japan, late 19th century (?)
11″ × 3½″

Time was and is
when a craftsman knew—
knew fabric as fleece,
as dried grasses or slivered reeds
as the magic of interlaced
basketry braids and blankets

For after leaves and skins
interlacing was
early man's first raiment
first container
oldest shelter shoe sling
sail pot and trap

For a very long time now
these multifarious interlacings
have been foreign to each other
so separated by use and form
construction and market
that we are deprived
of their essential connections

Let us know the *whole* of fabrics
not just the look of them
the luster nub slub
grain and cord of them
but their pattern and form
and the relationships between them

Above all, honor the structures:
those ancient orders
almost as elemental as fire,
more universal and sometimes
earlier than the wheel.
These structures, now our legacy,
also shall be our bequest.

Now, when all joinings are hidden,
more often adhesive than cohesive,
it is imperative we assume
a high vantage point
where we can view the relationship
of the parts to the whole

There perceive that each puzzle piece fits
—even the bizarre exceptions.
When all parts are in place
we shall *know*
and this knowledge will become
an aspect of our innermost experience

Jack Lenor Larsen

5
Pensée Perovienne de Patak, 1978
Guy Houdouin, France
1/1 plaiting
paper
15¾" × 16½"

In his studio near Paris, Guy Houdouin plaits small, flat filigrees remarkable for their unprecedented forms and complex color nuances. While modulating justaposed weft colors is common in woven tapestries, his medium permits the introduction of new tonalities in both directions. The chance crossings of these shades produce the lively "pointillist" fusion.

His work testifies to the awakening that, even in two dimensions, plaiting permits freedoms of form, scale, and materials not available to weavers, and that the loom—invented to increase uniformity and productivity—greatly limits one's options.

The premise

INTERLACING is the term for all fabric constructions in which each element passes over and under elements that cross its path. It is both a concept and a system—or, rather, a system of systems.

INTERLACING IS

Knotting	*Plaiting*	*Weaving*
nets	mats	textiles
mats	braids	
	baskets	
	bobbin lace	

INTERLACING encompasses an extreme diversity of structure and form. It is the quintessential construction common to weaving, braiding, and plaiting. Many knots, baskets, and laces also fall within its parameters. Materials as dissimilar as wire, bamboo, soft fiber, clay, and dough may serve as elements. Interlacings embrace a vast range of scale, from Victorian jewelry braided with single strands of hair to industrial blasting mats plaited with a ton of steel cable. Completed forms may be two or three dimensional, rigorously geometric or softly organic, limp or rigid.

Scholarship has specialized in ever-narrowing fields for nearly a century. Even popular how-to books limit themselves to a single technique and its variations. A sweeping view and survey of interlacing in all its forms is needed.

INTERLACING is one of the earliest and most universal of all inventions. Its various structures have been devised countless times in every part of the world and every culture. After the invention of the loom, and particularly since the Renaissance and Industrial Revolution, weaving has so dominated fabric production that we have forgotten its roots. Weaving is only one, relatively recent, facet of interlacing. This book embraces the *whole* of interlacing, concentrating on those interlacings that are not loom woven; loomed fabrics are touched on only to explain their relationship to the whole.

To weavers who have for centuries limited their thinking to vertical/horizontal structures convenient to loom production, coming upon the broader concept of interlacing is like discovering a new continent. For an increasing number of craftspeople, the potential for both freedom and discipline in plaited structures will incite and direct energies somehow inhibited in the mid 1980s. As shown in these pages, the early manifestations are in the form of individual exploration and expression. The influence of these will expand, to finally make an impact on industry and market and build pressures to devise machines capable of producing a broad range of interlaced forms.

In a short quarter-century, fiber artists have covered, recovered, and discovered more ground than in most eras of the past. With that Art Fabric revolution a part of the past, the call is for discipline and structure, for systemic thought—the requisites for working within a given order. This book is an attempt to classify and interrelate several heretofore separate bodies of knowledge and technical vocabularies—to juxtapose rare instances with everyday examples, to acknowledge the contributions of past and present, to present contemporary exploration of INTERLACING techniques and thus indicate a future.

Sage Reynolds interlaces paper strips through "warps" of slit paper to achieve an amazing play of pattern. His variety of high and low contrast is consistent with the oriental form of this piece.

6 |
Kami Kimono, 1985
Sage Reynolds, U.S.A.
plaiting
2SOE, various H-V
paper
60½" × 57"

Sherri Smith's long series of plaited hangings are extraordinary for the precision of their dye-patterned elements and the symbiotic relationship of color to relief. While the relief highlights color progressions, the hues accentuate the optical boxes characteristic of this interlacing. Her zigzag form echoes the serrated edges.

7 |
Cogs, 1985
Sherri Smith, U.S.A.
3SOE, 2 obliques + horizontal
cotton tape
4'6" × 7'

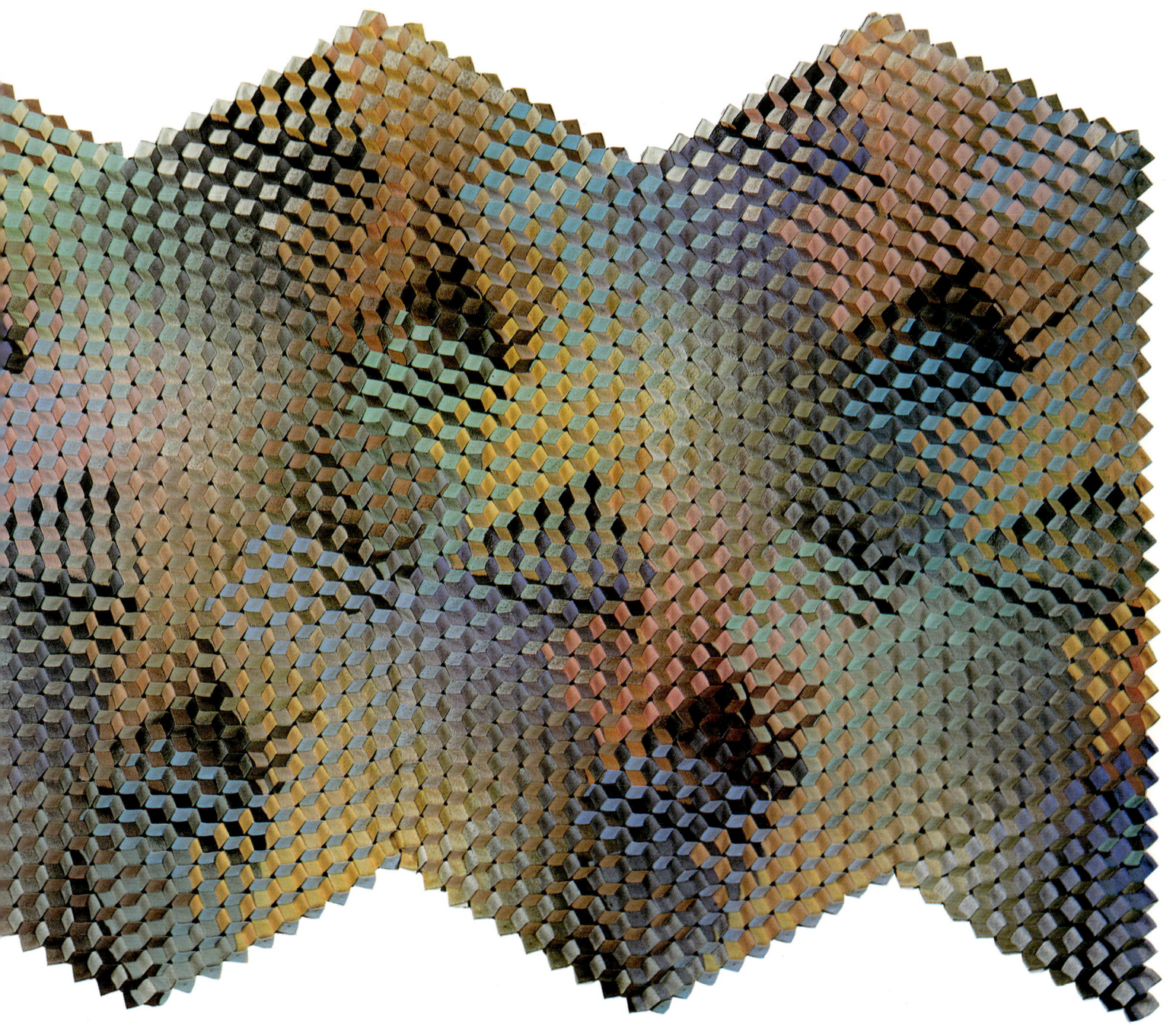

8 |
At the Fulongguan Monastery near Chemgden in China a tree has been plaited into a diamond grill. European gardeners "espalier" rows of branchless saplings into a similar form known as a Belgian fence.
Copyright Huxley 1980.

Arline Fisch's loaf of bread is of interlaced silver bands, with a "raised" top crust.

9 |
Bread Basket, 1978
Arline Fisch, U.S.A.
2 SOE, 1/1
sterling silver, copper
2″ × 3″ × 4½″

Although we associate plaiting with fiber, linear elements of any material can be used. Rina Peleg plaits large baskets of leather-hard clay elements—often with ceramic supports made rigid by prefiring. Like basket makers through the ages, she combines plaiting with twining.

10
porcelain structure, 1980
Rina Peleg, Israel (lives in New York)
plaiting, twining
2SOE, 1/1 H-V
porcelain
63" × 30"

If the versatility and ingenuity of Mexico's *patate* plaiters is legendary, none of their mats or brooms have quite the virtuoso quality of the life-sized *bandolero* figures. Actually, most of their components are plaited flat, then fastened on one side with an oblique casting stitch of the same material. Note the twisted fingers, the twined cartridge belts.

11 |
bandolero
2SOE, 1/1 oblique
bast
H. 6′
Mexico, 1984

1
Origins

While preparing for the first presentation of interlacing as a concept—at The Banff School of Fine Arts in the Canadian Rockies—I came across networks of conifer roots lying fully exposed over alpine boulders measuring a thousand feet across. Often as not, these roots interlaced over and under each other like overscaled darning. Remarkable! Craft in the order of plants? I was well aware of the weaver birds' nests and the instinctive, fine craftsmanship of mud wasps, spiders, and paper-making hornets—but plants!

A park naturalist explained that, with no possibility for striking a tap root, this was the tree's defense against the hazards of winter gales combined with heavy burdens of snow. Ascribing root interlacing to the "survival of the fittest," he said that this tendency is most common to tree stands of the virtually soilless upper altitudes. An analogy became obvious to me: just as interlacing has enabled these trees to survive under the most challenging conditions, it has been basic to human survival.

Of mankind's major systems, interlacing is certainly one of the earliest, in most cases predating ceramics. "Earliest," of course, is a relative term. Rudimentary knots, braids, and other plaiting must have been developed in hundreds, perhaps thousands, of times and places. Some forms occurred early in one area but did not come into use until much later in another. In almost every culture, some form of plaited tools preceded, then accompanied initial experiments with agriculture, animal husbandry, and navigation.

Interlacing is not only ancient, but universal. No other group of related technologies encompasses such widespread utilization—not chipped stone, not metalwork, nor even ceramics. Interlacing is more common than the wheel. If we question why these particular methods of interworking elements occurred so frequently for a wide spectrum of human requirements, the answer is that no other structures serve so well or in as many capacities. Each method is versatile, with unlimited applications. Many and various forms have strength without great weight, are usually portable, and can be produced with few or no tools. Easy access to a wide range of materials, and the relative ease of preparing these materials, contribute to the universality of interlacing. Plant and animal materials are combined with relative ease into workable elements and, of course, are universally accessible.

Transference of the necessary skills was fostered by contacts with neighboring peoples and, on occasion, through the practice of taking artisans as captives. This adoption of interlacing technology has continued into the present, where Western artists are plaiting plastic film in the same manner as "stone age" artisans of the South Pacific work stripped leaves.

Even more curious is the spontaneous generation of identically interlaced structures among widely separated peoples. For instance, a rare braid made by the Maoris of New Zealand is also known to the Indians of Guiana. This book illustrates many such parallels.

Baskets, The First Tools

The roots of interlacing lie buried in the shadowy recesses of prehistory, perhaps as deep as the earliest vestiges of human existence. While we can make informed guesses about the great antiquity of interlacing, it is difficult to point a finger at hard evidence. Because the first experiments in fiber structure turned to dust tens of thousands of years ago, it is stone artifacts that have furnished the support structure for most theories about our earliest tools and lifestyles.

Recalling that "lithic" means "of stone," we are reminded why periods of human development were named Paleolithic, Mesolithic, and Neolithic, followed by the Bronze and Iron ages. Anthropologist Adrienne Zihlman explains, "Plant remains and organic tools preserve less readily, and we must therefore realize that the paleontological and archaeological records are biased in the evidence they preserve."

In recent years, however, the focus has been shifting away from those stone tools. Zihlman and others have come to startling new conclusions about protoman's lifestyle and its effect on the first tools. We learn of the possibility that not only was basketry the basis for one of the first tools, but that humanization developed with and through the basket. Glynn Isaac, archaeologist at the University of California, Berkeley, has said that *the watershed achievement of all time was the invention of the basket*. This tool enabled protoman to develop into modern man.

Richard Leakey, who has spent his career studying archaeological finds of the earliest human traces (first under the tutelage of his renowned parents and later on his own), says that we would be more accurate if we described ancestral hominids as "gatherer-hunters" instead of hunters or even hunter-gatherers. His insight is partially based on comparative studies of the contemporary "stone age" !Kung San nomads of southern Africa showing that their gatherers provide approximately 70 percent of the daily diet, far outweighing contributions of the hunters. Except for similar societies in the extreme arctic, this proportion has been found to be the rule, not the exception.

He also cites research employing electron microscopes to reinforce his thesis that the earliest hominids were not primarily meat-eaters. The extreme thickness of the enamel and scratches on their teeth indicate a diet consisting mainly of vegetables, roots, and fruits that require much grinding. Scavenged meat probably provided only an occasional repast, he says.

The first tools invented were "*not for hunting* large, swiftly moving, dangerous animals," says Zihlman, "*but for gathering* plants, eggs, honey, termites, ants, and probably small burrowing animals" (her italics). These implements were probably the gatherer's sharpened digging stick and a container to hold the numerous, usually small food items. The concept of the container altered our ancestors' lifestyle, says Leakey. Containers meant that fruits and vegetables could be collected, carried home by the gatherer, and shared with family or tribal unit. *Sharing* is the quintessential act. This behavior not only revolutionized human relationships, as Zihlman points out, but it also forms a major distinction from apes, who eat their food when and wherever they find it.

What can we deduce about these first containers? That "utility is the mother of invention" was particularly true in the beginning, when gargantuan efforts were requisite to scant survival. At first only pressing needs existed; there were no prototypes to imitate, nor techniques to be adopted. It is reasonable to postulate that a Stone Age genius may have interlaced grasses into a protobasket. Certainly, for mothers who had to grasp or carry their infants while gathering, containers would be the means by which they could hold an armload of nuts or fruit *and* a wriggling child. A simple construction of interlaced grasses could have served. Ed Rossbach calls them "temporary baskets," created to fulfill an instant need and as disposable as today's fast food containers. He writes in *Baskets as Textile Art* that such baskets persist in many parts of today's world. The temporary basket in Plate 2, interlaced from palm fronds, is the echo of this technological milestone—and a tribute to the brilliance of its creators. The creation of these earliest baskets would have triggered the expansion of the protohuman brain.

The premise that some of these earliest containers were *interlaced* does not seem unreasonable when we consider that, according to Richard Leakey, gorillas and chimpanzees are known to plait their sleeping nests of twigs and leaves. He also mentioned that orangutans, bored in zoos, have been observed interlacing straws. A beaver dam or the randomly interworked nest of the weaverbird could have stimulated human experiments with plaiting. Perhaps the fabriclike bark of certain palms served as inspiration. The inner bark of the *Lagetta lintearia* palm contains laminated fibers so similar to fine lace that the governor of Jamaica is said to have sent Charles II a cravat and ruffles sewn from it.

There must have been many trials and failures. Which branches, grasses, or roots were sufficiently strong and supple to be interworked but not break down when dry? What technique would make a container sturdy enough to hold large fruits but would inhibit small seeds from falling between the cracks? Occasionally the response to need must have been a rudimentary technology providing a solution sufficient to sus-

12–13. Temporary baskets continue one of the oldest interlacing traditions. Often made on the spot when the need arises, they become brittle and useless when the material dries out. The burden basket below utilizes two palm fronds; a bark strip attached to their stems serves as a tumpline. The raincloak opposite is similarly interlaced—and as quickly.

12 |
burden basket
2 (2SOE), 1/1 oblique
palm fronds
26" × 17"
Auca people, eastern Equador
collection: Glenbow Museum, Calgary

13 |
raincloak
2SOE, 1/1 oblique
palm fronds
Guiana
collection: Smithsonian Institution, Washington, D.C.

20 Interlacing

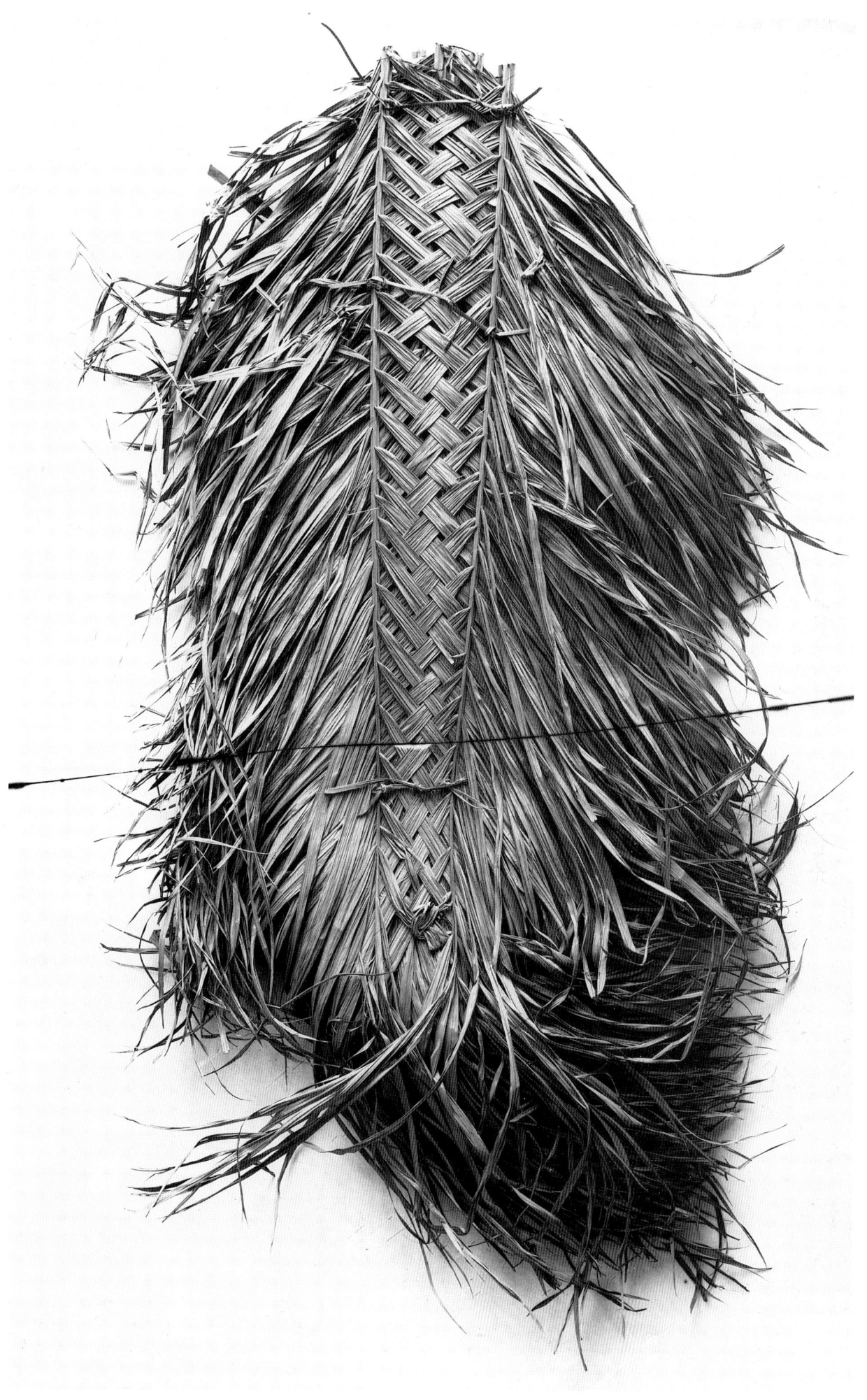

tain the body and to encourage the mind to come up with improvements. What could be done to make the interlacing stronger, more resilient or less cumbersome, lighter and more durable? What would make it easier to hold and carry?

The major advance achieved through the development of such "composite tools" as flint chips inserted along a groove in a wooden shaft or at the ends of arrows has long been identified with hunters. In *The Neolithic of the Near East*, James Melaart writes that during the Upper Paleolithic era (20,000 to 16,000 B.C.) these tools could have been employed as reaping knives as well as spears. "Such reaping knives may well have been devised for cutting reeds and tough grasses, to be woven into mats for shelters or baskets for gathering," he said. "Such usage would produce a silica sheen on the tool's cutting edge, as would the reaping of wheat and barley." A site from 14,000 B.C. on the eastern shore of Lake Tiberias in Israel has produced a tool with a silica sheen, as well as a grinding slab and a large mortar. The combination of these tools suggests the preparation of grain for food. The container used to collect and store these small grains could have been, as Melaart suggests, a basket. The plant fibers and the need were both at hand.

The second innovative phase involved *adaptive use*: what other purpose could a gathering basket serve? When did a basket become a hat? Out of adaptive use came modification and specialization. This can be seen as a "family tree" with each tier bringing forth an increasing number of branches. The container serving so well for gathering and, with a hang strap, carrying, could be made shallower to serve as a drying tray. Then, with the need to store and protect, when did an inverted tray become a top for the first covered basket?

What accident revealed that a satiny surface, less harsh to the touch, could be achieved by rubbing a mat with smooth stones? It seems likely that such developmental changes grew out of what *served* best: traps that yielded a better catch, baskets comfortable to carry, and mats smooth to sleep on. And which autumn, with enough food gathered to engender some sense of security, did an early maker discover embellishment: a twill reversed in direction to form the more satisfying chevron; fresh strands combined with those darkened by smoke to produce a pattern of contrasts?

Those who would attempt to reconstruct a picture of life in Paleolithic eras must proceed with the deliberate caution of an archaeologist who has uncovered fragments of an ancient vase. From these small shards he endeavors to restore the subtle curves and overall surface of the original. However, his is not the task of a free imagination; he is not creating in a void—similar vases are available for comparison. In the same way, today's remaining gatherer-hunters are studied for clues to their counterparts, our distant ancestors. Archaeologists are using this data to test their theories. Like the pot restorer, they attempt to reassemble a representation of the unrecorded past. We have used many of the same small pieces of information to formulate our conclusion: *the roots of interlacing trace back to the first tools used by* Homo sapiens.

Thirty years ago anthropologist Gene Weltfish came to similar conclusions about the great antiquity of interlacing by

14 |
mat with Chinese fret or Greek key motif.

15 |
decoration on bracelet found in Mezin, USSR (after Abramova, *Paleolithic Art in the USSR*).

taking art as her source material. Comparing paintings and engravings of Paleolithic societies with art of today's isolated cultures, her theory states that the chevrons, triangles, lozenges, rectangles, and hatched ribbons inscribed on bones by late Paleolithic peoples are imitations of the patterns produced by mat-making. "Basketry designs are ubiquitous," she states. "Everywhere a common type of basketry and matting is made, basic characteristics of art styles are traceable to this source."

Taking a special interest in the squared-off meander motif commonly known as the Chinese fret or Greek key, Weltfish traced its nearly universal employment as a border pattern to the roots of Greek ceramics (Pl. 16) and architecture, then back to the earlier rock-cut tomb of Thutmos III of Egypt. She discovered the same motif engraved on a fifteen thousand-year-old mammoth tusk found near Kiev. "Can it be that the Greek key is actually a mat-weaving design (Pl. 14) copied in many versions and wherever it occurs (Pl. 15) we should look to mat weaving for the orginal?...There is a close relationship between art and industrial production," she says. "Art emerges not as an abstract vision, but a celebration of the skill of work well done and enjoyed."

14–16. The rim of an early Attic run illustrates the Greek key motif anthropologist Gene Weltfish believes to derive from twilled mattings. The diagonal hatching and especially the chevron were probably adapted from the same source.

16 |
funerary krater detail, black-on-red geometric style
Greece, 8th century B.C.
collection: Metropolitan Museum of Art, Fletcher Fund

The Agricultural Revolution: From Gatherer-Hunter to Sower

By the sixth millennium B.C., many nomadic peoples had ceased their wanderings. Spurred on by primitive agriculture, settlements were initiated across the Fertile Crescent, Meso-America, and portions of southern Asia. Not only was food revolutionized in the transition, but food-related tools were also transformed. Long-term storage of seeds and produce in durable containers became both necessary and feasible. Since portability was no longer essential, restrictions on weight could be lessened or eliminated. Rather than making one implement serve multiple purposes, the gatherer-hunter-turned-farmer could now keep a collection of them, each designed for specific uses. Basketry adapted to the changing conditions.

Think of inventing sowing baskets and sewing ones, winnowing trays, sieves, egg baskets, the first fences to retain animals, or the first walls of wattle and daub. All utilize similar plaiting techniques, but specific materials, sizes, shapes, and tensions had to be selected to fulfill the different tasks. For beasts of burden, the tensile strength characteristic of braiding would be used in girth straps, halters, bridles, whips, and slings.

With a quantum leap in population, settlements became towns. Pooled resources meant that full-time craftsmen could serve full-time farmers. Improved skills and products would result from such specialization. Hélène Balfet, the French basketry researcher and classifier, says that mats, baskets, and traps were produced in nearly every Neolithic society, but we may be aware of only a small fraction of the techniques employed at that time.

Basket Maker Epochs

The common practice has been to name time periods within Eurasian and African prehistory in terms of stone, metal, or ceramic artifacts, e.g., Paleolithic, Neolithic, Bronze Age, etc. Fragile fiber, which generally disintegrates quickly, is never specified and seldom noted. A major exception is the ten thousand-year-old Jōmon culture of Japan, named for the characteristic cord-marking of ceramic vessels. Plaited mat-marked examples tend to be Middle Jōmon, about 2500 B.C. However, archaeologists writing about the prehistory of southwest North America from 10,000 B.C. to A.D. 600 have distinguished epochs that they call Basket Maker I, II, and III. The name is apt. Deep in the inaccessible recesses of caves and rock shelters in eighteen states of the American Southwest and Mexico, tens of thousands of complete and fragmentary bags, mats, and other basketry specimens have been discovered. Archaeologist J. M. Adovasio says that a piece-by-piece tabulation of the basketry finds from all the so-called Neolithic sites around the world would still be meager in comparison with the number of objects that have been found in this limited region of the Americas. "Basketry items represent one of the twin hallmarks of Desert Culture; they are the natural accompaniment of basic seed culture that was well established by 7000 B.C.," wrote Jesse

17–18. Technical sophistication combined with form variations testify to a long developmental period for prehistoric baskets of the American Southwest. The small basket at left is interlaced of yucca leaves still attached to their stems, which, in turn, form a finial. Note the eccentric pitch in the upper section and the reverse direction in the center band.

The container below was plaited in two parts then stitched together. The concentric diamond twill pattern of the base is known to weavers as "bird's-eye"; the oblique twill of the upper section switches from a 3/3 interlacing to 2/2.

17 |
small basket
1SOE, 2/2 oblique
yucca
3″ × 1¾″ (top D.)
Kiet Siel, Arizona, A.D. 900–1200
photo: Arizona State Museum

18 |
basket container
1SOE, 2/2 and 3/3 oblique
yucca
D. 6¾″, H. 4⅔″
White Canyon, Utah, A.D. 900–1200
photo: Arizona State Museum

Origins 25

Jennings, pointing up the remarkable antiquity of many of these finds. Metal was rare or unknown in these times, often termed the "preceramic period."

The explanation for the abundance is that extremely dry, wet, or cold environments prevent disintegration of fibers. Almost all this ancient basketry from the Southwest was preserved in the stable conditions of arid caves and shelters.

In a special report written to the authors of this book, Dr. J. M. Adovasio, anthropologist at the University of Pittsburgh, pushes back many of the traditionally accepted dates for plaiting and horticulture in the Americas. He says that "twining was long thought the oldest basketry manufacturing technique represented in the New World. It now appears, however, that plaiting is equally as old, if not older, at least in some areas.

"Perishable remains of any kind are extremely rare in Paleo-Indian contexts east of the Rocky Mountains. To date, the oldest reliably dated, unequivocal specimen derives from middle Stratum IIa at Meadowcroft Rockshelter, Washington County, Pennsylvania. The item is a wall fragment of simple plaiting with a 1/1 interval and single elements. It is bracketed by radiocarbon dates $10,850 \pm 870$ B.C. and 9350 ± 700 B.C. The specimen lacks selvage, shifts, splices, and decoration. While the 'finished' form of the plaited fragment cannot be ascertained, it was manufactured (as with all Meadowcroft basketry) of a cut, birch-like bark."

Adovasio says that on Petit Anse Island, Louisiana, "A single specimen of plaited matting was discovered near the surface of a salt dome but below the tusks and bones of a 'fossil elephant.'... The fragment is twill plaiting (2/2 interval) with several perhaps intentional 2/3/2 shifts. The specimen probably represents a portion of either a large burden basket or mat and does not exhibit selvage or decoration.... A late Pleistocene ascription would not be out of place given the demonstrated age of Meadowcroft plaiting." Other plaiting from Texas is dated at 7550–6050 B.C., and in Coahuila, Mexico, simple and twill plaiting have been found from the same period.

"It is interesting to note," he continues, "that wherever early examples of plaiting occur in some quantities they are already well-made examples of the craft. They are not rudimentary in any sense. This suggests that this technique, like twining, is of very great age in the New World. Perhaps like twining, it was part and parcel of the perishables technology known to the first New World migrants who passed over the Bering Straits land bridge.

"Whatever its ultimate origins may be, the appearance of plaiting in much of Formative America north of Mexico seems to be related, as suspected previously, to the horticulture out of Mesoamerica.... Virtually all of the later plaiting in the American Southwest postdates or is contemporaneous with the appearance of corn, bean, and squash horticulture.

"Finally," he concludes, "it should be noted that the earliest examples of plaiting cited in this summary presumably constitute the oldest examples of plaiting not only in the Americas but also in the rest of the world."

"During the pre-Columbian era, every culture within the Western hemisphere produced simple interlacings ranging

The relief pattern on one side of a Neolithic baking plate was probably impressed when, still damp, the plate was placed on a plaited floor mat.

19 |
earthenware plate
(impressed pattern) 2SOE, 1/1 H-V
Switzerland, 3000 B.C.
photo: Schaffhausen Museum, Switzerland

from 1/1 horizontal/vertical to the oblique wickerwork," writes O. T. Mason. It is the Basket Maker II (A.D. 1–400) and III (A.D. 400–600) and the succeeding Pueblo periods that provide myriad specimens of skillfully interlaced objects; these were often enhanced with intricate twills and braided finishes.

Not only has this stunning profusion of basketry finds established a new set of terms for time measurement, their discovery has ricocheted into archaeological research methodology. Scholars are learning to recognize and record the varieties of interlacing, twining, and coiling techniques. Descriptive notation has helped to pinpoint universal similarities as well as small differences. In the manner of forensic laboratories studying criminal evidence, such minute details as flexibility of fibers, splicing techniques, and selvage type are now noted in the records. J. M. Adovasio, in his book *Basketry Technology*, refers to the quality of data that can be extracted from the smallest fragment, information that had formerly been glossed over, ignored, or described in terms such as "nice."

Adovasio's remarkable conclusion is that no two cultures have ever created basketry in exactly the same manner, whether the products were coiled, twined, or interlaced, the materials rigid or flexible. This holds true for ethnological as well as archaeological comparisons, he said. This would mean that cultures have established individual expressions in their basketry, each different from the others by some degree. When we are reminded that known remains are just a tantalizing glimpse of what was created through time, the number of technological innovations appears infinite.

Ramifications of this research can extend far beyond the "digs," university laboratories, or museum cases. Sharing, that trait initiated by the first humans, could serve to expand knowledge in the areas of archaeology, craft, and industry. If they are written in common terms, archaeological reports can introduce ancient techniques to new uses. In return, those who work in interlacing could aid researchers who have little or no experience in "making."

First Impressions

There are other, less tangible remnants of early plaiting. Just as botanists learn of the existence of long-extinct plants through fossils, archaeologists are examining clay fragments bearing impressions of basketry. These imprints with negative "molds" of fiber constructions were often derived from the practice of daubing baskets with mud to waterproof them. The clay withstood the moisture and decay that disintegrated the fibers. These fortuitous patternings must have had great appeal, since later potters introduced embossing stamps and paddles that replicate them.

Still other shards record the patterns of the floor mats on which new pots were placed while still damp (Pl. 19). Finer interlacing on some pieces also suggests the potter's age-old practice of wrapping damp pots in cloth to prevent the cracking common to too-fast drying. These clay fragments have provided some of the missing links in the chronological study of interlacing. For the northeastern and midwestern regions of the United States and Canada, as well as Eurasia, much of South America, Africa, and Australia, the only information about prehistoric basketry has had to be garnered from examination of impressions on pottery.

Among the oldest known evidences of plaiting is a clay impression of a mat found in Jarmo, Iraq, dated by the carbon 14 process as originating ca. 6700 B.C. (Mesolithic period). The Jarmo find is not an initial experiment, say the experts. The technology it represents is advanced, indicating a long period of prior development.

Neolithic clay impressions reveal a virtuosity of skills, replete with a variety of intricate twill patterns which succeeding generations have been unable to surpass. Besides simple plaiting, several twills and decorative alternations of these are not unusual in American shards. Chevrons are characteristic of the Palestine area; twilled crosses, rectangles, and meanders have been found in other localities.

Conclusion

This introduction to the origins of interlacing concludes with the comment that we can only partially agree to the conventional idea of evolutionary progression from simple to complex. It is true that many cultures progressed from interlacing loose strands, to working through a taut and aligned set of vertical elements, toward some simplified loom device. Nonetheless, in some cases simple techniques of knotting and braiding appeared and developed *after* loom weaving was considerably advanced.

We stress the similarity of technology, tools, needs, and solutions of *all* Stone Age peoples, whether at the dawn of history or those still extant. Learning from those living today is an invaluable aid to comprehending our ancestors. In this regard, we acknowledge that there are old and well-established cultures *without* weaving. The Polynesians and other Pacific Island groups had masterful interlacing and twining but no weaving. Maori fabrics (page 54) are a case in point. So is the interlaced house shown on page 247. Arctic peoples, too, used some interlacing, but for all their ingenuity in problem solving and their artistic achievements they had no weaving at all.

We argue that *in most cultures the basic "weaves" were developed prior to the invention of the loom.* The complex mat on page 55, for example, employs not only the patterns identified with satin weave, but combines them in the manner of damask.

Plaiting in systemic rhythms to achieve a regularity of form demanded such a strong sense of discipline that the development of interlacing may be considered as a symbol of human triumph over the vagaries of nature and life itself. Creating the means of patterning and its imagery required ingenuity and control. Development of the finished basket rim and the handle were supreme technical feats. Each transition increased the complexity of structure and form. Intellectual acumen and manipulative skills grew in the process.

Here, in the primal and primary knots, braids, mats, and baskets *is* the root on which "humanness" is based, and all human achievement. Counting could begin here and from it mathematics and other systems. This same elemental problem-solving process can lead from basketry structures to rudimentary dwellings and bridges, and out of such structures are born engineering and the design process.

These primary systems of interlacing were an early human effort toward organizing matter. The development of social organization paralleled the production of these artifacts.

20 |
Perhaps 5000 years old, some pots from the Ban Chang site in northern Thailand are stamped with several interlace patterns. Other early peoples used clay rollers or incised wooden paddles to achieve such patterning. That such effects are common supports the theory that early ceramics of many cultures grew from the practice of daubing baskets with clay to make them watertight.

2
The precursors

The last several decades have witnessed a broadening interest in all fabric techniques. Scholarly dissertations have gained a wider audience, popular books on the subject are more specialized and much more numerous. Simultaneously, artists and craftsmen have made serious investigations into crafts from other, often older cultures. Examinations of ethnic fabrics employing knotting, sprang, plaiting, basketry, felting, and papermaking led to the current revivals of these techniques. In the 1970s there appeared, for the first time, sufficient plaited work to include a section in *The Art Fabric: Mainstream*. Publication of *The Dyer's Art* and Alfred Bühler's *Ikat, Batik & Plangi* resulted in sweeping probes into ancient dye techniques, especially the resists, including such specialized studies as Yoshiko Wada's *Shibori* and Inger Elliott's *Batik*.

Among those who turned their personal research into books is Peter Collingwood, whose *Sprang* explained a rare technique so clearly and exhaustively that it stands as a model to other writers. Virginia Harvey shared fresh insights in *The Techniques of Basketry* and uncovered several obscure fabric structures; Ed Rossbach's *Baskets as Textile Art* and *The New Basketry* illustrated ethnic variations and a new attitude to observing them. Arline Fisch explored the application of fabric methods to nontraditional materials in her book *Textile Techniques in Metal*. Now there are others.

There have also been sporadic attempts to take an overview of fabric structures through classification. Undoubtedly this was initiated by a need to describe the expanding collections of ethnological material gathered in the nineteenth century for a new field of scientific study: anthropology. However, the characteristics of many fabrics have no Eurasian equivalents. Since the eighteenth century, botanists have been able to communicate in the Latin of Linnaeus (1707–78). Similarly, the exact sciences of mathematics, chemistry, and music have been abstracted to universal terms. In the textile world, different terms are used by maker and merchant, still others by the curator, while archaeologist and anthropologist have their own pseudo-professional jargon gleaned from a myriad of sources.

21

Maria Van Blaaderen of Holland has worked for some time in techniques between plaiting and weaving (*The Art Fabric: Mainstream*, p. 85). Here, through tensioned verticals, with one shed stick but no heddle, she is interlacing a horizontal that will be covered by the dominant verticals. The Basel School of fabric classification refers to this stage of development as "half-weaving."

The central motif of an interlaced square knot was first plaited and tied, then integrated into the great plane.

Hand-weavers and power-weavers use different terminology. Different textile trades have different terms for the same cloth.

Even within the textile field, identical weaves have names that vary with region and dialect, medium, and profession. Take the simplest and most common, *plain weave*. Handweavers are prone to call it *tabby*, power-weavers, *taffeta*. Others say *lattice, cloth weave, linen weave,* or *basket weave*, while basket makers would use *checker* or *checkerwork*, and in other instances, *wickerwork*. Still other, disparate terms are used for the same interlacing when it occurs in lace and embroidery.

Similarly, plain weaves with a supplementary weft are, in some circles, referred to as *overshot* or *laid in*, but *brocaded* in others. This language problem not only leads to confusion, it obscures both the fundamental logic of fabric structure and the application of methodology from one discipline to another.

It is unfortunate that with the vocabulary currently in use, neither layman nor professional perceives the root of textiles, the oldest and largest industry. Both speak of "basket weaving," which is not weaving at all, but plaiting—or, as likely, coiling or twining. "Basket weave" has been used as the term for a certain knit patterning, and even farmyard fencing—in other words, each misnomer begets further fallacies. This babble of words and definitions is all the more unfortunate because these terms are taken seriously. If fabric vernacular is colorful as a study, it is—scientifically—rather useless.

No classification has appeared that consistently and logically relates the weaves of textiles to other interlacings. Our classification is proposed as a further step toward the comprehension of all interlacings as a single entity, which can be described by one system of classification.

To comprehend interlacing, two components are vital. First, a classification that extends far beyond the narrow confines of weaving to one that will manifest relationships with other interlacings. Second, we need a common language. It is the author's intention to develop a terminology that describes the number of elements or sets of elements used and also their means of interworking. This provides a precise description of the physical formation of a fabric, not an ambiguous comparison to something it resembles. The author agrees with Irene Emery that the materials and methods of production employed play no role in the definitions and classification of fabric structure.

Unlike Emery's and others', this book is not concerned with defining all manner of interworked structures, but only with those that are *interlaced*—albeit the broadest, most diverse and most important group of the fabric structures. Although interlacings appear to defy quantification, they are sufficiently limited to be analyzed, classified, and charted.

In 1934, Raoul d'Harcourt's *Les textiles du anciens Pérou et leurs techniques* successfully analyzed a great body of pre-Columbian material, including gauze weaves, tapestry joinings, and plaiting. Perhaps more than anyone else, he advanced the classification of fabric techniques through descriptions so clear that they meet the needs of both scholars and laymen. His work remains a foundation and a standard for all writings succeeding it. Because the original edition was only three hundred copies, the wide distribution of the English language version has been all the more valuable. (It was while assisting Professor Grace Denny on the translation of d'Harcourt's work into *The Textiles of Ancient Peru and Their Techniques* and on her own unpublished classification of weaves that I first became concerned with analysis of fabric structures and with the relationship of woven cloths to the baskets and blankets of the Northwest Coast of North America.—JLL)

Although d'Harcourt's analysis was limited to the finds of a single culture and a specific time frame, his examination encompasses a broad scope of fabric structures. For decades, his meticulous descriptions and diagrams have enlightened even anthropologists who have never tried to weave and weavers without access to historical fabrics. D'Harcourt wrote, "I wish to describe in detail all of the ancient techniques that examination of Peruvian weaving, network, needlemade fabrics, and plaiting has revealed to me, as well as the techniques of embroidery, and to show to what extent they are connected with one another and can be grouped together. This study has been neglected up to now... it will serve as a trustworthy foundation for further comparative studies."

Certainly the most complete, most erudite fabric classification ever made is Irene Emery's *The Primary Structures of Fabrics*. She, too, was inspired by d'Harcourt. Although Emery defined almost every known technique, she concentrated on woven cloths, devoting only a single page to all the forms of oblique interlacing. She also defined plaiting—the primary emphasis of this book—as interlinking, which it is not. Plaiting encompasses all interlacings of one or more sets of elements that are not done on a loom. An interlaced basket or mat should be spoken of as being "plaited," but not "woven."

22 |
Typical of the mat makers of East Asia, this Nepalese man sits on his finished web. Because the passive verticals are already positioned and the active horizontals interlace through them, this represents an intermediate step between plaiting and weaving. The Basel School would refer to it as "half plaiting," i.e., fixed verticals interlaced without the aid of a shedding device.
photo: Musée de l'Homme, Paris

Precursors 33

Although not treated in her book, Emery recognized the need for terms that would "identify characteristics common to [bobbin] lace at one end of the scale of delicacy, and basketry and matmaking at the other, and in the many intermediary forms which cannot be considered basketry or lace." Near the end of her classification she notes, "Obviously, this does not solve the problem of how to define the distinction between 'basketry' as one fabric type and 'cloth' as a wholly different one. It indicates instead that a problem only arises because of what proves to be a false assumption, the assumption that the terms *basketry* and *cloth* refer to mutually exclusive groups of fabrics. *Both terms are broadly generic and actually refer to fabric groupings that overlap in so many areas that neither group can be properly studied or understood without reference to the other.** The relationships between them are far more numerous than the differences, and while it is often easy to distinguish individual examples as one rather than the other, separation of the two groups is necessarily arbitrary. The habit of treating them as disparate subjects for investigation has led unhappily to the use of different terms for identical structures as well as to frequent failure to recognize and record structural identity or similarities in closely related fabrics that happen to have been relegated to separate categories. Much information which would be useful and should be available for studies of the development and distribution both of techniques and of structures has thus been misplaced or fragmentized, and often invalidated."

The classification presented here is like Emery's in that it is concerned with the essential *orders* of interworking, not with the *methods* of achieving them. In this sense, both our classification and Emery's are at odds with those developed through the ethnographic museum at Basel, which are concerned with the *means* of creating preindustial fabric structures. In her paper read at the Textile Museum in Washington, D.C., in 1976, Annemarie Seiler-Baldinger of Basel stated this very well.

"There is scarcely another area of technology with a classification and terminology as confused as that found in textiles. Although glossaries and dictionaries do exist, they are almost all devoted to industrial processes and products (e.g., CIETA vocabularies, Schnegeleberg, 1971), and have no place in them for nonmechanized, purely handmade textiles and their techniques. No wonder that archaeologists, anthropologists, ethnologists, and art historians who mainly have to deal with such processes have been using inadequate or even incorrect terms for years. The first classification dealing with the subject was established by Kristen and Alfred Bühler-Oppenheim in 1948 and has since been recognized as standard terminology in all German-speaking countries. Their work remained for a long time the only reliable and consistent systematic order of textile techniques, until the publication of Irene Emery's fundamental volume on *The Primary Structures of Fabrics* (1966). Textile specialists and scientists of languages other than English and German will still be confronted with terminological problems,

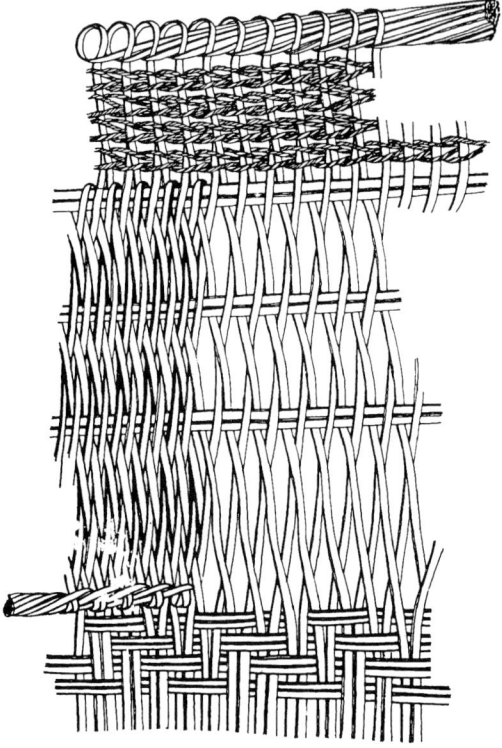
23

24

---

*The italics are mine and are consistent with my last conversations with I. Emery. She remained, then, strongly committed to limiting *textiles* to loom-woven fabrics, and *weaving* to interlacing on a loom.—JLL

since, with only a few exceptions in some aspects of textile manufacture, like 'basketry' or plaiting (e.g., Balfet, 1952), they lack satisfactory expressions in French, Italian, Spanish, and Portuguese. While I reworked and expanded Bühler's book, I made a special effort to compile the already existing terms found in these languages (Seiler-Baldinger, 1973). Even in the preparation of the English version of my text many new terms had to be coined, because our approach differs basically from Emery's. The distinction between these two classifications lies in Emery's being based on the actual structural makeup of the fabrics (1966, p. xi), whereas the Basel system is based on the very process of textile manufacture. Both methods have advantages and disadvantages and are best regarded as complementary rather than opposing systems. Emery's work is certainly more useful to the textile layman, because it is founded on the

23–25. From the eastern Himalayas through the highlands of Burma and Thailand, to Indochina, seminomadic tribal peoples employ particular skills in plaited bamboo basketry. Their round-rimmed burden baskets sprung from a square base—often footed as protection from the damp—have much in common.

Over a period of several years the National Institute of Design has researched this tradition in India's Northeast Provinces. Their appreciation includes a variety of interlacings used to meet specific needs. Grain baskets are closely worked; other types are quite open to allow circulation of air or to reduce weight.

Often several structures are combined, as in this yarn basket. Plate 24 shows how the base is twilled with paired elements, which interlace singly (and obliquely) for the side walls, then are constricted by several courses of twining before ending in a self rim (Pl. 25). The walls are reinforced with supplementary elements.

Plate 25 shows the geometry of a square-bottomed basket started at the center.

25
yarn basket
plaiting, twining
3SOE + 2SOE, 3/1 oblique-horizontal
split bamboo, smoked
Monpas people, Northeast Provinces, India
photo and drawings: National Institute of Design, Ahmadabad

analysis and aspect of the finished product and therefore does not require a thorough knowledge of technology. It can also be applied to any textile product, even if the process of manufacture is unknown, which is true of archaeological fragments and of many museum objects. But this means that one finds textiles that are made by entirely different means grouped together because their structures are the same or very similar, for example, plaiting, sprang, and weaving; linking and sprang; half-plaiting and twining; knitting and encircled looping. From our point of view, though, these differences are highly significant, as they express a certain level of technical development or achievement.

"So it mostly depends on the special interest of the investigator, whether he will use one or the other classification. Emery considers only woven fabrics as textiles proper (1966, p. 62), whereas we define textiles as surfaces formed by mechanically interworked elements. As it is impossible to deal thoroughly with all variations in such a general survey, special studies, which will furnish more detail and help to work out a finer order within a specific group or subgroup, are always welcome."

The authors sometimes quarrel with the English terms chosen by these Swiss scholars. Usually they are not coined, as stated, but appropriated words—with other meanings. We take exception to their exclusion of machine production from a "classification of textile manufacture." The bias of interpreting fabrics by the tools used in their creation has been avoided in this book primarily because, as Emery said, "Any classification based on means of production breaks down when means of production cannot be determined."

The scope of this book extends beyond an analysis of interlacing systems and their usage. The authors also want to demonstrate the breadth of interlacings—their adaptability to widely varied tasks, the frequency of their use throughout and well before recorded history. One explanation for the universality of interlacing and its accessibility to all cultures can be found in the vast range of materials employed, as discussed in Chapter VII.

Simple or complex, interlaced structures continue to present real challenges: they demand both discipline and manual dexterity. It is vital to recognize the axiom that plaiting—or interlacing other than weaving—is today the most procreant area for developing new fabric structures. These "Third World" techniques hold latent potential for commercial producers as well as artists.

So, this is a study about *systems* of interlacing in all their aspects, inclusive of those less apparent or removed from our experience by time and cultural distance. The author's concept is that—like geography, astronomy, and biology—the collected knowledge of interlacing can be charted to effect a thorough comprehension of its propensities and uses.

At the same time, the authors acknowledge that all these systems have a power beyond the sum of their parts. They comprise an entity rooted in age-old mysteries, a denominator of science and religion, of art and music and movement, and of everyday common logic.

26-27 |

The pivotal turn-of-the-century Bavarian architect Richard Riemerschmid envisioned large, vaulted structures made quickly and cheaply with plaited wood. About the same time, the Catalan architect Antonio Gaudi draped interlacings as studies for dynamic vaults.

Precursors 37

3

Meanings, modifiers, methods: the intangible tools

We begin with our title—what it is, and what it is not—and then define key terms employed throughout the book. (All terms are listed alphabetically in the Glossary-Index, p. 275). The meanings of these terms are the building blocks on which the classification is structured. Consider the modifiers as the clothes and flesh that apparently differentiate individuals. Once these are identified and stripped away, the common or skeletal structure is revealed.

INTERLACING   A fabric structure interworked so that each element passes over and under elements that cross its path—*without other engagements such as twisting or linking* (See Glossary-Index). In this sense, interlacing is the simplest form of interworking (Fig. 1).

The direction of crossing can be either oblique or horizontal-vertical (see definitions below). Since the principle of interlacing includes certain knots and all plaited structures plus weaving, interlacing embraces the largest, most widely distributed, and most often employed fabric structures. Fabrics not interlaced include *coiling* (Fig. 2), *twining* (Fig. 3), *linking*, (Fig. 4) and *looping* (Fig. 5)—as in crochet and knitting.

FABRIC   The generic term for all pliable planar structures worked with linear elements, plus such intermeshed fiber structures as felt, leather, and bark cloth. This definition also encompasses such nonfibrous films as plastic and rubber.

FABRIC STRUCTURE   The system by which linear elements or fibers are interworked or enmeshed.

INTERWORKING   The great umbrella term for all fabric structures created with linear elements—including, of course, interlacing.

MESH   A woven, plaited, knit, or knotted fabric so openly worked that it is transparent.

ELEMENT   A strand with the potential for being interworked to form a fabric structure. Elements are the basic components of all interworked fabric structures. The term *element* is an

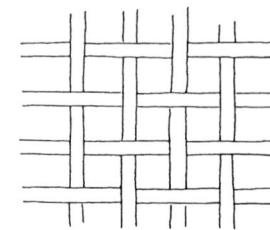

Fig. 1

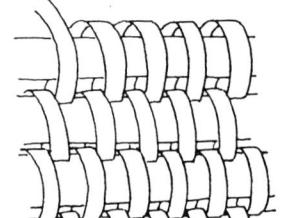

Fig. 2

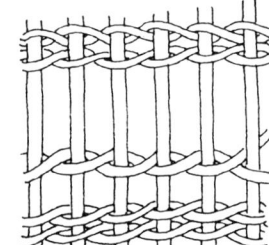

Fig. 3

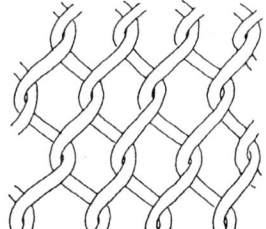

Fig. 4

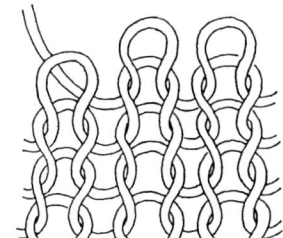

Fig. 5

Fig. 6

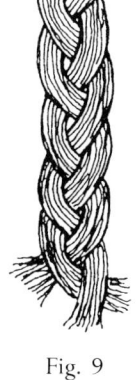

Fig. 7

Fig. 8   Fig. 9

Fig. 10

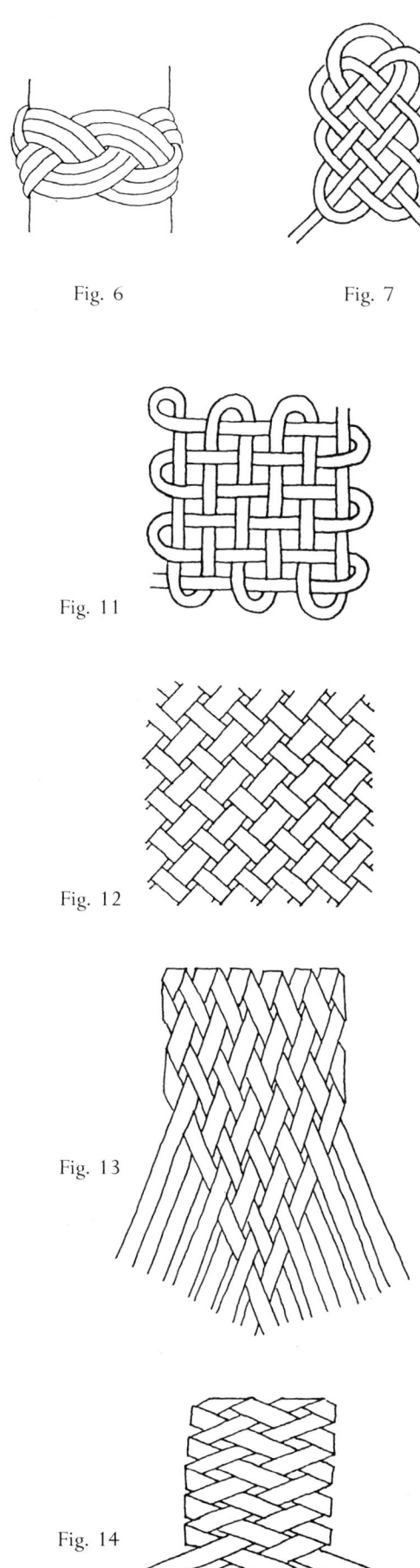

Fig. 11

Fig. 12

Fig. 13

Fig. 14

abstraction: physical characteristics of a particular element—such as its material, ply, size, or flexibility—modify a fabric structure but do not affect the essential order of its interworking. Today, fabric elements are most often yarns, but thongs, wires, tapes, and basketry materials are also used as elements, as are coils of clay or dough. Yarn is a typical *continuous* element; a slat or single strand of horsehair exemplifies a *discontinuous* element.

Note: Perhaps more than anyone else, Irene Emery has made us aware of the importance of classifying fabric structures by the number of elements or sets of elements employed. Because these essential terms are cumbersome when repeated frequently, they are abbreviated here to E and SOE.

SINGLE-ELEMENT STRUCTURES *(1E)*   A structure in which one strand circles about to interwork with itself. The Turk's head and certain knots (Figs. 6, 7) are classified as single-element interlacings. Because the largest portion of 1E fabric systems, such as knitting and crochet, are *looped* structures, they are not within the focus of this study.

ONE SET OF ELEMENTS STRUCTURES *(1SOE)*   Fabrics in which all strands interwork in the same manner. A simple braid (Fig. 8) is an example of interworking one set of elements (1SOE); most weaving employs 2SOE. In determining the number of elements or sets of elements, there should be no confusion between the term *element* and the visible strands. Two or more strands carried as one count as a single element (Figs. 9, 10). Although Fig. 11 can literally be interlaced with one element, it counts as 2SOE.

DIRECTION OF ELEMENTS   The orientation of worked elements in relationship to an edge. See below.

OBLIQUE INTERLACING   Structures that are plaited on the diagonal in relation to the outer edge (Fig. 12). Simple braids and frame braids are, by definition, worked obliquely.

PITCH   In oblique interlacing, the angle at which elements or SOE cross. Plaiting with strands of equal size *tends* to produce a 90 degree angle (Fig. 12); *steep* indicates a more vertical pitch (Fig. 13), *shallow*, a more horizontal one (Fig. 14).

Meanings, Modifiers, Methods 39

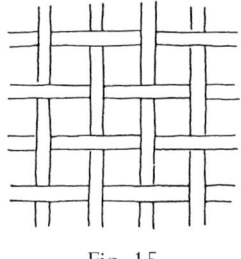

Fig. 15

Fig. 16

Fig. 17

HORIZONTAL-VERTICAL INTERLACING (H-V)   Structures in which one or more sets of lateral elements interlace at approximately 90 degrees to the selvage (Fig. 15). In wickerware, most interlaced baskets, and woven textiles, the verticals are created first. Although Emery and others use the term "right angle crossing" to indicate H-V structures, this phrase would also include oblique interlacings that cross at a right angle (Fig. 12). Because they are not synonymous, *these two terms cannot be interchanged.*

The terms *horizontal-vertical* and *oblique* are applicable to all interlacings. The terms *horizontal* and *vertical* preclude the use of "warp" and "weft" applied to basketry and other plaited structures. Admittedly, all these terms are awkward in describing radial interlacing (see below) or forms with curvilinear profiles.

SPIRAL INTERLACING   Work progressing in a circular direction rather than back and forth from edge to edge. Among 1E structures, this is exemplified by the Turk's head (Fig. 16), for 1SOE by tubular braids (Fig. 17). The monkey's fist (Fig. 18) is a three-dimensional (1E) example.

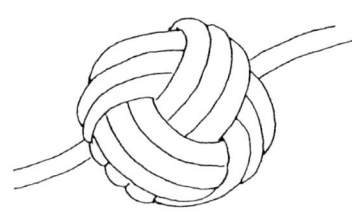

Fig. 18

RADIAL INTERLACING   A spiral course taken by an element or elements that pass over and under radiating spokes. This is common to 2SOE disc forms (Fig. 20) and fan shapes, as well as many cylindrical and spherical baskets.

MULTIDIRECTIONAL INTERLACING   Structures worked outside the systems just described, in manners varying with the number of elements employed. In carrick bends (Fig. 19), the interworking element must circle about to interlace. In some baskets, the interlacing of all SOE is multidirectional (see p. 7).

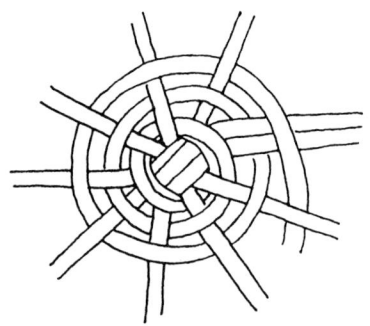

Fig. 19

ACTIVE AND PASSIVE ELEMENTS   Active elements may interwork with other active elements or around static (passive) elements. For instance, these terms differentiate obliquely plaited mats in which all elements are *active*, from wickerwork with its *active* horizontals interlacing over and under *passive* vertical spokes. Although the terms "active" and "passive" are used by some classifiers as universal substitutes for verticals and horizontals, such usage is misleading. On a loom, for instance, which SOE is passive?

Fig. 20

Fig. 21

Fig. 22

Fig. 23

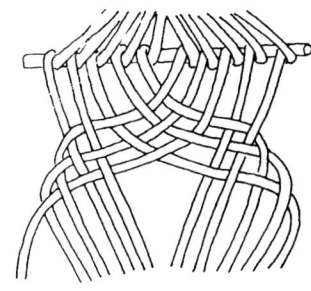

Fig. 24

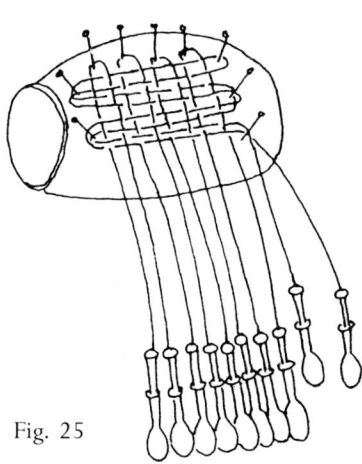

Fig. 25

ORDER OF INTERLACING   The *sequence* in which elements pass over and under other elements. To achieve universal terms, common to all structures and trades, orders of interlacing are designated by counting the passage of an element as it interlaces. "Plain weave," for instance, is a 1/1 interlacing: over one, under one (Fig. 21). The interlacing shown in (Fig. 22) is 2/2, or over two, under two. Orders of interlacing are further discussed on pages 50 and 56.

COMPLEX   Any basic fabric structure plus a supplementary element, elements, or set(s) of elements. If the suplementary element(s) are removed, the basic fabric structure would remain complete. Here, this term is never used in the sense of complicated or intricate.

COMPOUND   Any fabric structure interlaced with two or more layers. The layers are most often identical in material and interlacing, but need not be. Both terms, complex and compound, are parallel to grammatical equivalents used to analyze sentence structure.

PLAITING   Fabrics interlaced with one or more SOEs. This includes interlacings that are oblique, horizontal-vertical, spiral, multidirectional, or some combination of these. Although method cannot always be determined by the fabric, we exclude weaving from this definition (see p. 42).

BRAIDING   Oblique interlacing of 1SOE sharing a common starting point and worked with loose ends (Figs. 23, 24). Actually, the starting "point" may be a line, and the "loose ends" may be wound on bobbins. Braiding is the 1SOE form of plaiting. The resulting structure may be flat, round, square, or tubular.

BOBBIN LACE   One set of elements, wound on bobbins and interworked from a common starting line (Fig. 25). Constructions include braiding as well as oblique, horizontal-vertical, and hexagonal plaiting. Although bobbin lace can replicate 2SOE and 3SOE structures, it is indeed worked with 1SOE. Twining and interlinking may occur as well, often in combination with interlacing. Bobbin laces are often termed "pillow laces" because of the pillow on which the holding pins are inserted (see p. 93).

Fig. 26

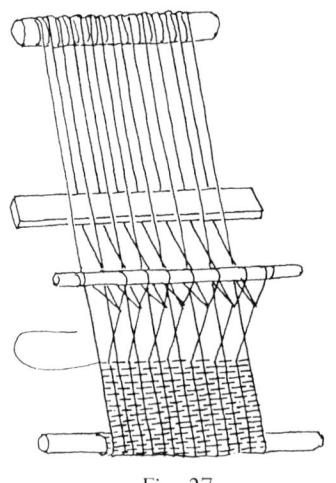

Fig. 27

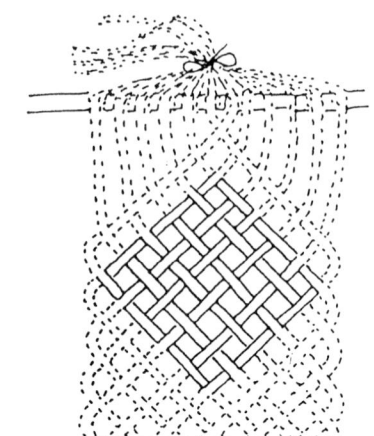

Fig. 28

FRAME BRAIDING   (interlaced sprang) One set of elements, stretched on a frame, obliquely interlaced in such a manner that both ends of the web are simultaneously duplicated (Fig. 26). All sprang is completed with a center horizontal that secures the structure. (Sprang may also be interlinked or twine plaited.)

WEAVING   Two or more SOEs interlaced at right angles on a loom (Fig. 27). Emery says that "weaving denotes warp-weft interlacing." Although all (and only) woven fabrics are *textiles*, normal usage limits the term to those that are pliable. Woven wire fencing would not be called a textile—although there are trades in which both wire meshes and screenings are called "hardware cloths."

The *warp* is the SOE running longitudinally on the loom, while the *weft* (filling) SOEs interlace through the warp. Both the warp and weft are each composed of parallel SOEs; the angle of their crossing is normally 90 degrees. Wefts not interlaced at right angles to the selvage are termed *eccentric*. Warp and weft are *weaving* terms; they are not relevant to describing the horizontals and verticals of plaited mats or basketry. A *shed* is the opening between raised and lowered warp yarns, through which the weft passes. It may be formed by a simple shed stick or by the loom.

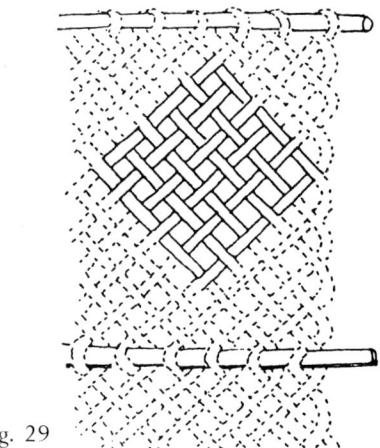

Fig. 29

Theoretically, the same interlacing can be either *oblique* or *horizontal-vertical*, and its structure achieved by various means. Even with a selvage to determine the direction of interworking, the method is not always evident. All of the following methods produce the same structure. It follows that *interlacing describes a fabric structure and NOT merely a means of interworking elements.*

A small "fragment" of 1/1 interlacing is shown:
(Fig. 28)   braided with loose ends
(Fig. 29)   frame braided (interlaced sprang)
(Fig. 30)   worked as bobbin lace
(Fig. 31)   darned with a needle
(Fig. 32)   woven with a simple shedding device
(Fig. 33)   woven on a loom with harnesses

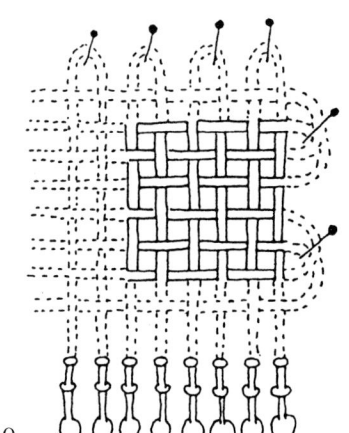

Fig. 30

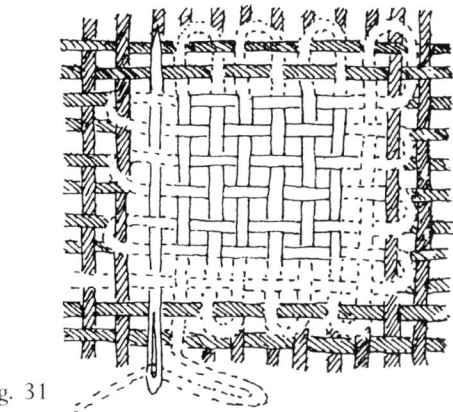

Fig. 31

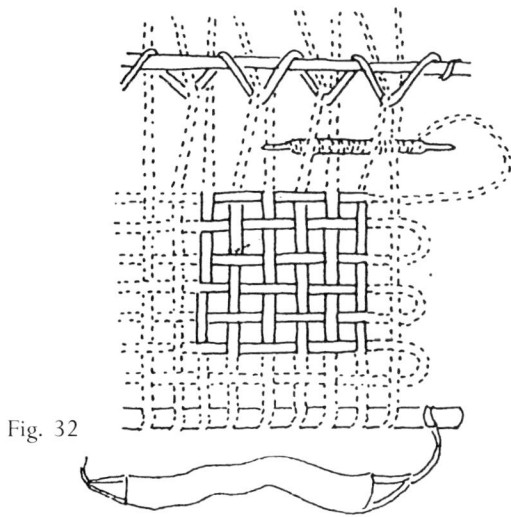

Fig. 32

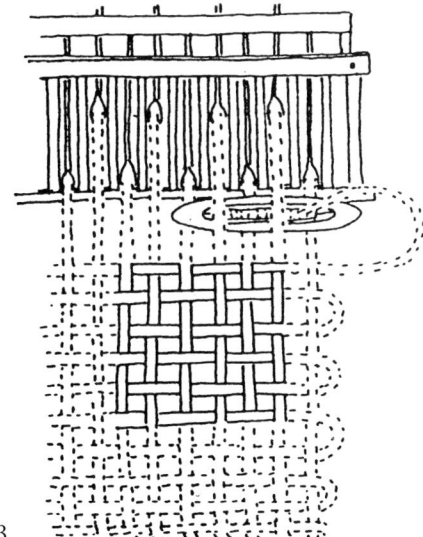

Fig. 33

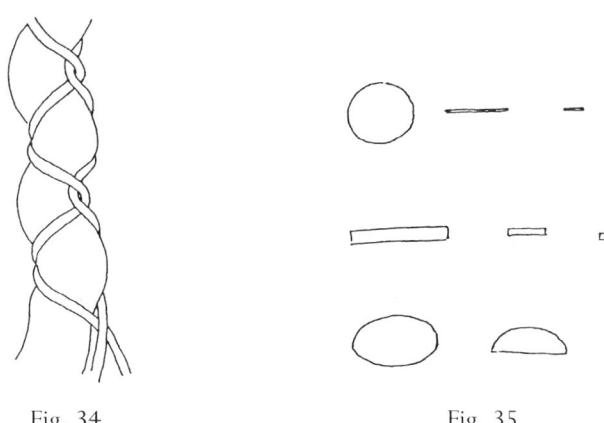

Fig. 34   Fig. 35

Modifiers

All interlaced structures are conditioned by various characteristics, here called *modifiers*. First are effects of the materials employed, including their size, form, and color. Second are *structural modifiers*, which condition the interworking through such variables as density and balance. It follows that the character of each interlaced piece is determined by several modifiers.

In discussing fabric structures, many specialists consider only the extremes as "modified," discounting the average as normal and implicitly "unmodified." Classifiers Emery and d'Harcourt describe a major category, such as "plain weave," then give equal value to subcategories of plain weave, such as "plain weave with paired elements." This approach impairs the direct simplicity of classification. Even more regrettably, it clouds the reality that *all* fabric structures can be modified by pairing elements, etc. Newer publications tend to use more accurate terms.

Materials as Modifiers

SIZE   Elements range in width from extremely fine to wrist-thick. Elements of different diameters may be combined within one SOE (Fig. 34), or interworked in opposing SOEs.

Even greater variations occur in the length of materials. *Discontinuous* strands of grass or hair are relatively short in comparison to *continuous* strands such as yarn. Although relative length modifies the appearance by the frequency with which strands are added by knotting or overlapping, this does not change the structure.

COUNT   The fineness or coarseness of interlacings is indicated by the number of elements in a linear or area unit measured in inches or centimeters.

SHAPE   In cross-section, elements may be round, rectangular, elliptical; any of these may be slit or flattened. Yarns and filaments typify round elements; slit bamboo, wood splints, and strips of leather or metal are usually rectangular or flat. Elliptical sections characterize interlaced grasses (Fig. 35).

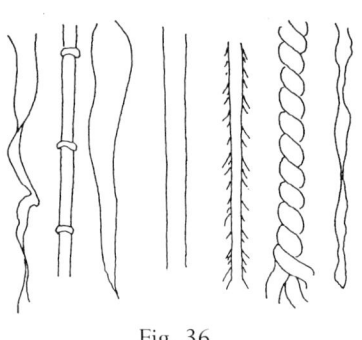
Fig. 36

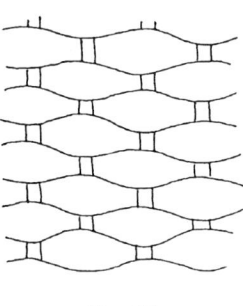
Fig. 37

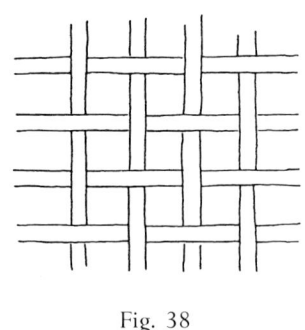
Fig. 38

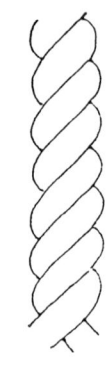
Fig. 39

The *longitudinal* profile may be thick or thin, smooth or rough, regular or irregular (as in the spaced nodes of grass stems, bamboo, slubbed yarns, or the slow taper of leaves). Plying may produce a round, smooth profile or the undulation of ropes and cords (Fig. 36).

BAST   The long cellulosic fibers derived from leaves, stems, bark, and husks. Basts are conventionally divided into those that are carded and spun, such as linen, ramie, and jute, and the hard fibers—sisal and coir—which are twisted and plied for cordage and matting. Such long, strong fibers as abacca, pina, or maguey may be used singly or as plied elements. Peculiar to the Third World, this last group of basts is extremely varied. Specific identification becomes difficult because these plants are known by dissimilar names in different geographic regions. Like many ethnographers, the author has employed the generic term *bast*.

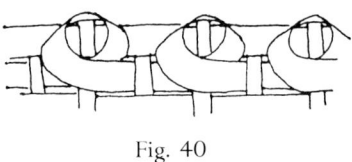
Fig. 40

SOLIDITY   Elements may be so soft that they compress at the point of interlacing (Fig. 37) or be hard and unalterable. Here relative weight or *specific density* is a factor.

FLEXIBILITY   Pliancy of elements influences the character of the finished work, particularly fabric density and balance. If all elements are extremely rigid, an open mesh with considerable body may be attained (Fig. 38); except for knotted nets, open meshes of pliable elements tend to be limp and prone to slippage. In wickerwork, the elements are so rigid that the horizontals must necessarily be relaxed by presoaking in order to make them undulate around the verticals.

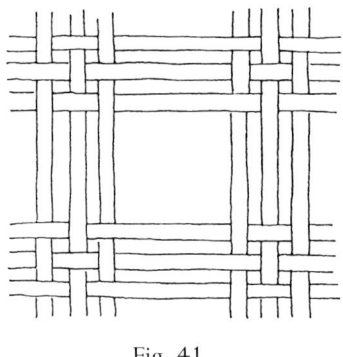
Fig. 41

TWIST   The torsion of an element or plied elements, which adds both strength and length; twist can affect other modifiers such as resilience. Two or more hues may be plied for color variation (Fig. 39). Flat elements may be twisted to produce an ornamental effect (Fig. 40).

RESILIENCE   The relative "stretch and return" of an element is determined by both the inherent nature of the material and such processing as twisting or plying.

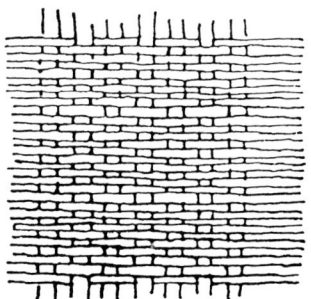
Fig. 42

GROUPING   Any one element may be made up of two, three, or more strands. For instance, each of the three elements of pigtail braids is composed of hundreds of strands.

It is useful to use the terms *paired* for elements composed of two strands (Fig. 10) and *grouping* or *grouped* for elements with multiple strands (Fig. 9). If different types of strands are combined within a single element or set of elements, it is vital to consider the characteristics of each (see Fig. 34).

Structural Modifiers

DENSITY   The degree of openness or compactness with which elements are worked is crucial in determining the character of fabrics. The flexibility of elements conditions the densities appropriate to interlacing them (Fig. 41).

BALANCE   The count of one SOE in relation to the count of another. When opposing elements or SOEs are equal in quantity and size, the structure has symmetrical balance. Asymmetrical balance may be achieved with opposing elements or SOEs unequal in size or number (Fig. 42). In the baskets on page 48, balance is achieved by opposing many fine, grouped elements with fewer large, rigid ones.

TENSION   The relative tautness with which the elements are worked is usually uniform throughout the structure—all of one SOE are relaxed or all tightly drawn. Occasionally, some elements within a set are taut, others not (Figs. 43, 44). In some flat braids, the active elements are pulled so tightly that they are hidden by the passive elements. This produces stripes or chevrons rather than the oblique "plaids" resulting from equal tension.

TAKE-UP   The degree of foreshortening caused by the undulation of elements during interworking. Take-up is affected by the solidity, flexibility, and size of elements, or by the tension under which elements or SOEs are pulled or weighted (Fig. 45). The ornamental loops or twists of some basketry and bobbin lace require considerable take-up.

PITCH   The angles at which elements are interlaced. While the pitch of narrow braids has no norm, it tends to be steeper than 45 degrees. For braids in which the outside strands interlace only from one side (as in the belt on p. 153), the pitch tends to be *shallow*. Some tubular braids, such as the manioc strainer on page 123, function through their ability to change pitch and—consequently—diameter (Fig. 46).

Most 2SOE interlacing is worked throughout with one SOE at right angles to the other. In baskets worked spirally over vertical spokes the incline is usually so gradual that it appears horizontal. The interlaced diagonal derived from *twill* progressions is not to be confused with pitch—the relationship of horizontal to vertical SOE is still a right angle.

COLOR EFFECTS   A term appropriated from the textile industry to describe sequencing elements of two or more color values to achieve a pattern. Often, as in stripes and checks, the color is sequenced independently of the order of interlacing. Contrasting a dark SOE against a light SOE brings out a pattern that is otherwise obscured. This is also true when light and dark elements are alternated within an SOE (see pp. 203–15).

Fig. 43

Fig. 44

Fig. 45

Fig. 46

The steep twill on an African box was influenced by the use of two materials with very different characteristics. The dark verticals are so hard and rigid that they deflect the soft raffia horizontals. Because of the long floats, the raffia also packs in the more closely, producing asymmetrical balance. The horizontal bands are twined.

28 |
covered box
2SOE, 5/3, 5/1, etc., H-V
bast
East Africa, early 20th century

The pitch (and thus the length) of this openly worked burden basket changes with gravity and weight. In this photograph, the angle of the crossing is approximately 90°. The basket elongates when suspended, making the angle considerably steeper. With a weighty burden, it becomes a long, pliable tube conforming to the body of the carrier. Compare with Plates 92 and 94.

29 |
basket with braided tumpline
2SOE, 1/1 oblique
rattan
approx. 20″ × 9″
Borneo, Indonesia
collection: Historical Museum, Bern
photo: Monique Jacot

46 Interlacing

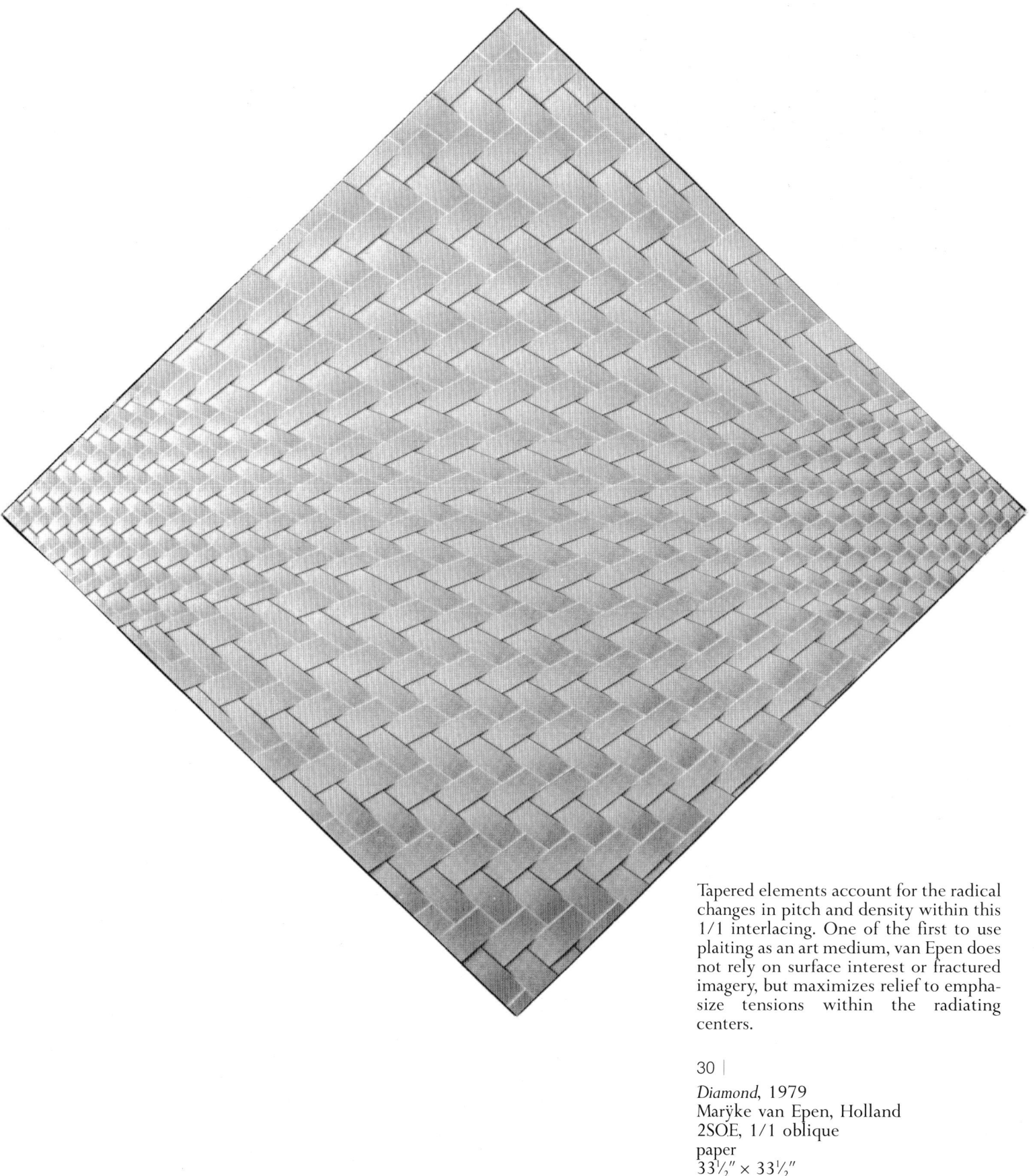

Tapered elements account for the radical changes in pitch and density within this 1/1 interlacing. One of the first to use plaiting as an art medium, van Epen does not rely on surface interest or fractured imagery, but maximizes relief to emphasize tensions within the radiating centers.

30

Diamond, 1979
Marÿke van Epen, Holland
2SOE, 1/1 oblique
paper
33½" × 33½"

Meanings, Modifiers, Methods

31 |

This Polish marketing bag is stronger than its few horizontal crossings would suggest, not because the rush itself is so durable but because of the balance of verticals and horizontals. The elements that support weight are many; those that only bind, few. As important, the crammed verticals form a stout defense against abrasion: like the proverbial bundle of faggots, there is safety in numbers.

photo: Edward Koprowski

The patterning of this mat is achieved with areas of discontinuous interlacing, a technique similar to slit tapestry. The rigid verticals were first positioned with rows of twining.

33 |
mat (detail)
2SOE, 1/1
rattan
Africa

In the hand, this small hemispherical scoop feels balanced, although there are nearly 40 radial elements for every lateral one. Flexibility of the grouped laterals permits an asymmetrically balanced form that is dense, rigid, and durable.

32 |
scoop
2SOE, 1/1 radial-lateral
split bamboo
5″ × 6″
Southeast Asia, c. 1975

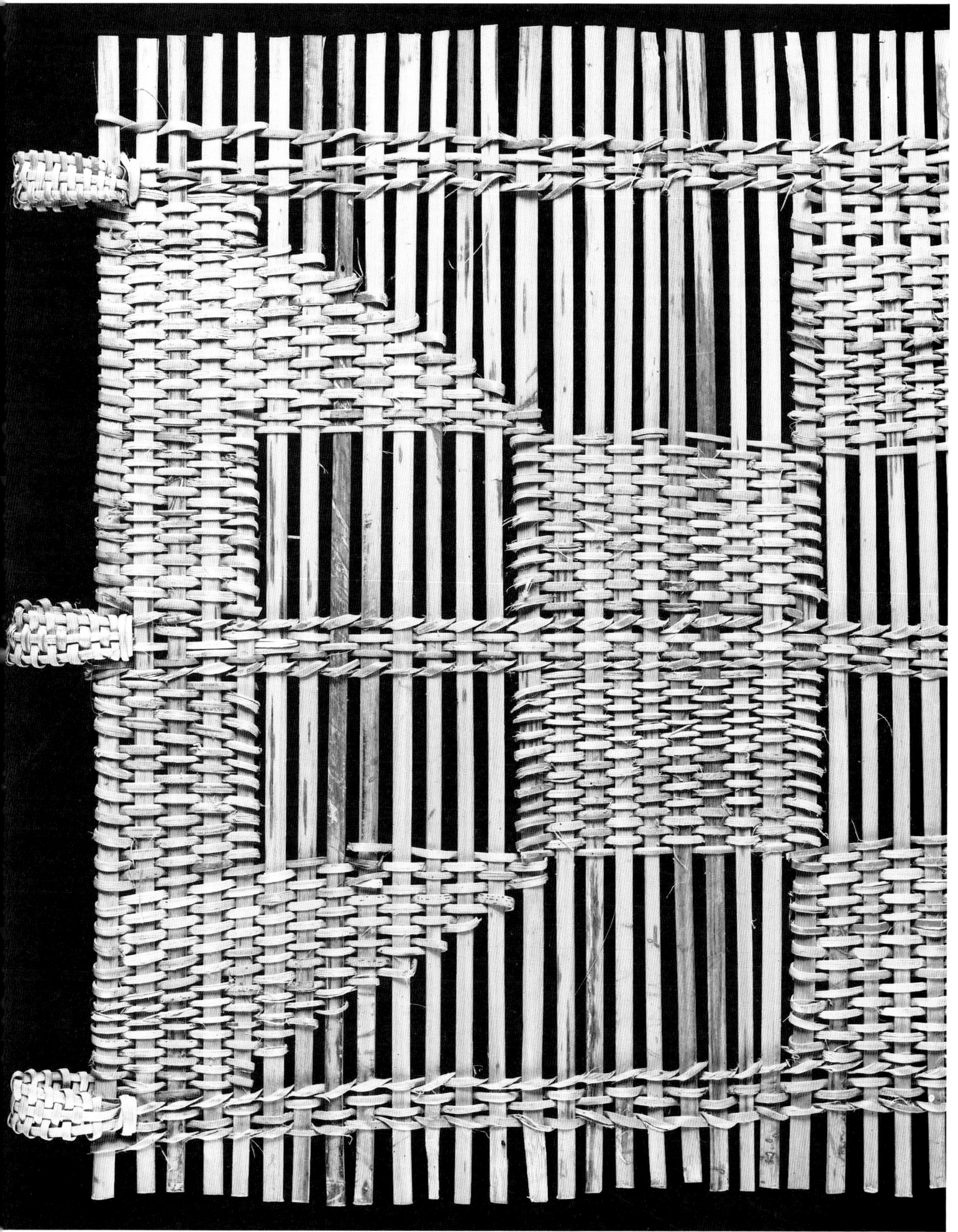

Orders of Interlacing

An order of interlacing is defined in terms of the sequential path of one element over and under other elements. In Figures 47–49, for example, the path of each element is over one, under one. Such sequences are the denominator common to all interlacing. Passage of an element over two or more opposing elements is described as a float (Fig. 50).

While establishing this classification, the authors considered the old maxim, "There are only three weaves: plain, twill, and satin; all others are derived from them." Although an oversimplification, it is close to the mark. This is now reduced one more step. *The immense scope of all interlacing may be classified into two groups: those based on the 1/1 order, and those incorporating floats.* When one considers that most interlacings are 1/1, this further simplification does not seem so extreme. This premise is further supported by Irene Emery's conclusion: "The frequency with which *satin weave* is described in terms of twill…and certain *twills* in terms of satin weave…strongly suggests that the structures of *satin* and *twill* belong to the same basic class of weaves."

In determining an order of interlacing, it is vital to consider not just one, but both *faces* or sides of the structure. Although the faces are often alike, they may be dissimilar or reversed in some manner—a fact too often overlooked. Whether twisted, looped, or flat, supplementary elementary elements may conceal a basic structure only revealed on the other face.

The difference between faces of one structure may be caused by a reversal in the direction of the float. This occurs when floats of one SOE predominate on one face while floats of the other SOE dominate the opposite face. We describe these as *face reverse structures* (Figs. 51, 52). The 2/1 twill of denim is typical.

Face reverse patterns are formed when floats of opposing SOEs dominate in alternating areas of *one* face (Figs. 53, 54). Damasks are a familiar example.

We may now conclude that the enormous diversity of the work described in this book is a multiple of:

count of elements
X
orders of interlacing
X
modifiers (including materials and color effects)
X
form (including size)

It is this multiplication that produces variants numerous as the stars, with many as yet untried. The interaction of these factors allows infinite options that permit creative expression within ancient and familiar structures.

Fig. 47

Fig. 48

Fig. 49

Fig. 50

Fig. 51   Fig. 52

Fig. 53

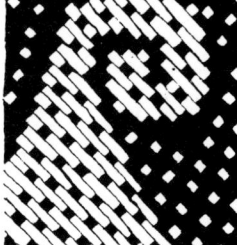
Fig. 54

In woven textiles this construction would be called satin damask, but the author proposes *face reversal pattern* as a term common to mats, baskets, and textiles. The float structure here is a *stepped progression* (twill). The faces reverse from 4/1 to 1/4.

Note the decorative attachment of the rattan edge reinforcement.

34 |

envelope
2SOE, 4/1 and 1/4 oblique
rattan peel
The Philippines, c. 1975

The soft patterning of an African cap combines twills in several orders of interlacing. The large 2/2 areas, most often separated by 4/4 bands, are themselves interrupted as the ribs change direction.

36 |

cap
2SOE, 2/2, 4/4 oblique, etc.
bast
6″ × 9″
provenance unknown

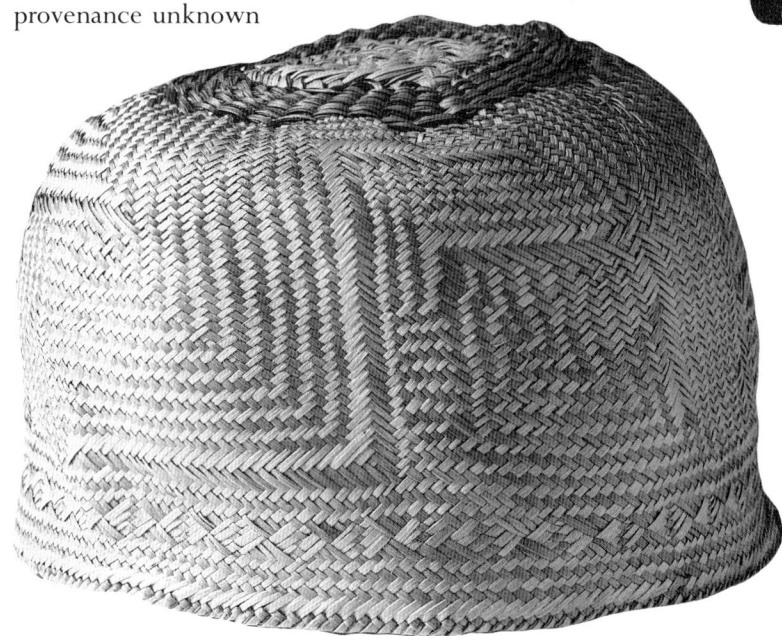

A diamond motif in the same *face reversal pattern* as woven damask is barely discernible in the photograph. Note the interlaced motif on the wrapped base, also the fine braided bandings. The raised base and the cover sliding on a carrying strap are typical of Southeast Asia.

35 |

covered basket with shoulder strap
2SOE, 4/1 and 1/4 oblique
rattan peel
The Philippines, 1970s

Meanings, Modifiers, Methods 51

The 5/2 twill of this tray is as handsome as it is unusual. Verticals interlace over 5, under 2; horizontals over 1, under 1, over 1, under 4. Like tiffin trays of China, the twilled matting is stretched on a bamboo frame.

37

tray
2SOE, 5/2 H-V
bamboo
c. 13″ × 13″
Japan, 19th century
collection: University Ethnographic Museum, Zurich, Spoerri Collection
photo: Pierre Germond

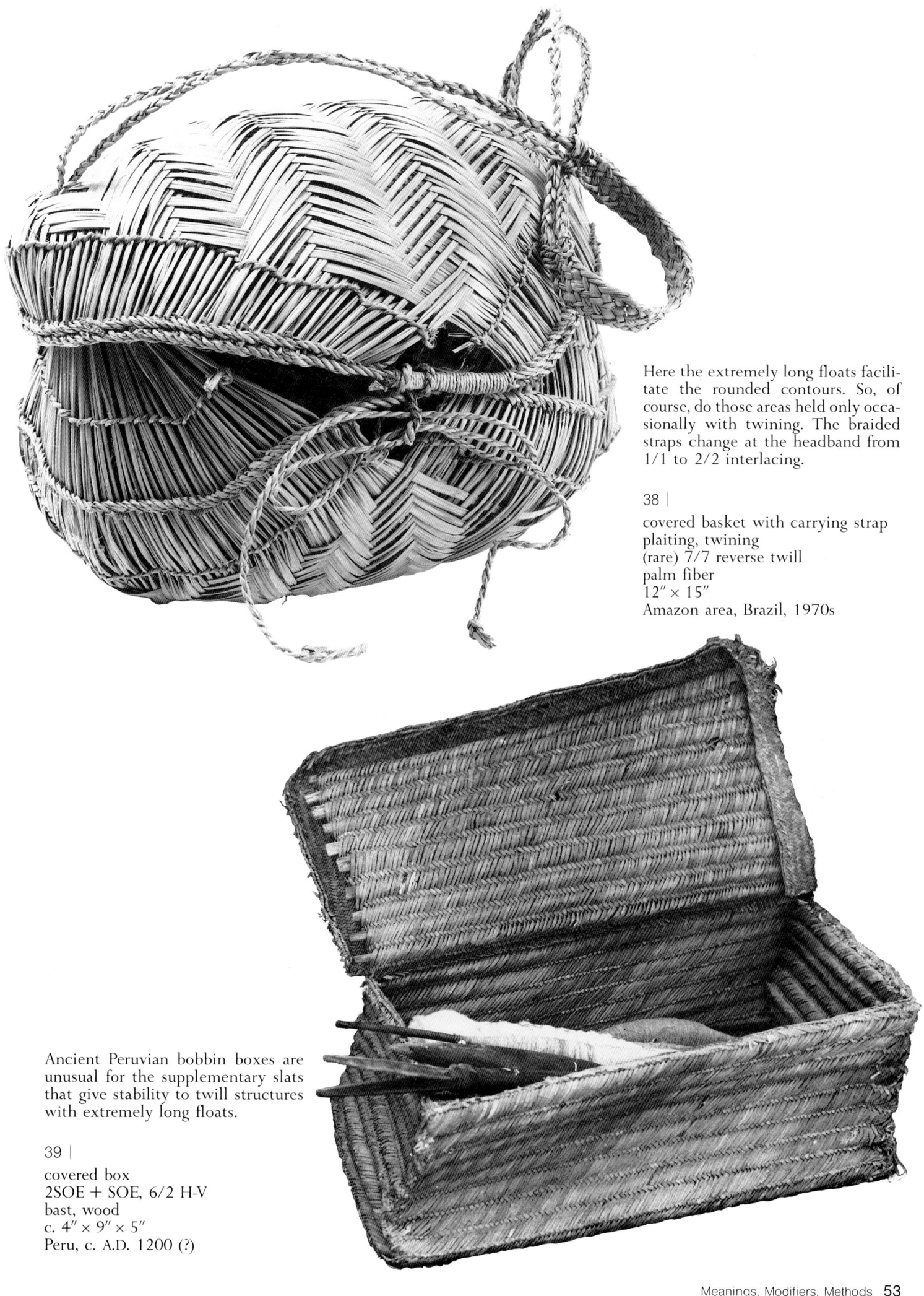

Here the extremely long floats facilitate the rounded contours. So, of course, do those areas held only occasionally with twining. The braided straps change at the headband from 1/1 to 2/2 interlacing.

38 |
covered basket with carrying strap
plaiting, twining
(rare) 7/7 reverse twill
palm fiber
12″ × 15″
Amazon area, Brazil, 1970s

Ancient Peruvian bobbin boxes are unusual for the supplementary slats that give stability to twill structures with extremely long floats.

39 |
covered box
2SOE + SOE, 6/2 H-V
bast, wood
c. 4″ × 9″ × 5″
Peru, c. A.D. 1200 (?)

Meanings, Modifiers, Methods

40–41. Although the Maori of New Zealand did not develop weaving, their twined and plaited fabrics are remarkable. Many of the face reversal pattern structures are similar to those of Borneo (opposite). The mat work of Kalimantan and Sarawak on the huge island of Borneo has without doubt the most highly developed plaited patterning in the world today. Worked either obliquely or on the horizontal-vertical, the face reversal patterns contain a broad range of symbols. The dot patterns on them, resulting from working with high contrasts of dark and light, recur in similar motifs on the warp ikats of the same areas. This leads to the conclusion that the plaited mats were developed first, the woven ikats, after (see *The Dyer's Art*). Compare with the baskets on pages 51 and 161.

40 |
mats
2SOE, 6/1 oblique or H-V
bast
Sarawak
photo: British Museum, London

41 |
bag (detail)
2SOE, 3/1 oblique
bast
Maori people, New Zealand
photo: Wool Secretariat, New Zealand

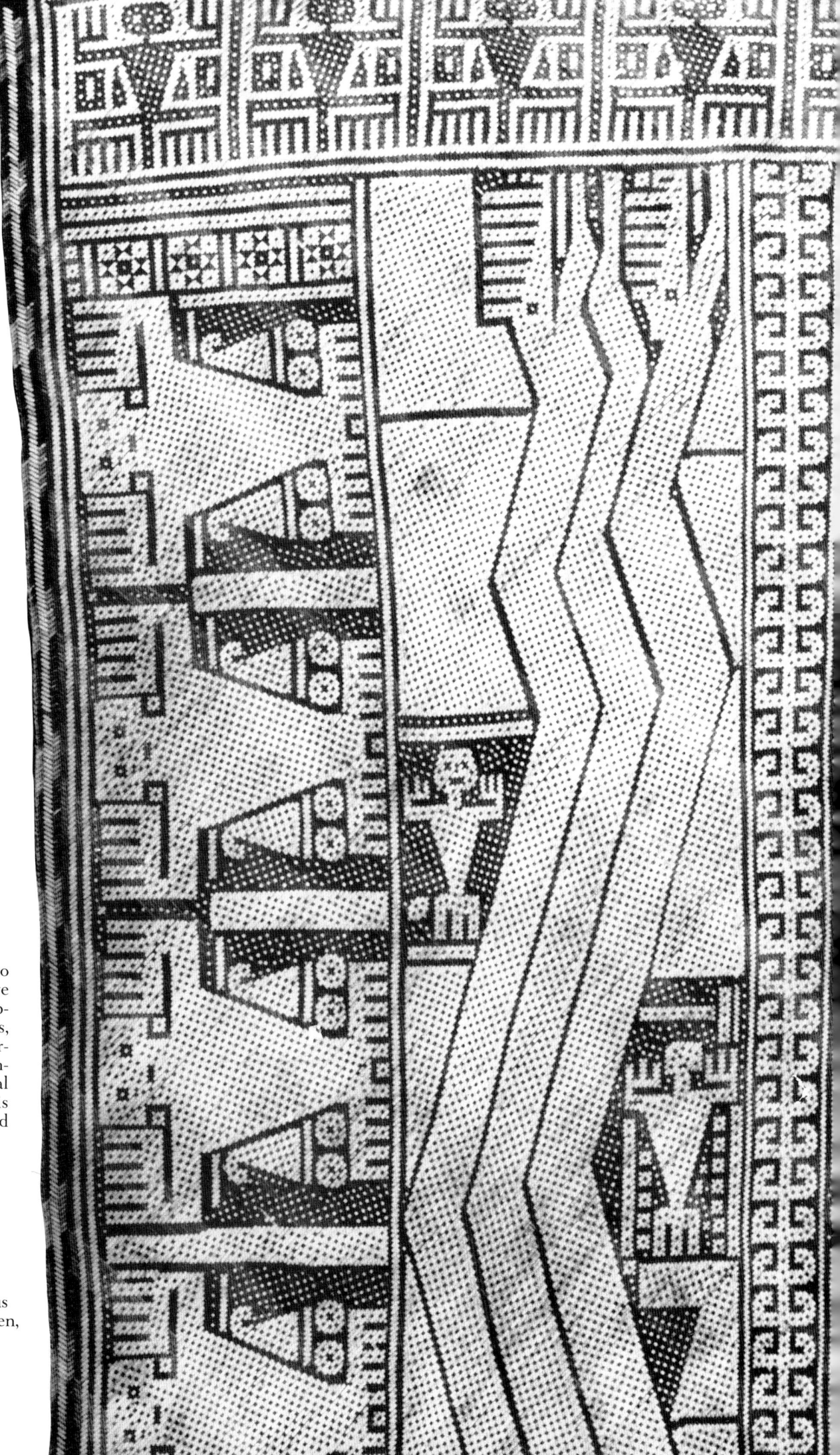

The large mats of Borneo are even more figurative than the small ones (opposite). Within borders, the typical motifs are serpents (*nagas*) and humanoid figures. The diagonal striping of one SOE is common, often in red and green.

42
mat (detail)
2SOE, 6/1 oblique
bast
Danum people, South Borneo
collection: Anita Spertus and Robert J. Holmgren, New York

Orders of Interlacing

	1E	2E	1SOE	2SOE		3SOE
1/1						
2/2						
3/3						
				face reverse structures		
1/3						
1/4						
				face reverse patterns		

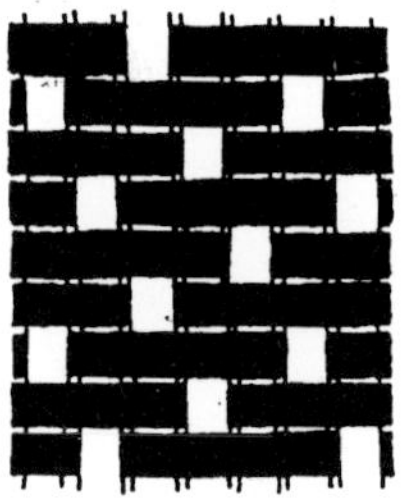

56 Interlacing

Olga de Amaral continues to create the type of plaited hangings first shown in *Beyond Craft* and *The Art Fabric: Mainstream*. In her mid-1980s work, subtlety of color prevails, with an enrichment of applied gold leaf. Note the transition from H-V to oblique interlacing and her typical ingenuity in the top and bottom edge finishes. Frame-braided Columbian bags (Pl. 101) influenced this work.

43

Tejido Policromo #2, 1985
Olga de Amaral, Colombia
top: 2SOE, 1/1 H-V
below: 1SOE, 1/1 oblique
woven horsehair tapes, gold leaf
5′ × 4′

Meanings, Modifiers, Methods 57

A plaited panel from Papua New Guinea is patterned with single courses of twining then polychromed with mineral pigments.

44
panel (detail)
plaiting, twining
2SOE, 1/1 oblique
palm fiber
Papua New Guinea

The exuberant plaited mats of Mindanao are unique in both their tapestrylike joinings and their combination of interlacings. Here 1/1 areas are juxtaposed with 3/1 and 1/3 twills, plus two other patterns created with floats (see the mat in Pl. 217).

45
mat (detail)
2SOE, oblique
palm fiber
Mindanao, The Philippines, 1980

46–47. For a number of years, Susan Jamart has tested her sanity by employing "mad weave" to plait various directional forms. The woven and braided ribbons she uses lend clarity to her jewel-tone colors. The similar technique in Allan Greedy's flat piece is enriched by the ombré striping of his twill-woven tapes.

46 |
form, ca. 1975
Susan Jamart, U.S.A.
hexagonal plaiting
3SOE, 2/3 vertical-oblique
grosgrain ribbon (rayon)
H. 14″

47
Interruption, 1980 (detail)
Allan Greedy, U.S.A.
hexagonal plaiting
3SOE, 2/3 vertical-oblique
woven tapes

Japanese three-dimensional star puzzles are related to origami, but more intriguing in their structure and combinations of color and pattern. Sixteen paper squares are first folded into parallelograms, which become the discontinuous elements of the star. Then each is interlaced through two points. In learning how to make them, students develop dexterity, concentration, and color sensitivity.

48
puzzles, 1980
Haru Wakisaka, Japan
1SOE, 1/1 oblique
paper
2½″ × 2½″, 1½″ × 1½″

Meanings, Modifiers, Methods

Dorothy Gill Barnes's baskets are compelling for her sensitive handling of found and prepared materials in multiple layers (see page 111).

49 |

basket, 1985
Dorothy Gill Barnes, U.S.A.
6SOE, horizontal, vertical, oblique
mulberry bark (vertically slit),
matchstick bamboo
17" × 8" × 4½"

A superb modern basket reflects Southwest Indian traditions of form, patterning, and coloring. While most Southwest baskets are densely coiled, this one, plaited in the manner of wicker, achieves great strength and rigidity, with bold stripes of alternating colors.

50
basket, 1980
Jonathan Krout, U.S.A.
2SOE, 1/1 H-V
rattan
10″ × 25″

51

Sherri Smith combines two devices to control the color of a braided hanging. Both special techniques are known as "Chinese braids." One is the diagonal shift of elements to achieve a join of parallel narrow braids. The other, in this book called "wraparound braids," involves alternately, from left and right, bringing one strand around the selvage and over a group of then passive strands to cross at center. With this braid form in two colors, Smith is able to build small chevrons of pure color. Like slit tapestry joins, the long slits effectively separate color areas. Note the variations in density.

52

As an outgrowth of braiding the long silk fringes of his ikat, Richard Sauer made this brilliant small (H. 8″) fetish. The hundred silk yarns grouped in each strand are dye patterned as a unit. The slits at the top and bottom control color areas; so does the covering power of the dominant verticals at center.

64 Interlacing

4
Classification

The chart on the next page provides a broad overview of interlacings, extending from knots tied with a single element to structures with four or six sets of elements. In this classification, the various types are both distinguished and related. Here, seemingly disparate structures are brought together in much the same way as a family tree, which demonstrates how distant cousins, aunts, great-grandfathers, etc., are related by consanguinity or marriage.

Although formulated in arithmetic steps, the classification should not be considered as the outline of an evolution from simplest to most complicated. For example, decorative knots tied with a single element may challenge the dexterity of the most adept seaman, and Japanese braiding with but one SOE has attained staggering levels of intricacy. In contrast, because of the simplicity of their construction, 3SOE structures are commonplace in many regions. As with biological classifications, there are varying levels of complexity in each division. Nor is this a historical progression; the chapter on Origins referred to many archaeological finds of intricate interlaced structures well outside the scope of present-day craftsmanship.

It should be noted that the descriptive examples in each category of the following subdivisions are not to be considered as exhaustive; someone else could propose equally applicable structures without making the classification invalid. The selections are intended to be representative; it is impossible to be all-inclusive.

NOTES ON THE CLASSIFICATION
Knots

A knot is a tied structure composed of one or more flexible elements. It is usually worked by passing a free end back over and under itself.

Knots are defined as interlaced when they are worked with an over/under sequence. The carrick bend and mat "weaves" are such explicit examples that they could be considered the very symbols of interlacing.

Classification of Interlacings

	single unit	linear	planar	3-dimensional
1E and 2E	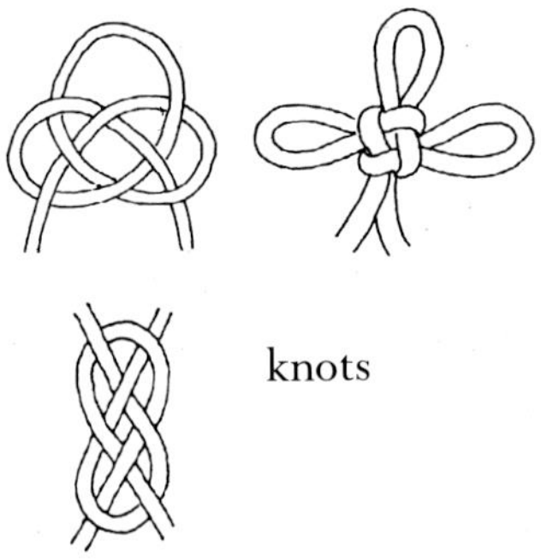 knots	 macramé knot	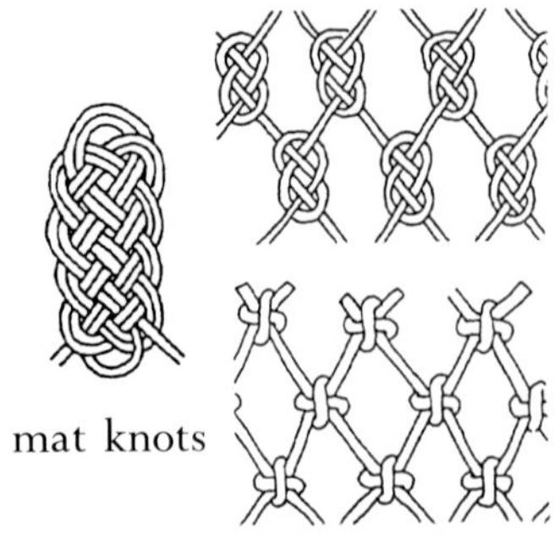 mat knots nets	 knots
1SOE		 braids	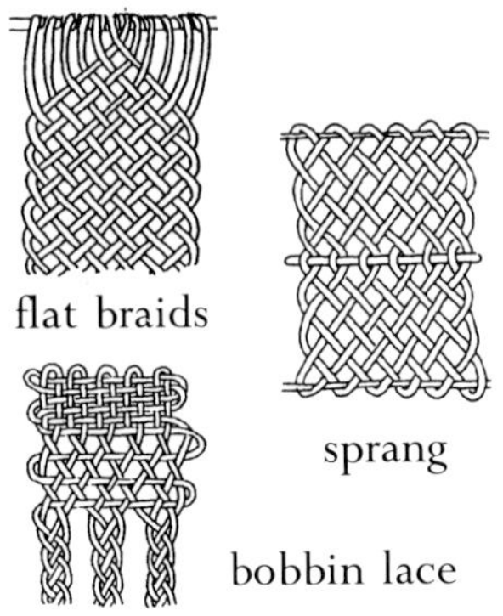 flat braids sprang bobbin lace	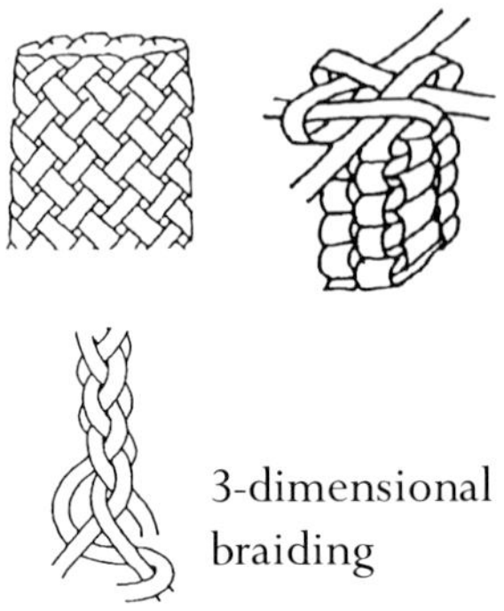 3-dimensional braiding
2SOE		 woven tapes	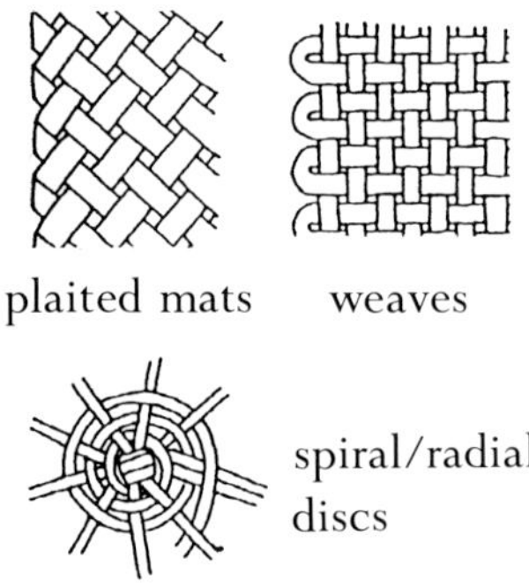 plaited mats weaves spiral/radial discs	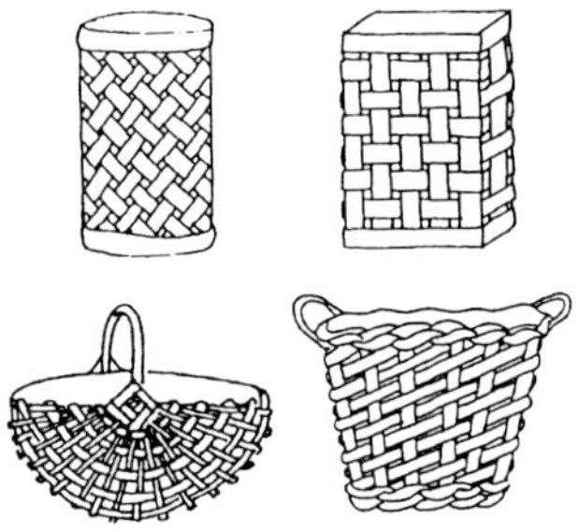 basketry
3SOE			 hexagonal plaiting	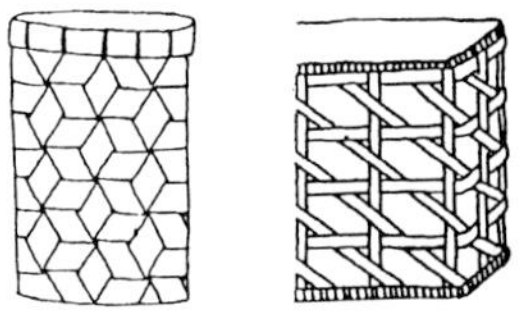 basketry
4SOE			 caning	 basketry
6SOE				 basketry

66 Interlacing

Although sailors, hunters, and herders have all used knots, it is doubtful whether these were ever limited to utilitarian tasks; early on, knots acquired esoteric meanings. In cultures around the world the visual appeal of curvilinear rope patterns often transposed these mundane structures to arcane levels. Similarly, knot makers have frequently been attributed with magical powers.

Some of these structures became fetishes with which sorcerers were believed to transcend such uncontrollables as violent storms or male potency. The heraldry established in medieval Europe incorporated carrick bends and overhand knots into familial escutcheons. In the final chapter we will examine the underlying symbolic, cultural, and ornamental aspects of these ubiquitous knots.

Admittedly, inclusion here of these particular knots may be startling to those unaccustomed to thinking in terms of fabric structure. But, without examining a correlation between simple knots and more recognized interlacings, the fundamental position of knots remains obscure. In a sense they are as basic as one-celled organisms are to the life sciences. Just as those invisible phenomena became fundamental to the comprehension of life or to any modification of life structures or processes, understanding of simple knots and primary interlacings is requisite to interpreting other fabric structures—even to potential processes for postindustrial fabrics.

A sculpture in miniature combines simple oblique plaiting with the crisp folds peculiar to coated paper.

53 |
soft box with stairs, 1980
Leonard Bentham, United Kingdom
2SOE, 1/1 oblique
paper
c. 8″ × 8″
courtesy: 4th International Exhibition of Miniature Textiles 1980, organized by British Crafts Centre
photo: Richard Davies

Classification of Interlaced Structures

I. WITH INTERLACED KNOTS
   A. worked with one element (1E)

   1. distinguished by dominant direction of interlacing

      a. in primary, single knots

         i. oblique

carrick knot

flattened Turk's heads

         ii. horizontal-vertical

Japanese crown knot

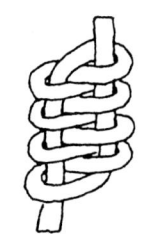
good luck knot

      b. linear: series of knots

         i. oblique

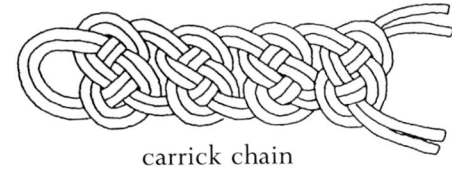
carrick chain

         ii. multidirectional

side-locking carricks

68 Interlacing

1E Knots

Knots worked with two elements are not necessarily more intricate than those with one; many structures can be formed with either. Two ends of the same element are sometimes counted as two elements.

Since knots are most often entities unto themselves, they are first considered here as single units. Continuous repeats form a linear series.

The dominant direction of the interworking provides a basis for classification of all interlaced structures. This direction is determined by the relationship of the interlacing to the outer edges of the structure (with woven cloths, these are the selvages). This invariable avoids confusion when studying two views of the same subject.

The *carrick* is known in macramé as a Josephine knot, knitwear manufacturers call it a split knot, while rangers prefer the term cowboy knot. To sailors, it is a warp knot—although usage at sea is severely limited by the difficulty of untying it when wet. While the carrick embodies both function and ornament, its form is quintessentially decorative.

In the *Japanese crown* (or good luck) knot, a single element works both horizontally and vertically. In tying, it appears to be diagrammatic of a 2SOE structure. When tightened, this knot has an H-V configuration on one face, but is oblique on the other.

Although the *carrick bend* has been classified as an oblique knot, with a lateral series it can become multidirectional.

The decorative quality of interlocked carricks has enticed the imaginations of diverse peoples. This knot is the basis of epaulets, oblong mats, and circular wreaths. As connected links forming chains, carricks have been fashioned into delicate necklaces or enlarged to create room dividers.

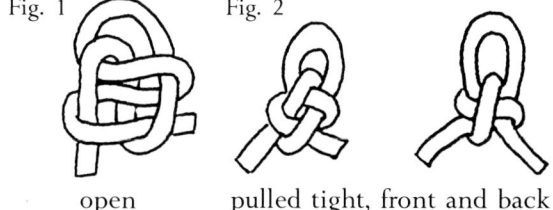

Fig. 1 open
Fig. 2 pulled tight, front and back

c. planar: knotted fabrics
   i. oblique

carrick mat

Chinese mat

   ii. horizontal-vertical

Turkish mat

   iii. multidirectional

sailor's breastplate

d. three-dimensional knots
   i. oblique
      (a). tubular

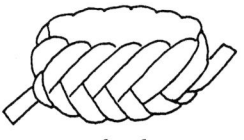

gaucho knot

      (b). spherical

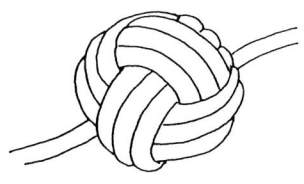

Chinese button

Worked as a plane, multidirectional knotting has the fascination of a labyrinth. The lacy rope patterns fashioned by bored seamen are instances of this virtuoso knotting. So are examples worked by the Moors of medieval Spain, who gave us the term macramé. Easel painters, unrestricted by the mechanics of physically controlling convoluted cords, have elaborated even further on the theme of decorative knotting. In a remarkable departure from his usual art, Albrecht Durer drew a series of knotwork patterns for embroidery—all based on engravings from the academy of Leonardo da Vinci (p. 264). Centuries earlier, Irish monks fused Coptic and native Celtic interlacing into the strapwork patterning identified with such early Christian manuscripts as *The Book of Kells*.

The single element that traverses the entire course of carrick mats distinguishes them from mats worked with a set of elements. Although this one or the flattened *Turk's head* could have been done with multiple elements, repeating the path with a single element solves the problem of finishing off numerous loose ends.

In the eighteenth century, when ornamental knotting reached its apex as a seaman's pastime, the carrick bend served as one of the basic units for virtuoso mats, bunk pockets, and picture frames.

For the *Chinese mat*, loops are overlapped and then united by being interlaced with the active ends. For many of these decorative knots, both concept and craft are so neat as to obscure methodology.

The *Turkish mat* "weave" is not, as it appears, a simple back-and-forth interlacing over opposing "elements"; its working requires six directional changes for a single element to accomplish this illusion.

Imagine the pleasure experienced when someone "invented" three-dimensional carricks. This probably occurred thousands of times as a center was accidently pushed out and tension rearranged. Often worked with wire or gimp cords, carrick knotted jewelry in the form of tubular rings, *monkey's fist* and *Chinese buttons*, or Turk's head bracelets are found throughout the world.

All of these knots, however intricate, are considered to be simple knots because they are independent entities. A complex knot consists of a knot plus a supplementary element, such as a suspended loop, or a "nonelement." By definition, the supplementary element can be removed without changing the basic structure of the knot. For instance, the *gunner's knot* is a carrick tied onto two support rings.

A single paired element forms the rigid plane of this traditional rug beater. The stress and tension of the circuituous interlacing adds considerably to its strength; so does the integration of the beater with its handle.

54 |
rug beater
knotting
1E, 1/1 multidirectional
rattan
W. 10″
The Philippines

A single element interlaced as a flat Turk's head knot and held within a circular frame becomes a serviceable trivet. Grouping small strands (in place of a single larger one) has made the disk flatter, firmer, and more elegant. 1E structures must be grouped by retracing the same path in successive courses—not, as in most interlacing—by working several elements simultaneously.

55 |
trivet
knotting
1E, 1/1 multidirectional
peeled cane
D. 6″
Japan, c. 1970

A hemispherical headhunter's cap from Borneo is similar to the ball (below) in size, form, and material, but the groups of single elements split into two elements, and the orders of interlacing vary.

56 |
cap
knotting
1E (and 2E) 1/1 or 2/1 or 2/2 multidirectional
rattan with argus pheasant and hornbill feathers
D. c. 9″
Borneo, late 19th century (?)
collection: Field Museum of Natural History, Chicago
photo: Ron Testa

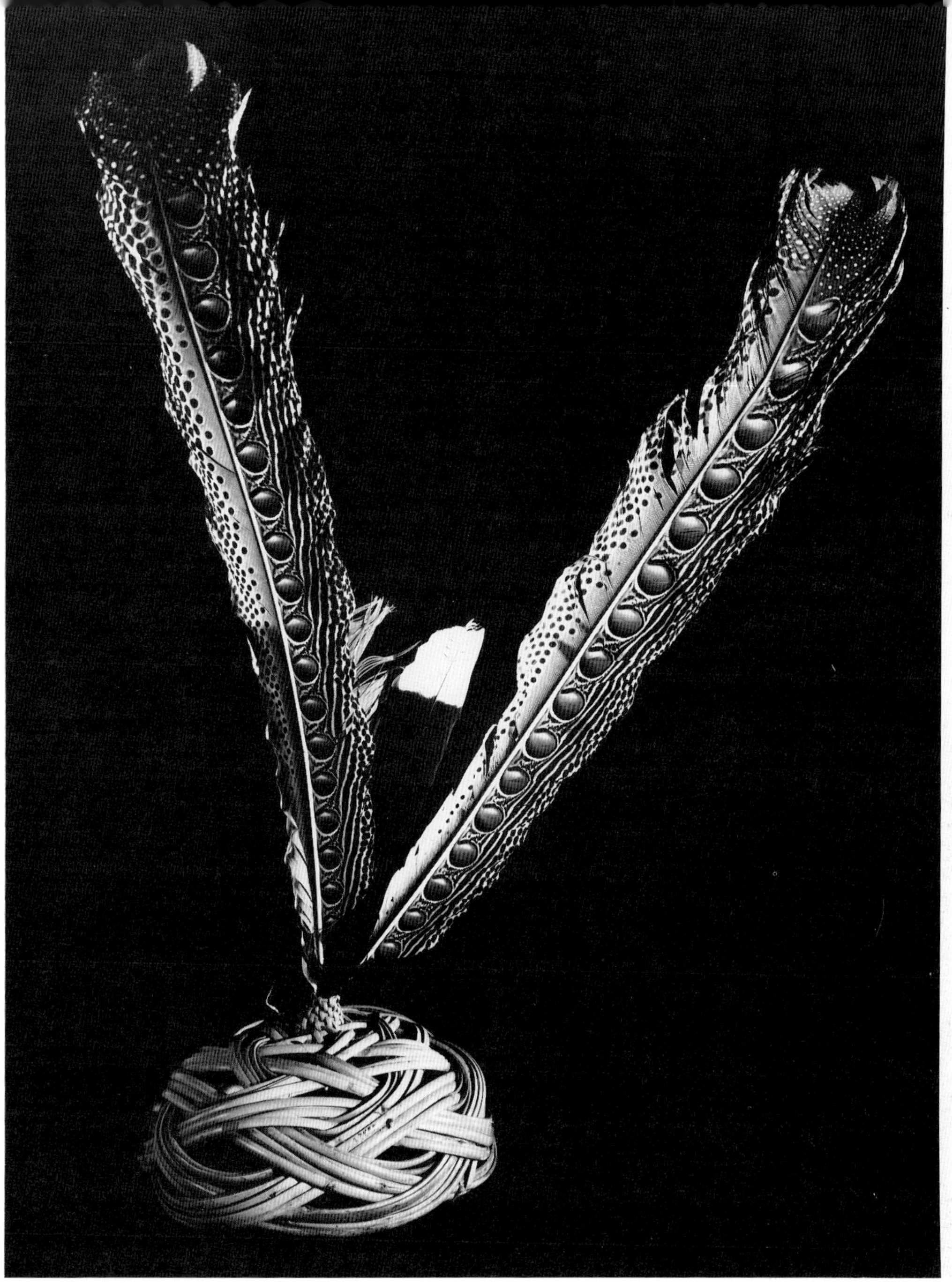

A traditional Southeast Asian ball game involves keeping such balls in the air with the knees, ankles, or heels. Although the rigid, durable structure resembles a 1E Turk's head knot, it is worked with six elements, each redoubled to read as nine strands across.

57 |
ball
knotting
6E, 1/1 multidirectional
rattan
D. 5″
Thailand, c. 1975

Classification 73

ii. horizontal-vertical

monkey's fist knot

2. distinguished by structure of interlacing

   a. simple (1E)

carrick knot

   b. complex (with supplementary element[s])

      i. primary, single knots

         (a). worked around passive "nonelement" (1E + X)

gunner's knot

         (b). worked around a core (1E + E)

Turk's head

In a rare structure (shown front and back), an active element first wraps around the crossings of two sets of passive elements then interlaces at the interstices. In a sense, the passive SOE are supplemental (1E + 2SOE), but their removal would result in serrated tapes.

58 |
covered box (detail)
knotting
1E, 2SOE, 1/1 oblique
slit palm fronds over split palm ribs
provenance unknown, c. 1980

Two Chinese finals effectively work silk braids in simple interlacing. At left, a "*good luck*" knot incorporates single picotee loops. The *Turk's head* (right) is applied in the manner of a lanyard. The spectacle cases are (left) silk tapestry and (right) satin stitch embroidery over satin, bound with a space-dyed flat braid.

59 |
(left) finial
square braiding
1E, 1/1 oblique
silk
c. 7½" × 2"
China, 19th century

(right) finial
tubular braiding over core
1E, 1/1 oblique
silk
c. 8" × 2"
China, 19th century
collection (both): Fashion Institute
  of Technology, New York

In her discussion of knotted fabrics, Irene Emery introduces two useful terms relating to complex knots. She says *suspended knots*, such as overhand ties or hitches, are used to secure an element around the *passive pendant loop* of a previous row—net making is an example. When the pendant loops are not actively engaged, the knots are not totally secure. However, she points out, *fixed knots* (such as the *carrick bend* and *Japanese bend*) actively engage the pendant loops (p. 78). Since both elements are active in fixed knots, we have included them among 2E structures.

This can be explained in the following terms:
  1E = a simple knot
  2E = a bend

A fabric mesh can be formed by suspended knots repeated at regular intervals. Typically, it is an open filigree.

By definition, all compound structures are two-layered. The intricate route traced by a single element to produce this double layering must have appealed to the Oriental imagination. The *Chinese temple knot* (p. 76) is found on cords suspending antique Chinese mirrors or carved ivories.

Classification 75

c. compound (with two layers) $\begin{pmatrix} 1E \\ 1E \end{pmatrix}$

(open)   (pulled tight)

Chinese temple knot

B. worked with two elements (2E)

1. distinguished by direction of interlacing

   a. in primary single knots

   i. oblique

      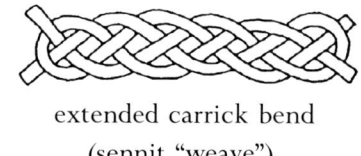

   carrick bend   extended carrick bend (sennit "weave")

   ii. horizontal-vertical

   Japanese bend

   b. linear: series of 2E knots

   carrick bend chain

76 Interlacing

Of the fabric-making knots, none is more satisfying than the *double carrick bend*. More often than square and granny knots, the carrick is worked sufficiently open to "read" the implied symbolism of its interlacing. At once simple and intricate, each is a perfectly integrated entity. Multiplied, the knots suggest cellular units—equal, undifferentiated, and interdependent.

This Philippine basket possesses a mystery and a sense of harmony not apparent in a two-dimensional photograph. Also obscured is a rigidity of form derived from the stress-tension of interlaced rattan. Note the bracing of the integrated handle.

60 |
basket
knotting
2E, 1/1 multidirectional
split rattan
24" × 12"
The Philippines, mid-20th century (?)

2E Knots

Two-element knots are frequently indistinguishable from their one-element cousins. As noted earlier, a bend joins two cords; the term is derived from the same root as "bind." The *carrick bend* and *Japanese bend* are typical.

Four projecting ends (instead of two plus a connecting loop) constitute the essential difference between the 1E and 2E carrick bends. The sennit "weave" example may be compared with the slit leather that was braided from two directions (p. 145).

The ornamental 2E Japanese bend achieves special color effects when connecting two silk cords of different hues. It, too, results in four "ends."

Series of 2E carricks are the essence of much decorative knotting. Known as Josephine knots, they provide one of the basic units for the limitless intricacies of macramé. In a series, they may be worked vertically, horizontally, or diagonally, then interrupted by single knots or untied segments.

c. planar: 2E knotted fabrics

   i. oblique suspended knots

carrick bend netting

   ii. horizontal-vertical

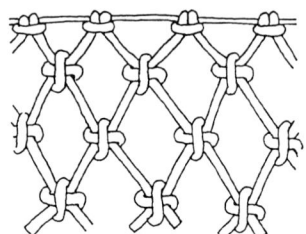

Japanese bend netting

d. three-dimensional

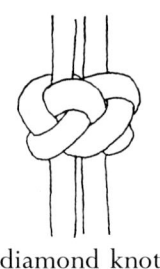

diamond knot

2. distinguished by structure of interlacing

   a. simple knots (2E)

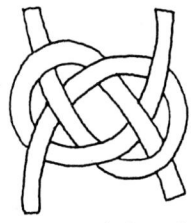

carrick bend

   b. complex knots

      i. with "nonelements" (2E + X)

carrick bend series with supplementary element

The planar knotting of macramé, employing many pairs of elements, might appear to be worked with one SOE; both the line of its start and the number of loose ends at the working edge are comparable to those of wide braids. Pins, often used to aid macramé construction, also bring forth associations with bobbin lace (1SOE). However, the 2E designation is correct: the individual unit is 2E, and so is its repeat.

Decorative fringes of macramé have been uncovered in ancient Babylonia and Assyria. An Arab-Moresque style flourished in medieval Spain and from there migrated to Italy and the New World. The ornate character of this knotting was revived for lacy trimmings of Victorian parasols and lamp shades; the mid-twentieth century has seen another revival.

Carrick bends can be used in netting. When Japanese bends are employed, one face would be H-V knots, the other oblique. Nets are typically worked from a foundation cord with elements passing around a simple tool, called a mesh stick, to obtain uniform spacing before tying each knot. Successive rows are tied into the pendant loops, producing a *diamond mesh*.

Filet lace is worked by embroidering (sometimes called "darning") across the openings of a netted mesh. Silhouettes of flowers, animals, or geometric shapes are filled in square by square, like images on a transparent graph paper.

Worked by discontinuously interlacing over a knotted net, filet laces have been made in many cultures.

61 |
filet lace (fragment)
1E + knotted net, 1/1 H-V
cotton
c. 10″ × 15″ (shown)
Sicily, 17th or 18th century

II. WITH ONE SET OF ELEMENTS: BRAIDING

A. flat braiding (1SOE)

1. distinguished by direction of interlacing

    a. linear

       i. oblique

          (a). symmetrical: two oblique lines of working

             [1]. elements worked from sides to center

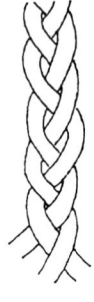

             [2]. elements worked from center to selvages

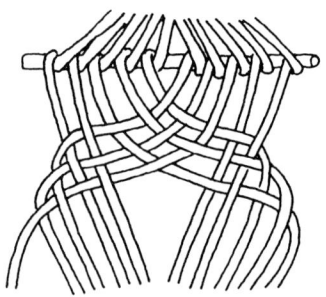

          (b). asymmetrical: one oblique line of working
               elements are worked from only one side

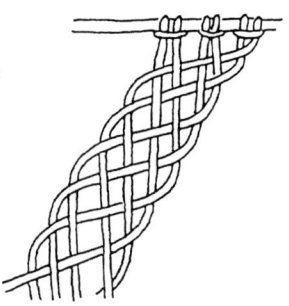

    b. planar: fabric-making braids

       i. wide braids

80 Interlacing

Braiding (1SOE)

In the Glossary, braiding is defined as the "oblique interlacing of one set of elements sharing a common starting point and worked with loose ends." If these ends are wound onto bobbins or looped into bundles to facilitate their interworking, this does not alter the basic technical concept.

Braids and braiding are terms that have become so generalized as to have almost lost significance. Dictionaries give such vague definitions as "narrow bands" or "decorative trimmings," implying all manner of passementerie.

Here, braids have been allocated to two major categories: *flat* and *three-dimensional*. Three categories are used by some classifiers, the third often being delegated to twined narrow bands.

Too frequently bizarre exceptions have also been given equal standing in other classifications. Since truly nonconforming examples only "muddy the waters," they are discussed separately in Chapter 5, which is devoted exclusively to braids. In the interest of clarity, only the basic forms have been represented here by diagrammatic examples.

Surveying this classification, braiding specialists might conclude that we have omitted two major flat braid structures. First there are the Peruvian repp braids, given so much attention by d'Harcourt and practitioners of so-called "finger weaving" or Indian braiding, and secondly, the structures called "running sennits" in Raoul Graumont and John Hensel's *Encyclopedia of Knots and Fancy Rope Work*. Both of these structures are discussed in Chapter 5.

In flat braids, the course of the interlacing elements is an oblique path to the selvage and then back to the opposite edge. The term "flat" indicates that the work takes place on a level plane, i.e., elements do not move in a circular path or in eccentric crisscrosses.

Flat braids have been divided into two general types: *symmetrical* and *asymmetrical*. The first group is subdivided into braids with outside elements alternately interlacing toward the center and those in which the center elements interlace outward to the selvages.

With more emphasis on methodology than structure, some specialists differentiate between braids with *odd* and with *even numbers of elements*. Their thesis is that in those with an odd number of strands, both outside elements first pass over then under the adjacent strands to create a symmetrical braid. With an even number, one outside element first passes over/under and the other side commences with under/over, which is asymmetrical. But is a three-strand braid truly symmetrical?

There is no debate, however, about obviously asymmetrical constructions, such as those braids continuously interlaced from one side only.

Wide braids have no limits to their proportions when they are worked from a line with loose ends. Plaited mats, worked similarly, could even be considered to be braids.

ii. interworked parallel braids

    (a). with exchanging elements

Chinese braiding

    (b). with interlinked elements

    (c). with interconnecting elements

neolithic braiding

    (d). with interlacing between braids

iii. intersecting braids

    (a). interlaced at meeting point

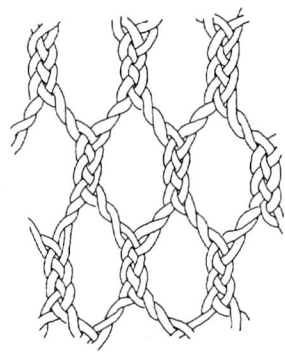

    (b). interlaced at crossing

The so-called *Chinese braid* becomes a slit fabric as adjacent SOEs intermittently split and rejoin (Pl. 51).

The difficulties of working a wide braid with numerous loose ends can be circumvented by several means. The most common method of forming a wide-braided fabric is additive: successive units link into adjacent braids at the selvages.

Crocodile ridge braids consist of two parallel braids that are linked while being plaited simultaneously. These are commonly made with leather thongs, which accentuate the central meeting line.

In the rare neolithic braid, joins are integrated into the construction. Unplaited elements, extending from each interstice, are successively incorporated into the interlacing of the adjacent braid.

62, 63, and 65.   The three elements of neolithic braids can be worked in a linear progression or as a plane. The flat disks of the market basket in Plate 62 are determined by circular frames. The bracelet (to protect against snake bites; Pl. 65) is densely worked, in a manner similar to handles of brushes for starching ikat warps in Borneo. In the early 1980s, Sherri Smith created large planar hangings in undulating neolithic braid technique combined with interlacing (Pl. 63).

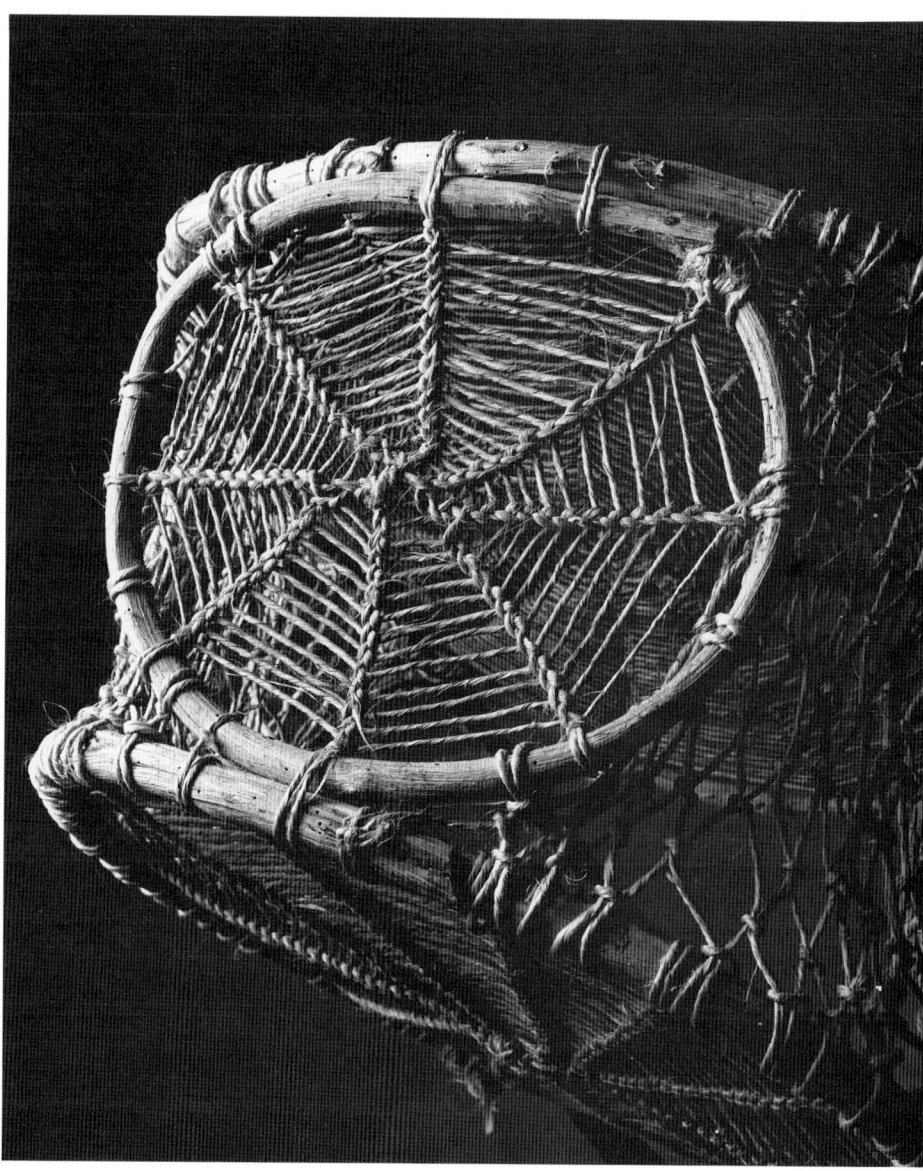

62 |
basket (detail)
1SOE, 1/1 radial
maguey
southern Mexico, c. 1975

2. distinguished by structure of interlacing

    a. simple (1SOE)

    b. complex

        i. with "nonelements" (1SOE + X)

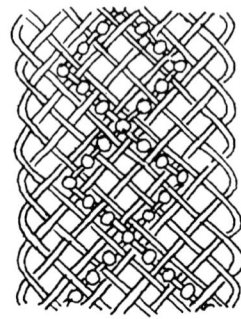

        ii. with passive supplementary element(s) (1SOE + E)

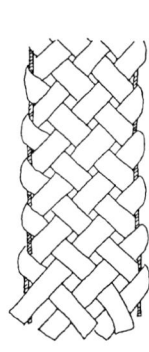 

        iii. with active supplementary element(s) (1SOE + E)

            (a). parallel to basic element

            (b). worked independently of basic elements

            (a)   (b)

    c. compound flat braids $\left(\dfrac{1SOE}{1SOE}\right)$

        i. layers connected only at selvages

        ii. exchanging layers

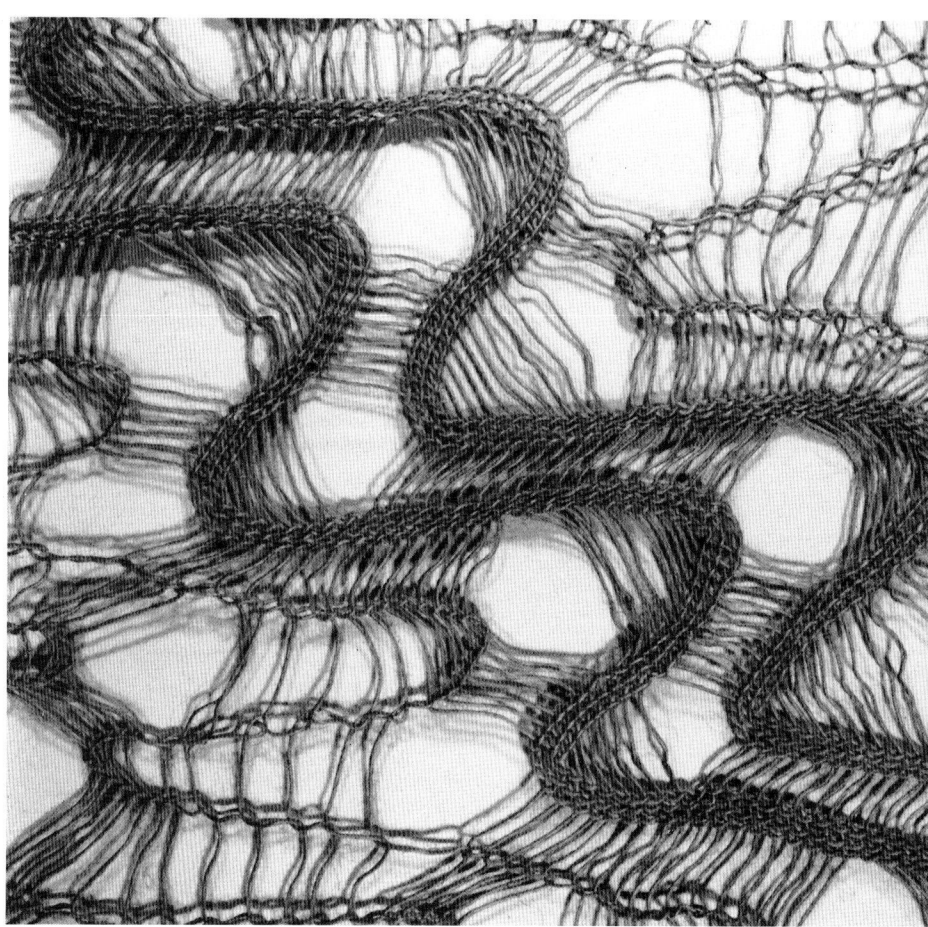

63 |
Meander, c. 1980 (detail)
Sherri Smith, USA
1SOE, 1/1 multidirectional
hemp

Graumont and Hensel's encyclopedia (p. 270) goes one step further by showing examples in which two intricate braids can be joined by interlacing—and all formed simultaneously, a tour de force available to anyone who can follow their instructions.

Braided mats are often the result of a series of narrow braids successively joined by interlacing around a common element. For some mats and baskets a single braid turns 180 degrees at the top and bottom edges and is connected to itself with a supplementary element (see African mats on p. 139). If this element was removed, a curving long braid would reappear.

Braids can also be joined by interlacing as they intersect, as seen in the Vietnamese hammock on page 137. In the Brazilian hammock on the same page, two braids engage so as to make a right angle turn.

In the nineteenth century, the Creek Indians of Georgia used small, white trade beads to outline the diamond repeats of their braided sashes.

Sometimes the supplementary elements, integrated into the structure of the interlacing, become, in fact, the raison d'être. For the fish trap on page 126, braiding anchors the verticals; both are interdependent for the gently sloping framework. Braiding around such stationary verticals may so resemble twining as to be mislabeled. Another instance occurs in braids used as edgings when the braiding elements are inserted into the border of a basket or hat.

For the broad compound structure, called *Mexican double braiding* by Mary Meigs Atwater in *Byways in Handweaving* (p. 62), the elements of each layer exchange positions at regular intervals to form an alternating diamond pattern (see p. 135).

B. three-dimensional braiding with elements encircling center: "hollow" braids (1SOE)

1. distinguished by direction of interlacing

    a. linear

       i. oblique: tubular

       ii. horizontal-vertical

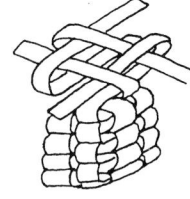

       iii. spiral

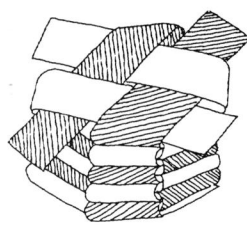

    b. planar (see notes on comparison with obliquely plaited baskets)

2. distinguished by structure of interlacing

    a. simple (1SOE)

An African baby rattle is remarkable for its rare instance of braiding with only two elements. As shown in the unraveled band at top, this is a fold-braid, possible only with flat material. The handle is a tubular braid. The rattles are interlaced of two elements with twisted strands at the corners.

64 |
rattle
(band) braiding
1SOE, 1/1 horizontal-oblique
palm fronds
West Africa, c. 1970

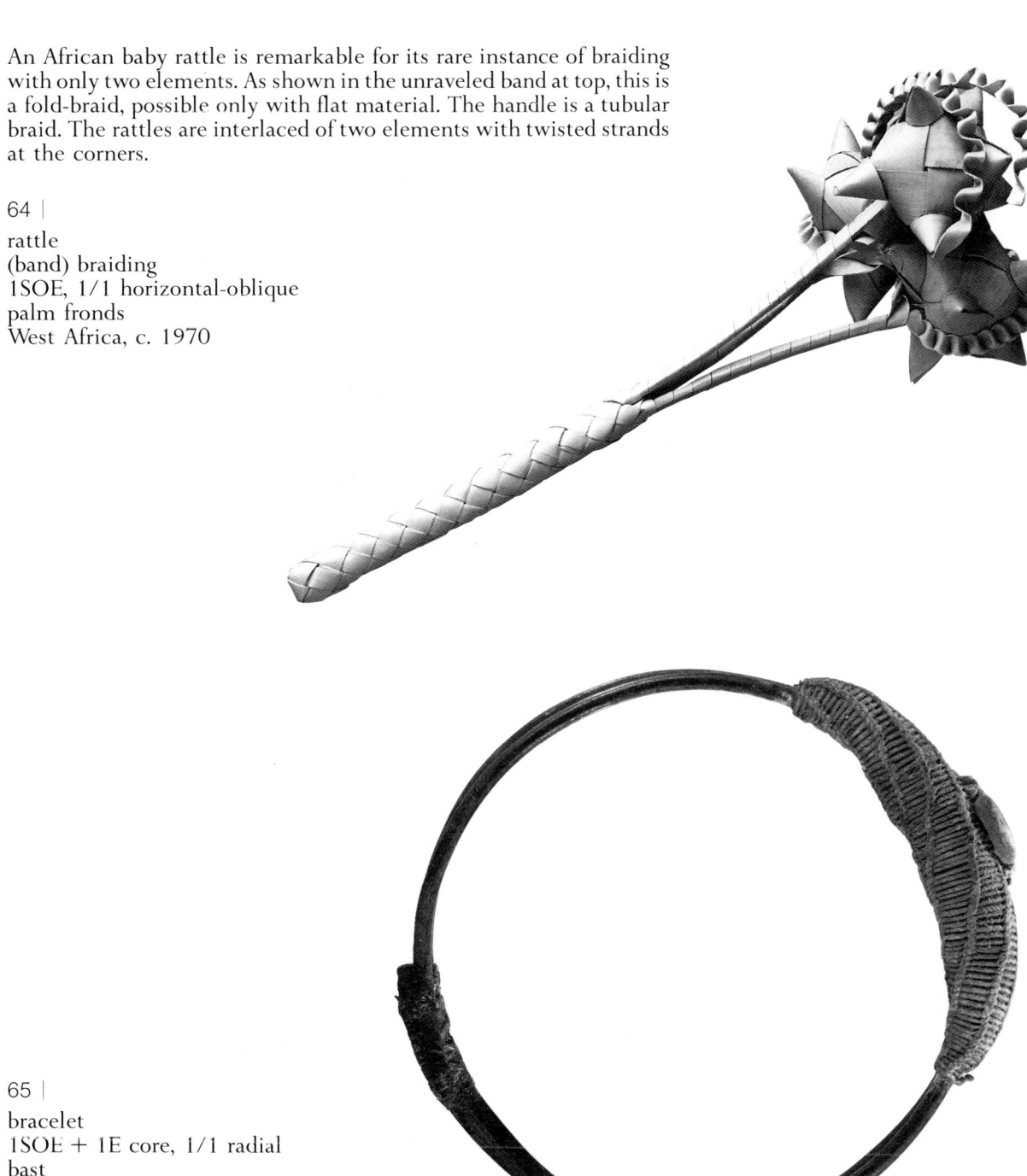

65 |
bracelet
1SOE + 1E core, 1/1 radial
bast
Guiana
collection: Musée de l'Homme, Paris
photo: D. Rousard

The key difference between the two types of three-dimensional braids is obvious in cross-sections showing the positions of the elements of each. In the first category, elements encircle the center, whereas elements of the second type cross the center to form so-called *solid braids*.

The "hollow" centers of *tubular braids* range from a potential in a seemingly solid section to a void of considerable diameter. The cylindrical wall of an obliquely interlaced basket is comparable to a tubular braid. In both cases, elements are worked around the circumference in right-hand and left-hand directions.

Each element of a *square braid* passes in both horizontal and vertical directions as it overlaps and folds. "Fold braids" and spiraling "corn dollies" are analyzed further in Chapter 5.

Classification **87**

b. complex, with core (1SOE + E)

　　i. oblique

　　ii. horizontal-vertical

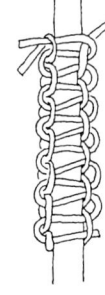

c. compound: $\left(\dfrac{1\text{SOE}}{1\text{SOE}}\right)$

　　i. active: braid in a braid

　　　　(a). both braids worked simultaneously

　　　　(b). outer braid worked around completed inner braid

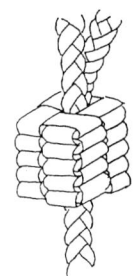

scout lanyard

　　ii. active/passive: braiding elements and core elements repeatedly exchange roles

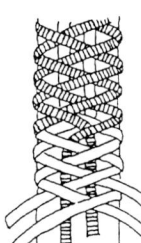

C. three-dimensional braiding with elements crossing center: "solid" braids (1SOE)

When a core is present, a braid is usually tubular. Although such braids may feel solid, the core is a supplementary element and removable from the basic tube. A maypole is such a typical example of complex braiding that the term is commonly applied to industrially produced braids worked around a core. For the lanyard, so familiar to boy scouts, a square H-V fold braid is worked around a completed round braid core.

A pre-Columbian zebra-striped braid has been the subject of many scholarly writings. The consensus is that, at times, the dark-colored inner elements serve as a core for the oblique braiding of the light-colored elements. At regular intervals the light and dark elements exchange positions—so that the passive elements become active to produce the striping. Adele Cahlander writes that there are five methods of attaining zebra-striped cords for slings; other techniques include spiral wrapping around the core, interlinking, wrapping of individual outer elements, and tubular 2SOE interlacing.

Compound (two-layered) braids can be formed when the outside turns of elements on both layers are linked to produce common selvages. However, flattened tubular braids such as shoelaces are NOT compound.

Effects similar to "double weave" can be achieved with compound braids. On page 103 of her manual, Noémi Speiser discusses vertical striping on narrow braids by continuous interexchange of two different-colored layers.

The simplest form of solid braiding involves a simple crossover at the center without interlinking or twining; the four-strand oblique braid is typical. A Jewish ceremonial candle made in this manner demonstrates that even brittle wax can adapt to this form.

Speiser has diagramed a hand-held Tibetan braid in which two opposing pairs of elements exchange positions, crossing the center. The braid is rotated 45 degrees, and the interchange repeated for the other two opposing pairs of elements. After each step, the loose ends are tucked under the lower fingers to maintain tension. The same braid can be worked with greater ease on a Japanese round stand for making *kumihimo*.

D. frame braiding: interlaced sprang

1. distinguished by structure of interlacing

   a. simple (1SOE)

   i. flat

   ii. circular "wrap"

   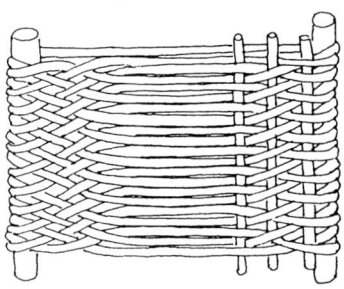

   b. compound: two layers $\left(\dfrac{1\text{SOE}}{1\text{SOE}}\right)$

Frame braiding (or *interlaced sprang*) is distinguished by simultaneous interlacing from both ends of a web, finishing with a central fastening line. The framework on which it is constructed solves the braider's quandry of how to prevent many loose ends from becoming entangled. The frame and fastening line also remove these structures from consideration as conventional braids.

For sprang, one continuous element is wound around two ends of a (usually vertical) "frame" in the same manner that a simple warp is wound on a frame; this is considered as one SOE. Unlike weaving, however, there are no horizontal elements. Each vertical is interworked successively over and under adjacent elements and thereby takes an oblique path to the selvage. At the same time that elements are worked at one end of the frame, a mirror image of the interlacing occurs at the other end. After each successive row, rods are pushed toward each end to retain the duplicate work. When interworking of the two end portions finally meets in the center, all rods are removed except for the central one. This is not pulled out until a join is chained off or another holding element inserted. If the central holding feature is removed, the entire structure returns to its original state of parallel verticals. Sprang may also be interlinked or twine plaited. Different methods can be combined in the same structure. Another variation, called "circular warp sprang" by Collingwood, is explained in Chapter 5. Collingwood also explains the technique for *double interlaced sprang* in his book *The Techniques of Sprang*. Back and front elements are exchanged in the manner of double weave.

E. bobbin lace (1SOE)

1. distinguished by direction of interlacing

    a. horizontal-vertical

    b. horizontal plus 2 diagonals
       (looks like 3SOE interlacing)

    c. oblique

this example includes a, b, c

2. distinguished by structure of interlacing

    a. simple (1SOE)

    b. complex (1SOE + E)

Bobbin lace is a 1SOE structure, yet it is—in actuality—an anomaly. While complying with the basic definition of a braid (all elements are positioned from a line or point and ends can be considered as "loose" even though they are wrapped on bobbins), the conformity stops there. Bobbin lace can take on the structures of 1, 2, or 3SOE interlacing, as well as twining. The enlarged photograph on page 94 illustrates these variations. Filet lace is sometimes done over a bobbin lace netting.

The border between 1SOE and 2SOE structures is not absolute; there are several borderline stuctures that do not fit into any one compartment.

Rope splicing, for instance, straddles the two categories. With an *end splice* (to prevent unraveling of a rope end), the several plies are turned back to interlace with the main body of the cord and would be classified as 1SOE. The same would be true with the looped single end of an *eye splice*. In the case of two rope ends joined by splicing (reciprocal interlacing), the designation should be 2SOE.

Two other structures fall into the gray area between 1SOE and 2SOE interlacing. First there is the question of obliquely plaited mats in which work commences from one corner with new elements added as the corner enlarges (left). Should this be considered as 1SOE since work progresses from a point, or 2SOE because there are two opposing "sets" of elements?

Derived from plaiting, a trick method of weaving triangular shawls involves cutting each successive warp element to interlace it horizontally as a "weft." This allows a natural diagonal selvage to emerge with two sets of free ends for fringes. 1SOE *becomes* 2SOE.

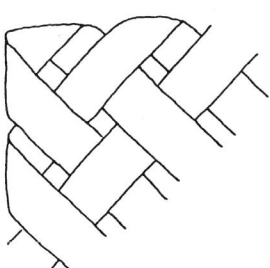

Fig. 3

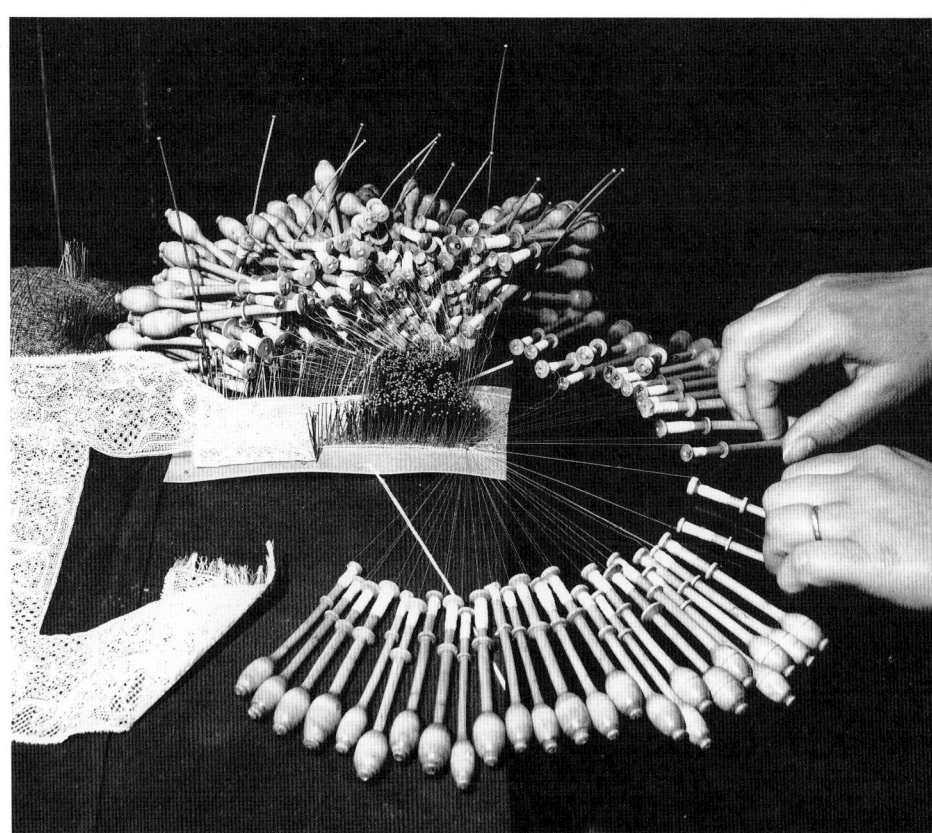

Bobbin lace is the most versatile of all interlacings with one SOE and, potentially, the most intricate. Several horizontal-vertical structures are used as well as oblique ones, plus interlinking, wrapping, twining, and knotting—in an extraordinary range of densities.

Here a border is being worked with more than 100 bobbins and a similar number of pins to determine the spacing.

66
border
bobbin lace
1SOE
linen
courtesy: Belgian Institute for Information and Documentation, Brussels

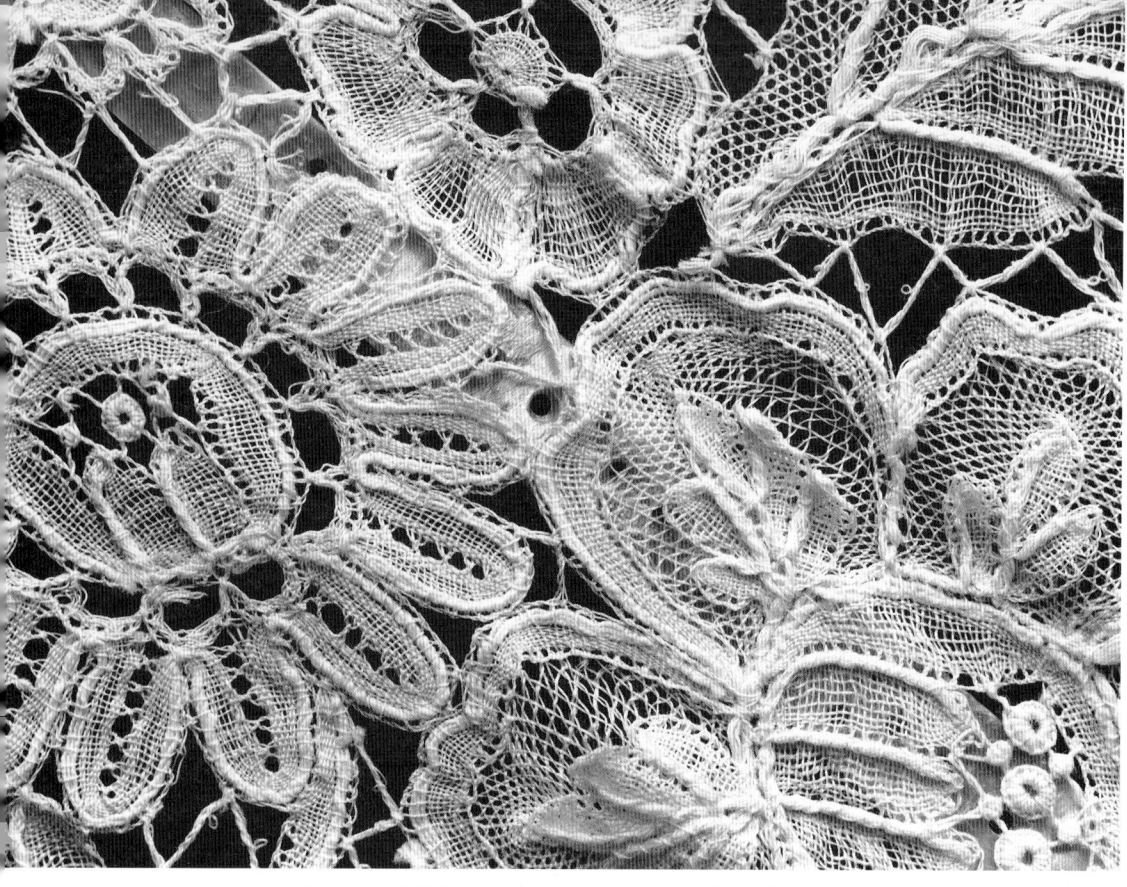

Bobbin lace, a 1SOE structure, can take on 2 and 3SOE configurations and can also be worked in nonlinear shapes and directions. This enlargement illustrates some of the possibilities.

67 |

fan (detail, enlarged 5 times)
duchesse bobbin lace
1SOE
linen
Belgium, late 19th century
collection: Mrs. Alfred Bellaire
photo: Peter Greenland

68–69. Of the modern masters of bobbin lace, none are so well known as Luba Krejci of Prague and Liselotte Siegfried of Zurich.

Siegfried is eclectic in her selection of a broad range of techniques, most meticulous in her execution of them, while remaining consistent in her miniature format and material. Compositions are asymmetrical and organic. The depth of her small reliefs is exaggerated by their play of highlight and shadow. Similar forms may be worked with bobbins or a needle, directly on the canvas or stitched to it later.

Since the 1950s, Krejci has included bobbin lace technique in large-format pictorial filagrees (see *The Art Fabric: Mainstream*, p. 87). Typically involving human forms in delicate balances of engineered structure and fine drawing, Krejci's work is extraordinary for its fragile power. In Plate 69 (opposite), a single figure, densely black, is entrapped as if by a cosmic spider.

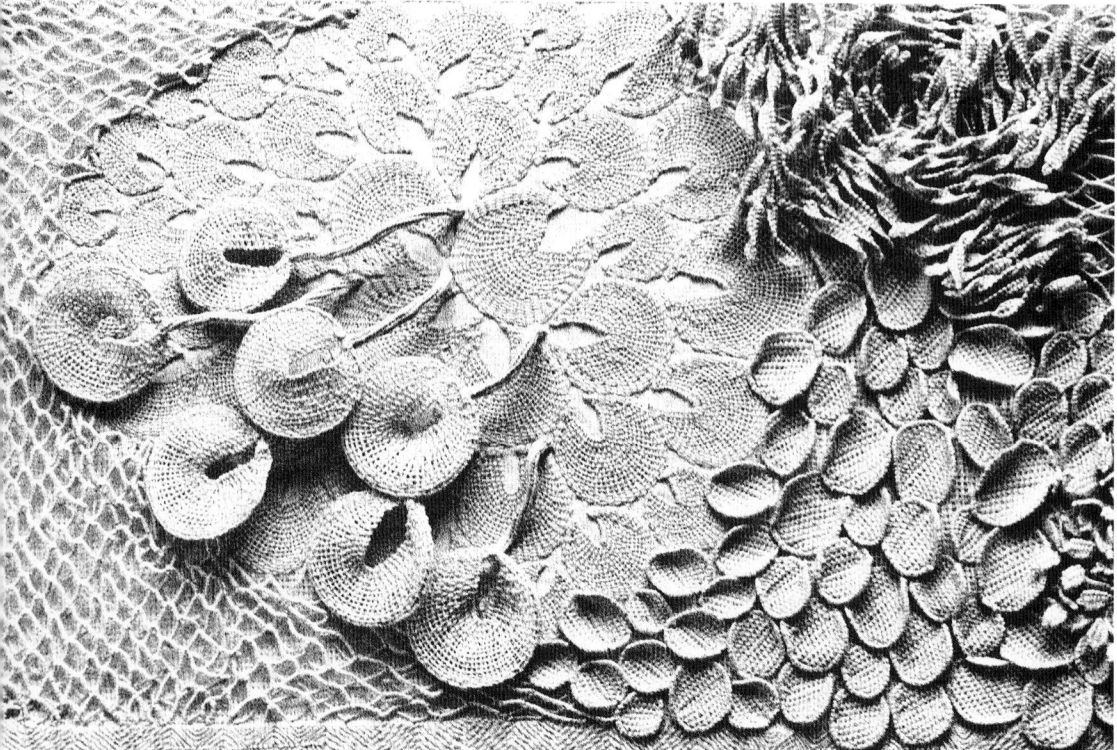

68 |

Der Teich, 1974
Liselotte Siegfried, Switzerland
embroidery and bobbin lace
linen
8⅝" × 26"
courtesy: Heidi Bauman, Kloten, Switzerland

69 |

Morpheus
Luba Krejci, Czechoslovakia
various interlacings
photo: Michal Krejci
courtesy: Jacques Baruch Gallery, Chicago

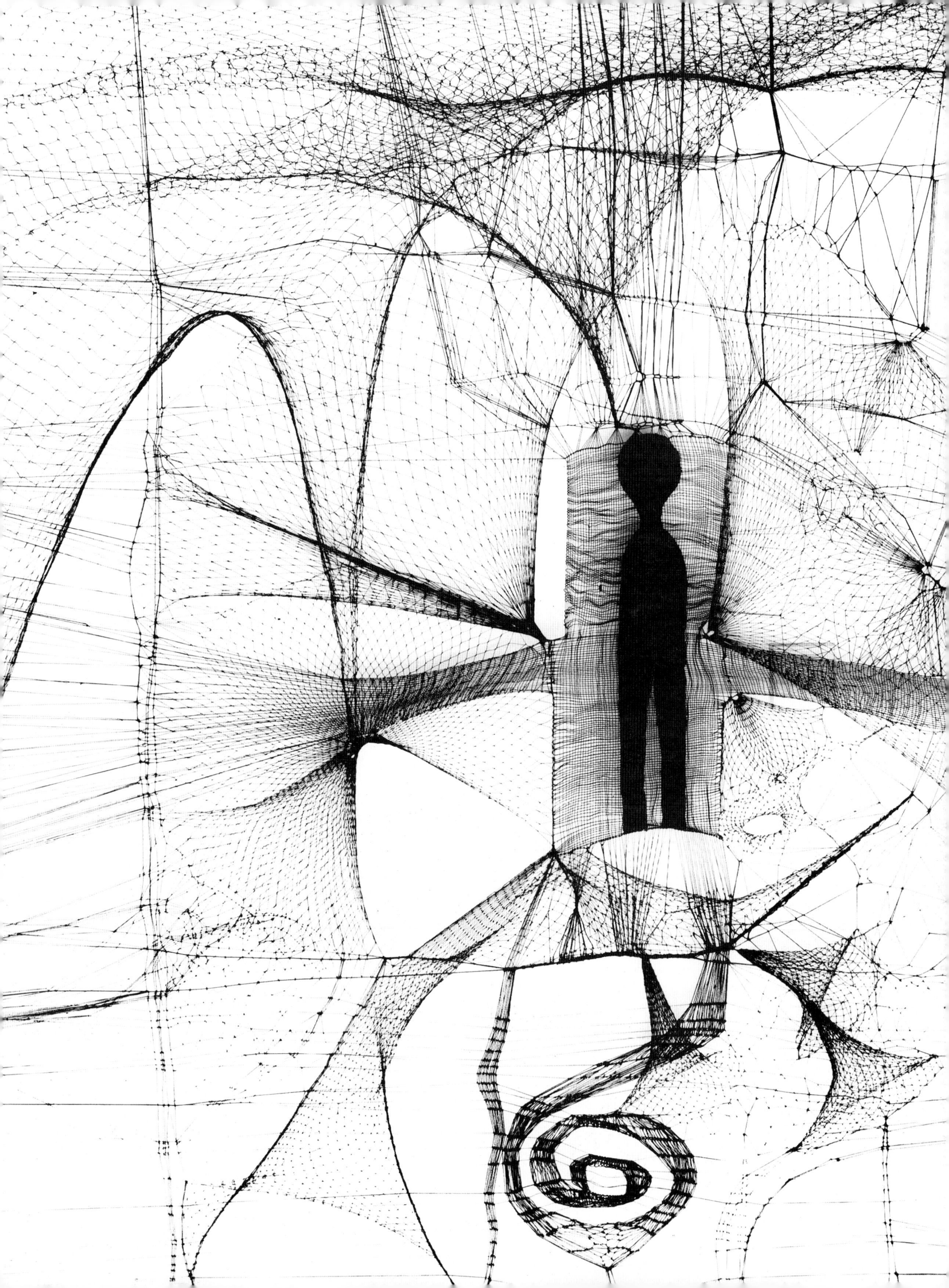

III. INTERLACINGS WITH TWO SETS OF ELEMENTS (2SOE)

A. distinguished by direction of interlacing

1. linear

    a. horizontal-vertical

2. planar

    a. oblique

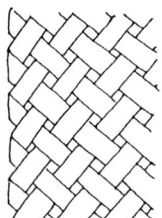

    b. horizontal-vertical

    c. spiral-radial

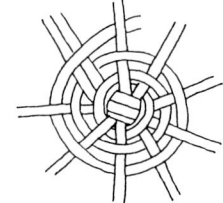

Two Sets of Elements (2SOE)

Structures with 2SOE are so dominant among present-day interlacings that an extensive explanation here seems unnecessary. While it is true that most other classifiers have laid their primary emphasis on woven fabrics, detailing the most minute differences, a glance at the chart on page 66 shows a new perspective: weaving appears as only one among numerous structures. Further, looms do not exist in some cultures; for others their use is extremely limited. Plaited 2SOE structures, on the other hand, have bordered on universality—for millennia. They are so mutable that they span the scale from inch-long plaited toys and miniscule baskets to architectural components (p. 247). Between the two extremes are a near infinity of applications, in a myriad of forms, materials, and interlacings.

As was mentioned in the section on 1SOE structures, H-V tapes should not be called "braids" merely because they are long and narrow. This misnomer is all too common in the textile industry. Although there are simple four-element structures in which a single element continuously interlaces across the other three, or both outer elements are interlaced through the same "shed," these still result in two differentiated sets of elements.

Mats are the most ubiquitous application of 2SOE oblique interlacing. They occur, with simple to intricate patterning, on nearly every continent—and throughout the centuries. As we discussed in the Origins chapter, impressions of such mats have been uncovered on Neolithic ceramic shards.

Some round mats and bases of baskets are examples of flat spiral-radial 2SOE structures. Work is usually done with an uneven number of spokes so that the over-under sequence can be repeated as the spiral progresses. This is achieved by pairing or splitting one of the radiating elements. An alternative method is to interlace simultaneously with two parallel elements, one passing over, the other under each spoke.

Horizontal-vertical 2SOE structures have diverse shape potentials beyond the familiar flat planes of loom-woven textiles. The flexibility of some basketry materials and rigidity of others permit inspiration from the curves and angles typical of ceramic containers; others are unique to fibers.

The first spokes of "melon" baskets are held in place with an *ojo de dios*, "eye of God"; interlacing proceeds around this skeletal hemisphere. *Ose*, or hen baskets, believed to date back to the druids, have their spokes forming complete circles with two round openings in the near-sphere to allow the arm to pass through for carrying.

Tubes and tubular rings form a third type of 2SOE spiral interlacing (see pp. 169, 175).

3. three-dimensional

   a. oblique

   b. horizontal-vertical

   c. radial

   d. vertical-oblique

B. distinguished by structure of interlacing

   1. simple

   2. complex

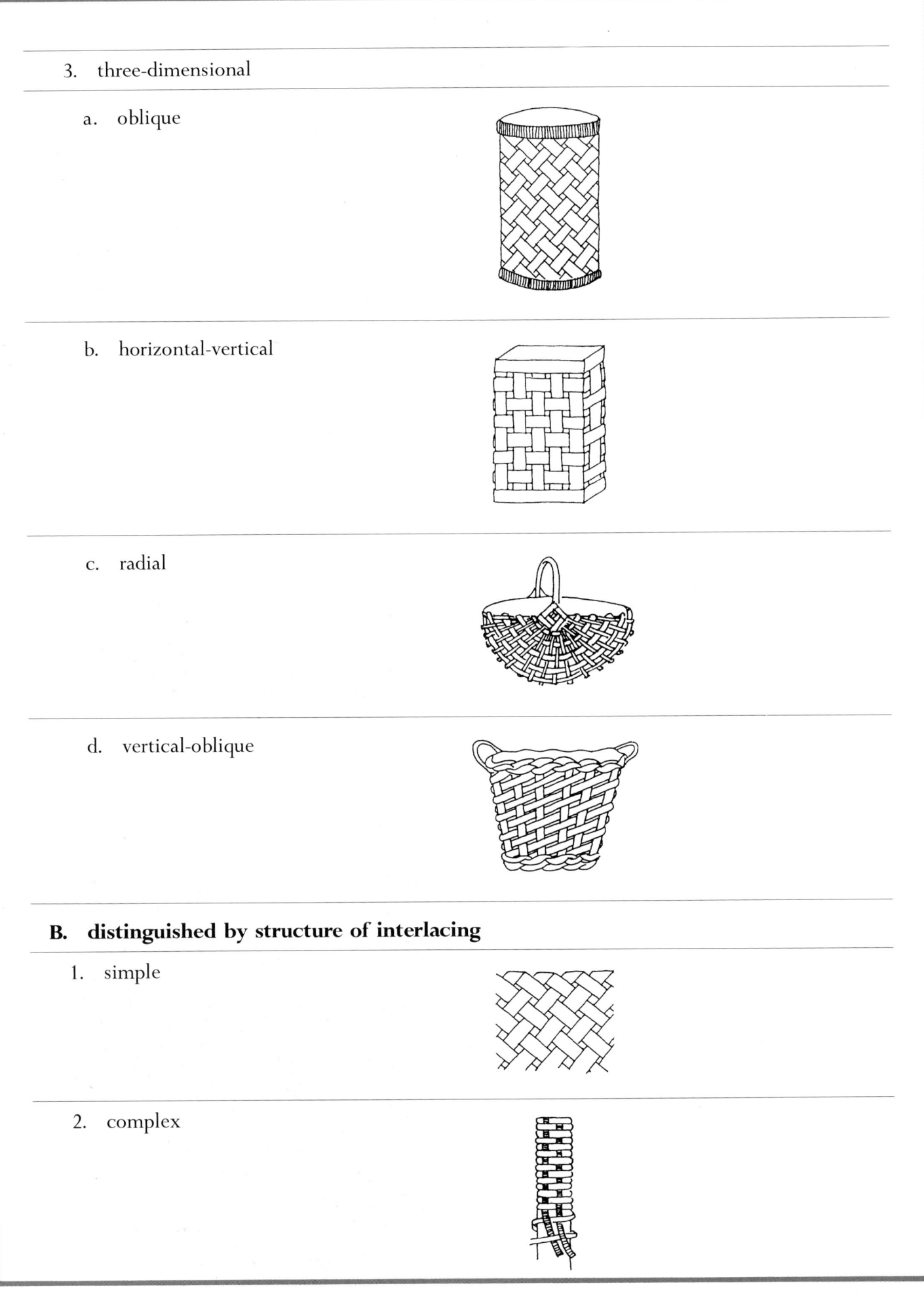

One particular 2SOE structure occurs almost exclusively with the rigid strands of wickerwork. This is shallow, oblique interlacing on vertical spokes. The course of each strand is shortened by this stratagem, since it is not forced to repeatedly encircle the entire circumference (as in H-V tubular interlacing). There is also less bending of rigid or brittle elements, and an unattractive overlapping at the joins of strands is avoided. The base of the vertical spokes is usually secured with several rows of twining, which this whole structure resembles at first glance. A wicker laundry basket is a typical example.

Supplementary "nonelements" like beads, feathers, and sequins are familiar in woven cloths; they are equally prevalent in other 2SOE structures. Such ornamentation does not affect the interlaced structure, but it may hide it completely.

Emery says that the term *brocading* refers to "patterning by means of supplemental wefts." Brocading, a textile term that is not appropriate to other interlacings, may also be formed by supplementary warps as well as by additional sets of warps and wefts.

Weft brocades, sometimes referred to as "embroidery on the loom," may so resemble embroidery that a definitive identification may require piercing the basic strands with a needle.

A rare old Japanese basket covers a flower container with a skeleton of horizontal twining over which finely slit and steamed supplementary elements interlace in oblique curves.

70 |
basket for *ikebana*
twining, plaiting
2SOE, twined H-V + 1SOE 5/5
bamboo
H. c. 9″
collection: University Ethnographic Museum,
 Zurich, Spoerri Collection
photo: Monique Jacot

a. with supplementary element (2SOE + X)

b. with supplementary set of elements (2SOE + 2SOE)

   i. carried with basic elements

   ii. independent of basic elements

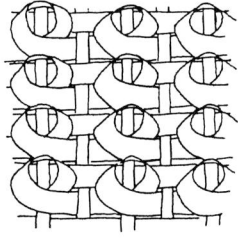

c. with supplementary sets of elements (2SOE + SOEs)
(supplementary SOEs worked in several directions)

3. compound: $\left(\dfrac{2SOE}{2SOE}\right)$

a. connecting layers

   i. joined at selvages

   ii. engaged intermittantly

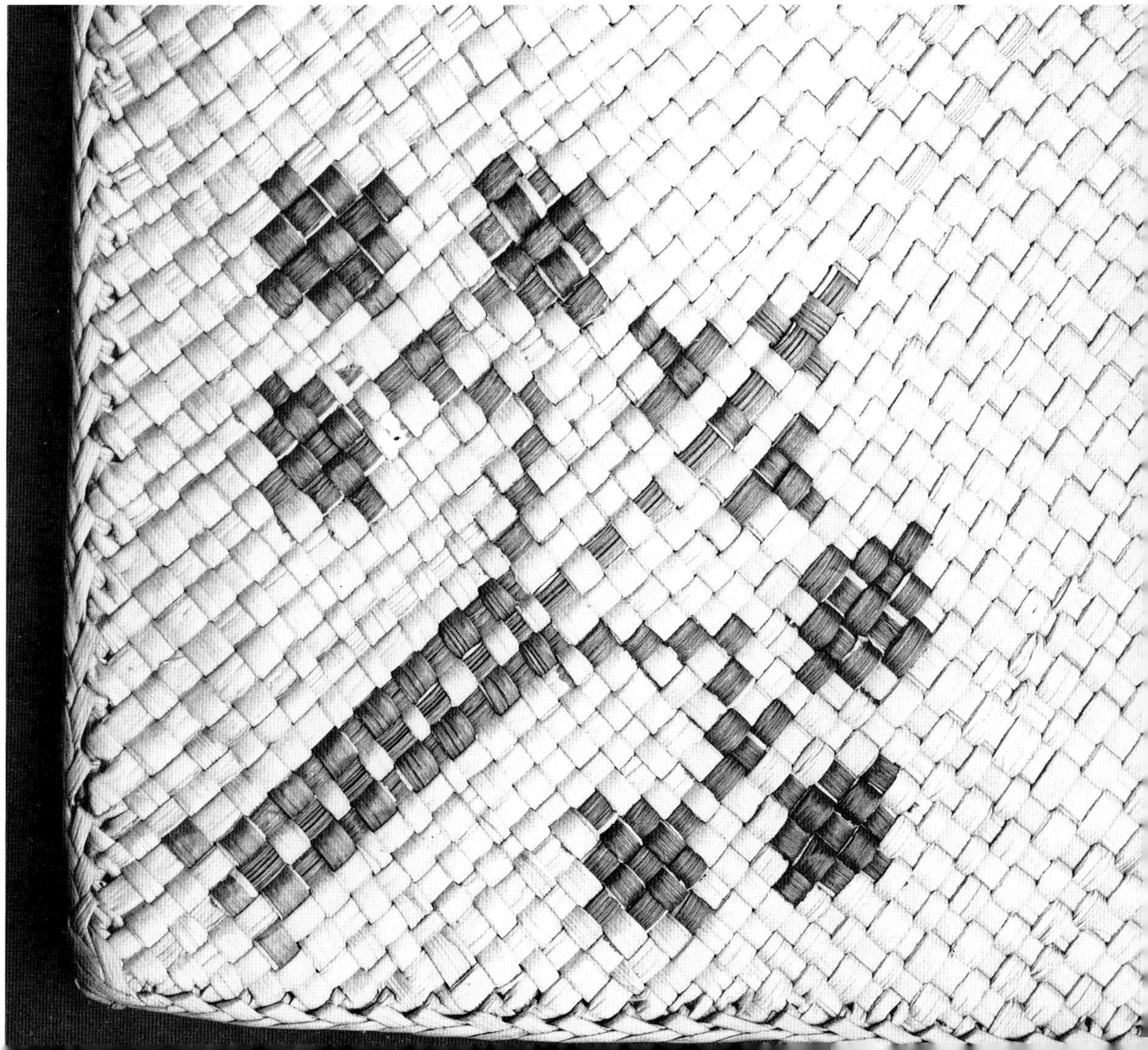

71–75. Although these examples of plaiting with supplementary elements vary in form, they have in common a supplement running in the same course as the basic structure. The Indonesian matting in Plate 71 has a set of continuous supplementary strands running in one direction only. The corners of a Philippine cushion, Plate 72, are patterned with discontinuous colored strands laced over the base, then discreetly clipped. The stars of a small basket from India (Pl. 73) are similarly worked. The cover is notable for its relief pattern of twisted stands.

The decorative loops of this Canadian basket (Pl. 74) formed with a continuous strand are interlaced over each basic horizontal. Roland Jung of Switzerland uses a similar technique on forms worked over and under a wire grid (Pl. 75).

73 |
lidded box
complex hexagonal plaiting
3SOE—3SOE, H-V oblique
palm fiber
India, ca. 1975

74 |
basket, 1980
Cecilia Thivas, Canada
2SOE + 1SOE, 1/1 H-V
wood
6" × 7"

102   Interlacing

Continuous supplementary SOEs may follow the course of the basic elements. Often their patterning is created with floats over the base structure—"spotting" motifs against a ground. They may be in several colors or materials.

In other instances the supplementary SOEs may be discontinuous, i.e., not extending from selvage to selvage, but—like tapestry—turning 180 degrees into the motif. Or, they may be worked only through the motif, using short strands.

Sometimes supplementary SOEs float over or under the base structure. These floats may be clipped closely, so that they are barely visible, or left long to form a fringe.

Those continuous supplements that are added after interlacing—to provide surface decoration—can usually be distinguished from paired or grouped elements.

Imbrication is a term for supplementary elements peculiar to patterning the flat strands of basketry. Derived from the pattern of overlapped roof tiles, the technique, although common to coiling, can also be applied to 2 and 3SOE interlacing (see pp. 102, 103, 180).

An oblique supplementary SOE can be interlaced over an H-V construction and vice versa.

75 |

Faltungen, 1985 (detail)
Roland Jung, Swtizerland
grid + 2SOE, 2/1 H-V
wire, plastic film

b. exchanging layers

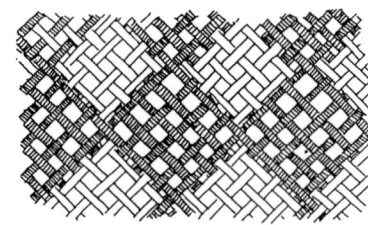

4. compound-complex

    a. two layers with supplementary element $\left(\dfrac{2SOE}{2SOE}+E\right)$

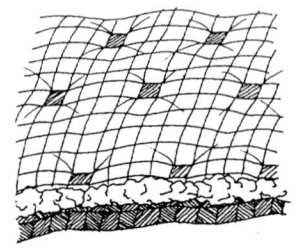

    b. two layers with supplementary sets of elements $\left(\dfrac{2SOE}{2SOE}+SOE\right)$

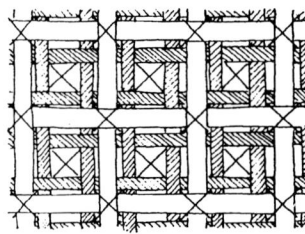

IV. INTERLACINGS WITH THREE SETS OF ELEMENTS (3SOE)

A. distinguished by direction of interlacing

1. planar

    a. two oblique sets + H or V

    b. one oblique + H + V

Compound layers may be connected by several methods. In the double cloth of weaving, the author agrees with Emery that if there is only one selvage join so the textile can be unfolded when cut from the loom, this is not a true compound structure.

Shereen LaPlantz gives directions for plaiting multilayered envelopes with each level connected on two adjacent selvages to produce an accordionlike effect. These would not be highly practical as containers, since half of the openings must always be inverted (see p. 100).

Compound structures may combine two different orders of interlacing, such as 1/1 with a 3/3 twill. The scale or density of the two layers may also vary. (Even the number of SOEs may be different; for example, 3SOE over a 2SOE. See p. 110.)

Typically, limited areas of two (differently colored) layers are repeatedly exchanged to achieve patterning. Those basketry materials that are colored only on one surface make these patterns nearly invisible on the reverse side.

Intermittent tie-downs are a method for obtaining more widespread interconnections between the layers.

When padding is the supplementary element added to the compound structure, it is usually passive.

While all pile structures involve at least one supplementary SOE, the velvet loom produces a compound-complex structure with a third warp working vertically between the two layers of cloth. The distinctive pile results when the layers are cut apart.

The diagram opposite (4b), after LaPlantz, shows an H-V open interlacing imposed on a more compact structure—all are secured with two oblique supplementary SOEs.

Three Sets of Elements (3SOE)

Interlacing with 3SOE may take one of several configurations. The most common version, utilizing two oblique sets plus a horizontal (or vertical) set, forms hexagonals interspersed with equilateral triangles. The open mesh and ease of working in a 1/1 interlacing make this practical for packaging, animal cages, and sieves. Conversely, hexagonally worked *mad weave*, with three layers of material throughout, is probably the most solid and compact of all interlacings—and, judging from its name, one of the most difficult to accomplish.

The asymmetrical structure produced with an H+V+one oblique is much rarer.

Sherri Smith has eliminated the open mesh typical of 3SOE in her hangings; instead her surface is contoured with tiny pyramids. By mathematically planned space dying of each set of elements, precise images are played against optical illusions (see p. 13).

The complex elements of 3SOE baskets may be spokes added to reinforce the openwork for a base structure, or broad, decorative supplementary elements that also provide greater solidity for the sides (p. 108).

In the interlacing of mad weave baskets, elements are often turned back at the edge and reinserted into the completed mesh. They follow the same path as the original SOE, thus producing six thicknesses (p. 108, top). This is not a compound structure because it does not produce two layers.

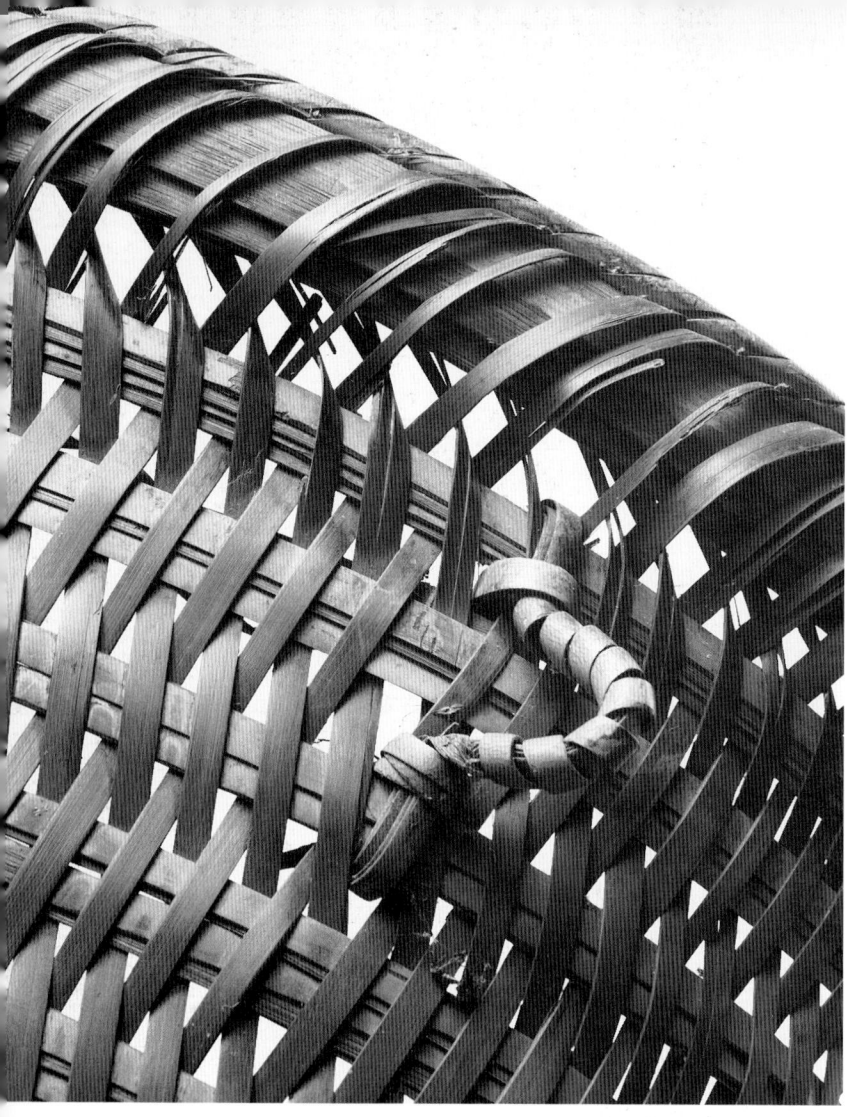

Although 3SOE interlacing is usually worked hexagonally with one material, basketry occasionally employs other forms. The burden basket in Plate 76—though simple—is remarkably engineered. The two sets of diagonals, crammed together towards the near conical base, add strength where it is most needed, while the four-fold horizontals are tension rings to offset lateral stess.

76 |

burden basket (detail)
3SOE, 1/1 and 2/2, oblique, horizontal
bamboo
26″ × 20″ × 15″
Meo people, Northern Thailand

For several years a traditional obi weaver working near Kyoto has been innovating new fabric constructions described in Japanese as "playing on the loom with a special tool Mr. Miyajima devised." Some are tubular, others without horizontal elements, and a few have vertical SOE that become oblique. The one shown has two diagonal SOE plus one horizontal SOE.

77 |

obi cloth (detail), c. 1980
Isamu Miyajima, Japan
3SOE, 2/1 oblique, horizontal
ikat dyed, plied silk
W. 13″
photo: Takeshi Fujimori

The vertical and diagonal spokes of the costly wedding basket from North India are interlaced with a pliable horizontal. Both spokes form a paired vertical at the base. Four steamed rattan corner posts with wooden feet add support and refinement.

79 |
wedding basket (detail)
3SOE, 1/1 H-V, oblique; 1/1 H-V lower band
rattan and bamboo
H. 22" × D. 24"
Bihar State, India

Elegant in form and exquisite in craftsmanship, these Watusi baskets are unique for their construction. The inside reveals a thin, solid wall of flat, passive, vertical elements almost covered with fine filaments spiraling around the circumference as they regularly engage the passive horizontals covering the outside surface. The pattern is achieved with discontinuous horizontals, neatly clipped.

78 |
covered box
3SOE, 1/3 H-V oblique
grass
5" × 3"
Watusi people, Rwanda, 1980

Of current basket makers, none approaches form with so broad a range of techniques as Shereen La Plantz. This composite form illustrates virtuosity in wrapping and looping and a rare combination of materials and interlacings. The cross-braced cubes involve a simple 1/1 form clad with bamboo splints, then bound and cross-braced with cord. The stepped, 3SOE bridge between the cubes reminds one of the glass-filled space frames connecting today's buildings.

80 |
untitled, 1982
Shereen La Plantz, U.S.A.
2SOE plus sup. elements, 1/1, H-V
(center) 3SOE, 1/1 H-V
paper fiber strips, bamboo, cord
10" × 10" × 20"

2. three-dimensional

a. two oblique sets + H + V (4SOE)

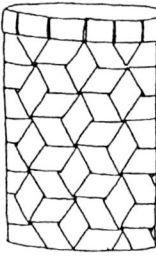

b. four oblique sets + H + V (6SOE)

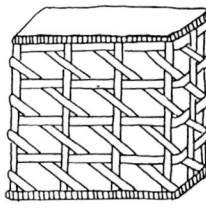

B. distinguished by structure of interlacing

1. simple (3SOE)

2. complex

a. with supplementary element

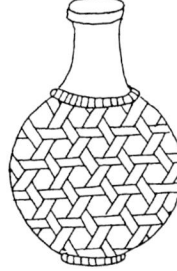

b. with supplementary set(s) of elements
(3SOE + SOE[s])
   i. carried with basic elements

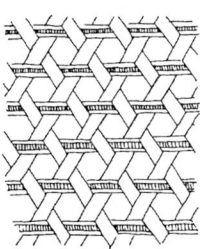

   ii. independent of basic elements

A display of Chinese crafts in the Chicago Field Museum featured minute, six-pointed stars emboidered into the mesh of a 3SOE fabric with openings of less than one millimeter.

Virginia Harvey has pictured three supplementary SOEs, inserted into the interstices of mad weave, yet each following an independent course (p. 108, bottom).

A diagram of a compound mesh with two dissimilar layers shows a 3SOE structure over a 2SOE one. The intervals are different sizes with the openness of the outer formation modulating the solid underpinnings (p. 110).

Occasionally leaves or other flat materials are sandwiched between two open-meshed layers of 3SOE. For Chinese "coolie" hats, this construction facilitates a lightweight protection against rain and sun. Made in a similar manner, the lid of the basket below is also a compound-complex structure.

Layers of compound interlacing may vary in orders of interlacing and in the count of elements or SOE. This basket lid with three layers is, on top (a), worked with two SOEs. The underside (b) reveals an openwork, 3SOE mesh supporting a middle layer of leaves that are overlapped to shed tropical rains.

Note the spokes added as the circumference enlarges. The light stripes centered on the spokes are outside bamboo peel that has resisted staining with smoke. The binding stitched through the edge of the three layers was braided as a ring.

81
basket lid
bamboo
D. 20″
Northern Thailand hill tribes

3. compound

a. two similar layers $\left(\dfrac{3\text{SOE}}{3\text{SOE}}\right)$

b. two dissimilar layers $\left(\dfrac{3\text{SOE}}{2\text{SOE}}\right)$

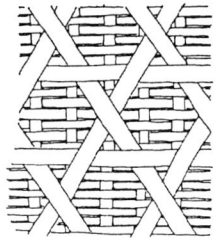

4. compound-complex $\left(\dfrac{3\text{SOE}}{3\text{SOE}}+\text{E}\right)$

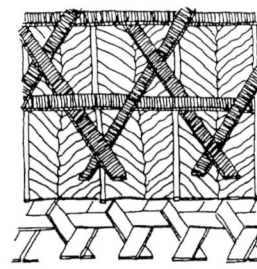

V. INTERLACINGS WITH FOUR OR MORE SETS OF ELEMENTS

A. distinguished by direction of interlacing

1. planar

a. two diagonal sets + H + V (4SOE)

b. four oblique sets + H + V (6SOE)

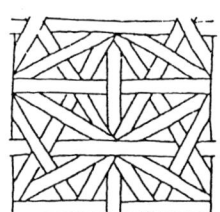

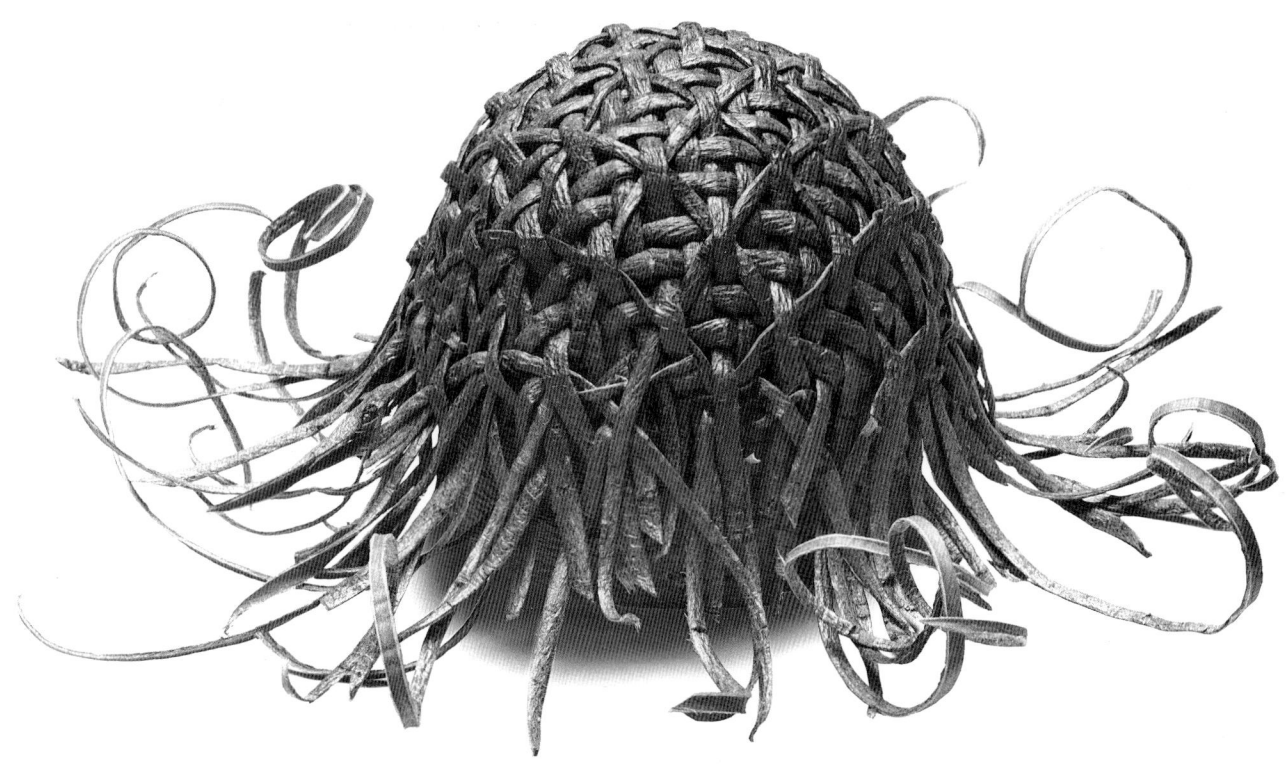

82–83. Dorothy Gill Barnes consistently plaits baskets with several sets of elements—often layered in different materials. The hemisphere (Pl. 83) is surfaced with a twill. Inside is a double armature of matchstick bamboo and bark strips. The object in Plate 82 is similar in form, but the four sets of elements are left untrimmed. (See her nest of footed baskets on p. 191.)

82 |
basket, 1982
complex plaiting
Dorothy Gill Barnes, U.S.A.
2SOE, 2/2 H-V
 + 2SOE, 3/2 oblique
mulberry bark
4½" × 9"

83 |
basket, 1982
compound plaiting
Dorothy Gill Barnes, U.S.A.
2SOE, 2/2 oblique
2SOE, 1/4 H-V
apple bark, bamboo
4" × 6"

Four Sets of Elements (4SOE)

Caning is typically done with a horizontal, a vertical, and two oblique SOEs. In most cases, elements are all of the same flat, semirigid material. This cross-bracing from four directions produces a stable structure.

The Indian wedding basket on page 107 has two distinctively different horizontal SOEs. An oblique set serves to lace elements together and secure the structure.

Five-SOE structures are extremely rare. The author remembers seeing only one, a Japanese basket that incorporated three oblique sets with the horizontal and vertical SOEs.

Classification 111

2. three-dimensional

    a. two oblique sets + H or V

    b. one oblique + H + V

B. distinguished by the structure of the interlacing: simple (4SOE or 6SOE)

Six sets of elements interlace to form the dome of a Thai food cover. At regular intervals, the density of the crossed strands creates a glistening hobnailed surface. The spherical Turk's head handle, worked from strands of rattan peel, is attached with neolithic braid (p. 83). In all, this rigid cover is lightweight, sturdy, and sufficiently dense to repel insects.

85 |
food cover (detail)
caning
6SOE (2H-V + 4 oblique)
rattan peel
D. 12″ × 26″
Thailand, c. 1980

A Papuan headband (right) appears as a twilled matting with a dark meander pattern of supplementary elements. The reverse (left) reveals a heavy plied cord stitched to the plaited foundation by means of a vertical set of elements.

84 |
headband
4SOE + 2SOE, 2/2 oblique, 1/1 H-V
orchid fiber
20″ × 2″
Papua New Guinea, eastern highlands, c. 1970

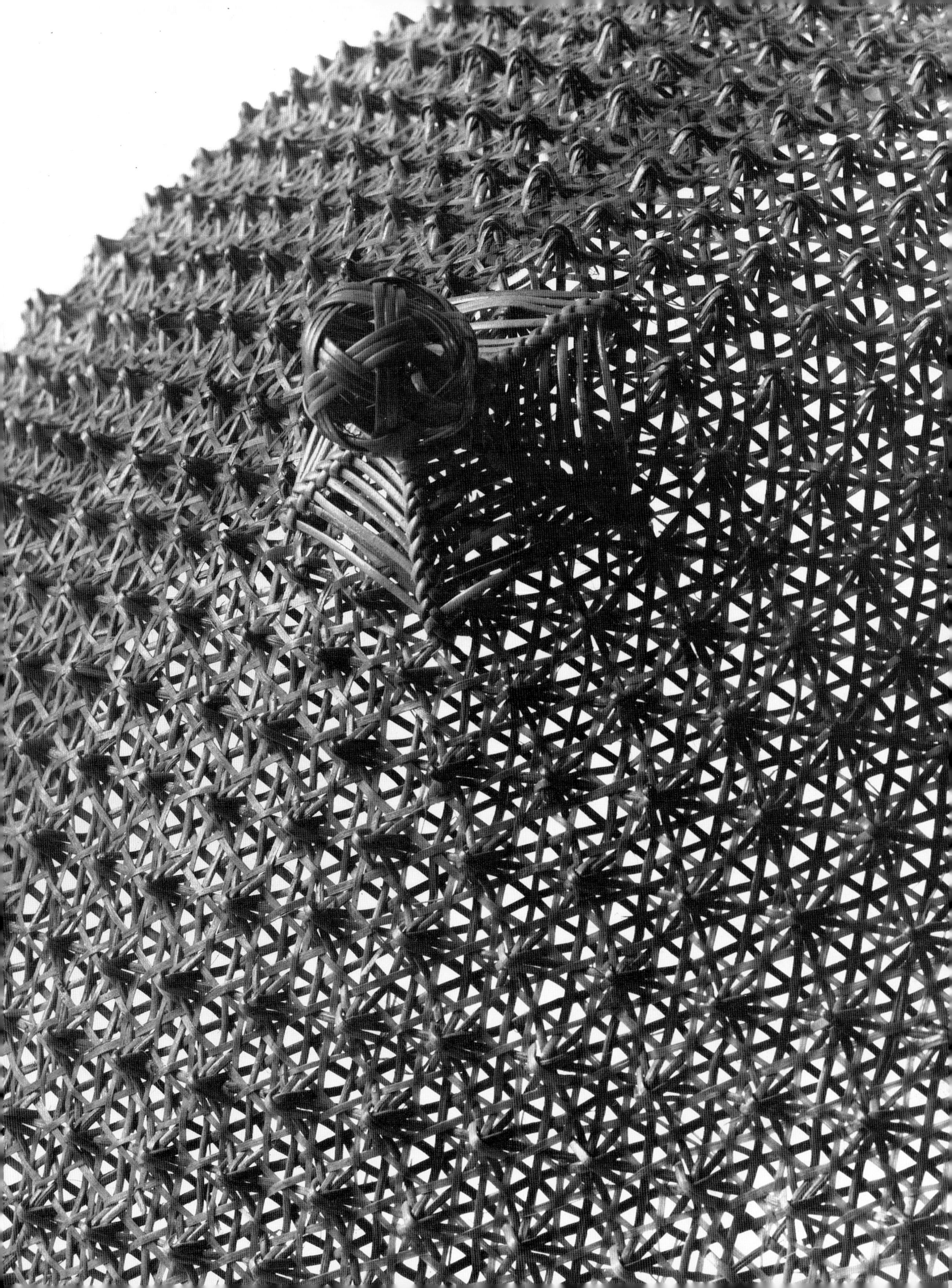

5
Braiding

In Chapter 4, familiar types of braiding were discussed, such as flat, tubular, and solid braids plus those worked around a core. Because there are diversifications that defy the limits of these categories, braiding assumes a unique prominence in this book; among all interlaced structures, it is the only one allotted a chapter.

Since most fabric texts either ignore braiding or relegate it to a minor position, a definitive study has yet to be written. Those few researchers concentrating on braids write on such specific aspects as the slings of the Andes, multicolored sashes from the Great Plains, *obi* ties of Japan, or the leather whips and lariats of the Argentine gauchos. Even those books promising encyclopedic coverage of braids are not exhaustive. And all too frequently their diagrams and directions are indecipherable or inaccurate.

Definitions

The terms "braids" and "braiding" would seem to need no definition to those whose daily life includes girls with their hair plaited into pigtails and boy scouts learning to braid lanyards. Braiding the tails of show horses into mud "knots" avoids tangles and expedites grooming. *Challah*, a braided bread, is as much an aspect of traditional Jewish sabbaths as are square-braided candles. Even today the tents of Lapland are fastened with brilliantly colored braids. Neolithic sandals with braided soles were forerunners of today's espadrilles.

Chapter 3 included our definition of braiding: the oblique interlacing of one set of elements sharing a common starting point and worked with loose ends. The resulting structure may be flat, round, square, or tubular, and the starting "point" may actually be a line.

"Braiding with loose ends" is included in our definition to distinguish braids from frame braiding. The weighted bobbins typical of Japanese *kumihimo* braiding are simply loose ends brought under control; wrapping and tying the loose ends in bundles or "butterflies" is so useful as to be common. The American Indians brought another solution to the problems of handling long strands: they started at the center of a braid and worked outward to the two extremes, thereby shortening the working elements by one-half.

Braiding is, of course, a specific type of plaiting. To circumvent the confusion that exists between the terms "braiding" and "plaiting," Emery wrote that "braiding should be limited to 'one-set' structures in which elements *interlace* with each other *obliquely*" (p. 61). Kate Peck Kent's definition is more explicit: "The interlacing of a single set of elements all tending in one direction from a point or line. Elements are not linked, looped, knotted, or wrapped about each other but simply pass over and under their neighbors, following an oblique course to the edge of the piece, where they turn back on the opposite diagonal.... Braiding may also be done around a core or in such a way as to produce round or square cordage, usually called sinnet" (p. 60).

It is useful to go further than Kent in indicating what is NOT braiding. Dictionaries too often give vague definitions encompassing "narrow bands" and "other ornamentation." This mistake is abetted by purveyors of woven "military braid." Emery regretted that the noun, "braid," was "used for general reference to a great number of narrow constructions, including innumerable varieties of round and square-braids, and many looped, interlooped, interlinked, and knotted structures of similar appearance and use" (p. 68). This broad interpretation of "braid" compared with her definition of "braiding" as "oblique interlacing" still confuses laymen, students, and especially translators. Braiding is a specific term, not an inclusive one.

We therefore disagree with Speiser, who includes interlinked, twined, and intertwined structures within her definition of braiding. Among the 402 sennit braids in Graumont and Hensel, those achieved by knotting and looping were probably included for their uncanny resemblance to oblique interlacing.

There is a real need for a common understanding of the meaning of the terms "braid" and "braiding." When NASA announced in December 1980 that the unmanned spacecraft *Voyager* had photographed Saturn, their scientists said that two of the rings around the planet were "braided." Braided? If the elements of a true braid interlace at regular intervals, do the laws controlling heavenly bodies comply with such a stricture? In actuality, the soft-focus photographs are unclear, indicating only vague curves that may cross over one another—more like the strands of a plied rope. In dropping their scientific terminology, NASA's use of the word "braid" was probably similar to the poetic phrases so frequently used to describe the constellations. But the imprecision surrounding the terms "braids" and "braiding" is not limited to scientists adopting words outside their field; for too long textile specialists have also distorted this terminology.

Although fold braiding is usually so densely worked that it is relatively heavy, this bracelet is open and feather light.

86 |
bracelet
1SOE, 1/1 H-V
bast
D. c. 3″
Colombia

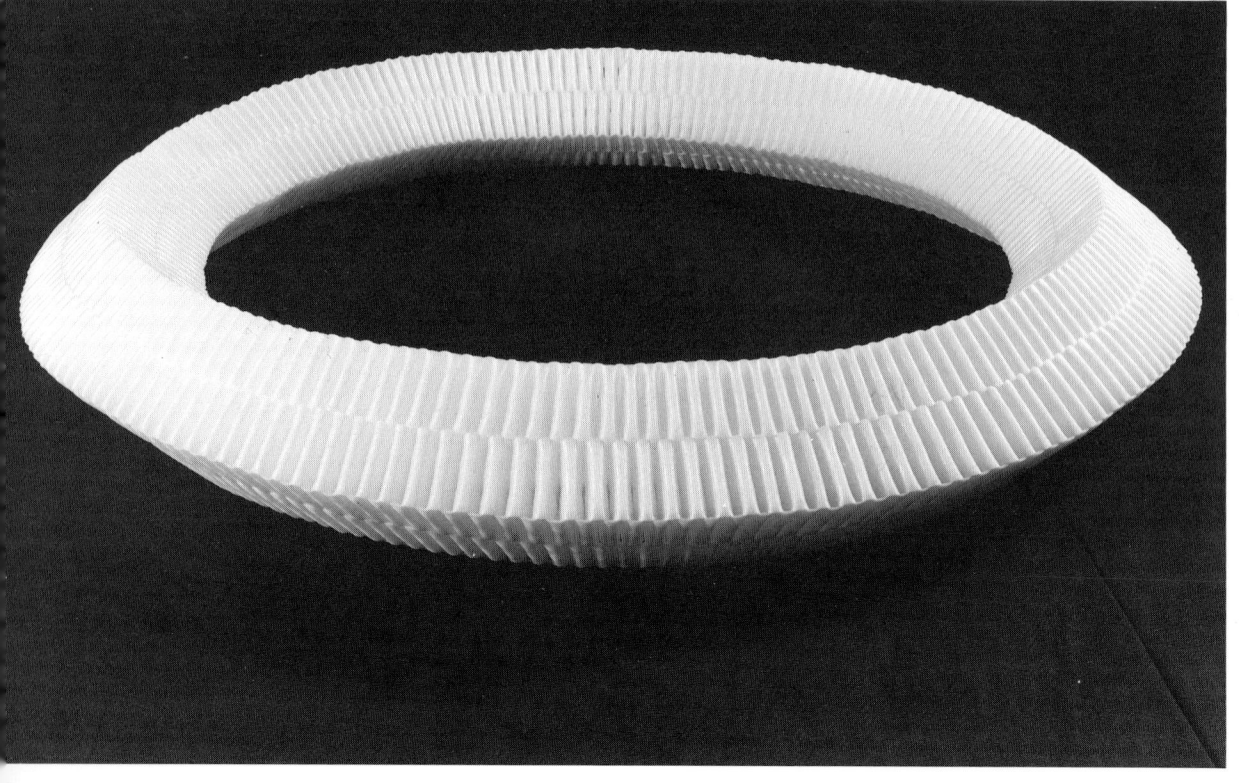

Although fold braids are most often in very small format, this one reads as minimalist sculpture in monumental scale.

87 |
untitled, 1984
Keiji Nio, Japan
fold braid
1SOE, H-V
plastic foam
c. 2′ × 12′ × 12′

The fold or squared braiding we learned as children is "as old as the hills." This structure provides an appropriate serpentine flexibility for the Roman necklace here.

88 |
necklace
fold braiding
1SOE, 1/1 H-V
gold
Roman, 3rd century A.D.
collection: Walters Art Gallery, Baltimore

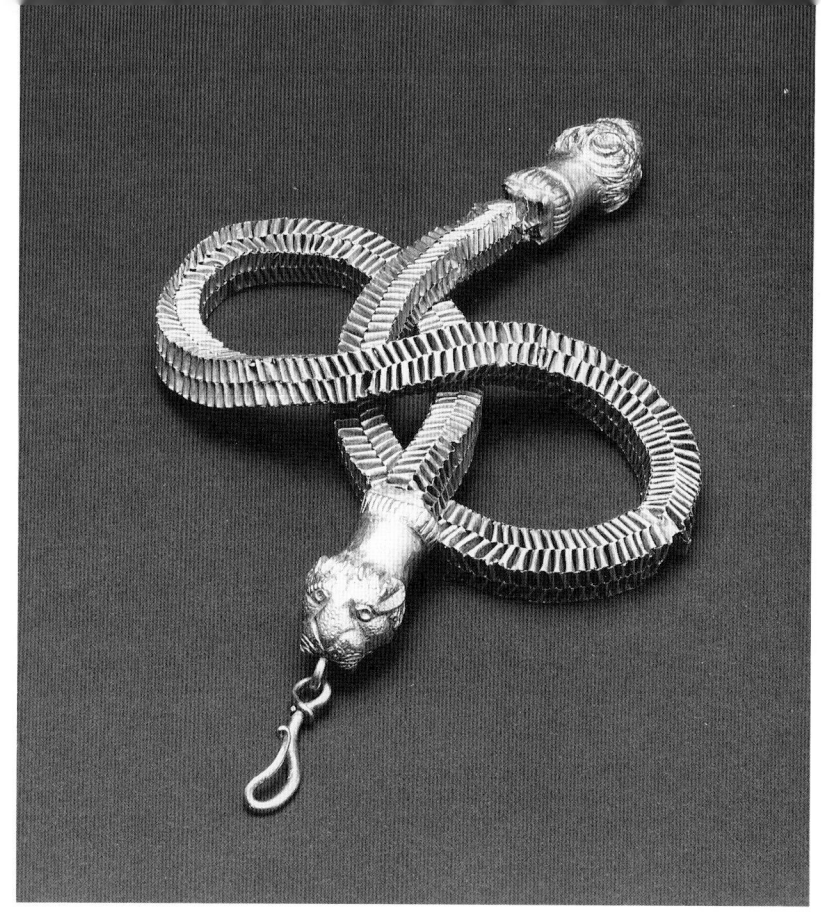

89 |
three rings, 1982
Arline Fisch, U.S.A.
fold braiding
1SOE, 1/1 multidirectional
silver
H. c. 2"

Fanciful dinner rings by Arline Fisch utilize fold-braids as their "jewels." Since these jewels do flex, they are wearable despite their extreme length.

Braiding 117

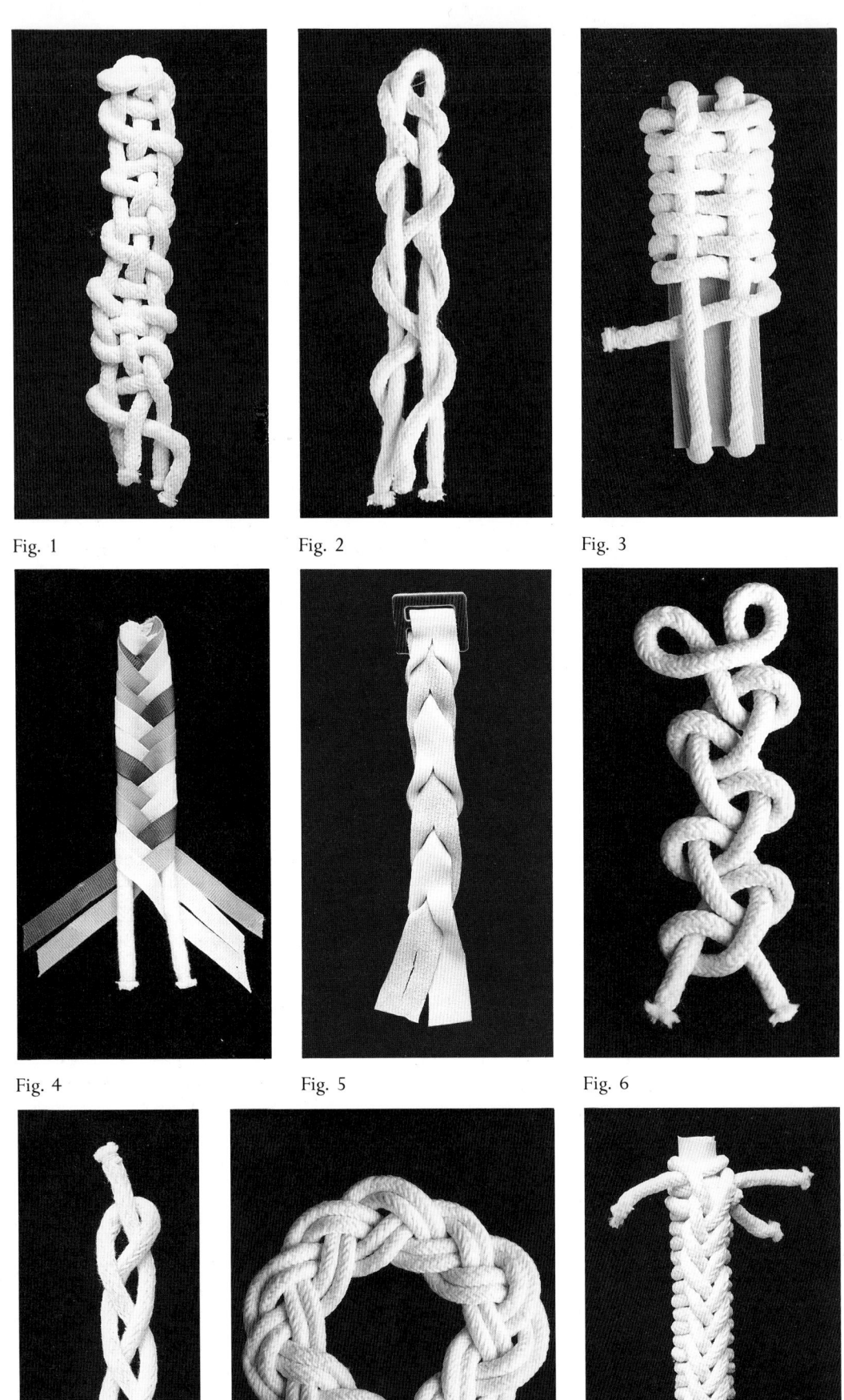

Fig. 1   Fig. 2   Fig. 3

Fig. 4   Fig. 5   Fig. 6

Fig. 7   Fig. 8   Fig. 9

Figs. 1–9. The terms "braids" and "braiding" are frequently misused in referring to narrow bands that are twined, wrapped, or knotted. Some other "false braids" are actually horizontal-vertical interlacing with 2SOE. Two trick "braids" (Figs. 7, 8) were worked with one element. They might be mistaken if only a fragment was seen. The structures illustrated here are NOT true braids.

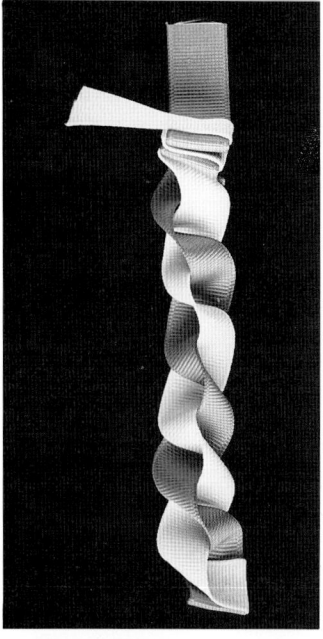

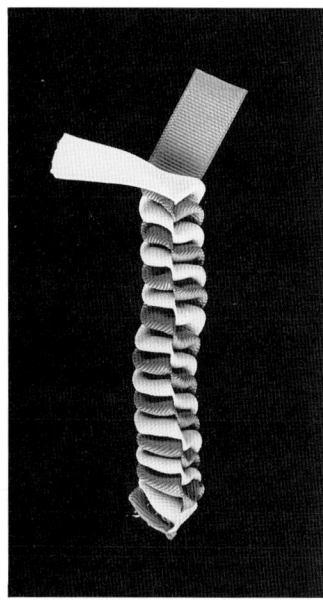

On Classification

In this examination of braiding, the hurdle of finding relationships within the universe of braid forms was simplified by concentrating on essential structures stripped of the appearances induced by materials and modifiers, discussed below.

In the classification in Chapter 4, braids were divided into two major categories: flat structures and three-dimensional ones. They were further broken down as simple, complex (with supplementary elements), and compound (two-layered). Although neither Emery nor Kent makes reference to compound braiding, Speiser recognizes two-layered braids as a distinct type.

The language problem arising from describing wide braids as "finger weaving" is aggravated by use of the terms "warp" and "weft" in the directions for braiding them. Weaving terminology is not applicable to oblique interlacing. "Active" and "passive" can be used to describe the working elements.

Those classifiers distinguishing braids "worked upward" from those "worked downward" seem astonished when they discover ethnic examples not conforming to this preconception. Differentiation by method is deceptive, since numerous braids can be worked in either direction. The similar problem of analysis based on tools has an exception in the case of the excellent classification of Japanese *kumihimo* by Mary Dusenbury that clearly identifies and describes each type in terms of specialized braiding stools. The Japanese system for diagraming intricate braiding methods is so easy to comprehend that it requires no translation.

"Fold braids" is a descriptive term adopted here for 1SOE structures worked with flat elements that can accept a fold. Leather, straw, leaves, and tapes are typical. The simplest fold braid, worked with one set of two elements, would resemble a twisted cord if yarn was used. The characteristic that places fold braids beyond the pale of Emery's definition is the direction of their interlacing: typically horizontal-vertical, not oblique.

However, the fold braid is a many-faceted performer that can assume different guises. Although usually square, the cross-section may be round, rectangular, have a central core, or a spiraling configuration (10–15, 18). A lanyard is an example of a compound square braid worked around a tubular one.

"Corn dollies" are typically worked with hollow grain straws in a spiraling fold braid. In such widely separated areas as Guatemala, India, Greece, and Scandinavia, they are made as talismans. When shaped into cornucopias, they are a feature of harvest festivals (p. 121).

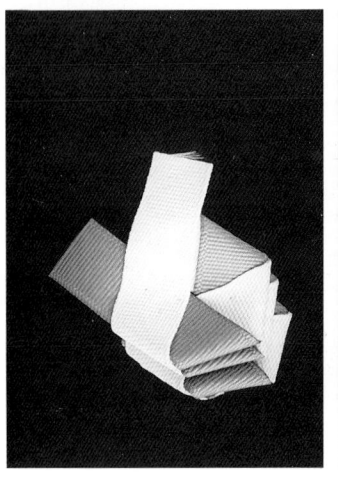
Fig. 12

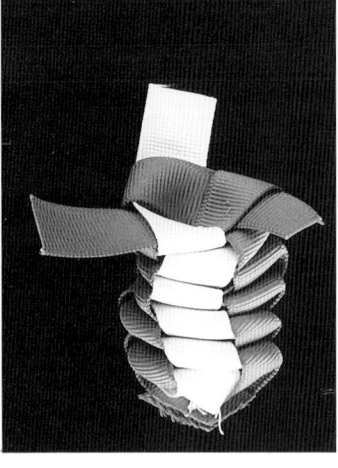
Fig. 13

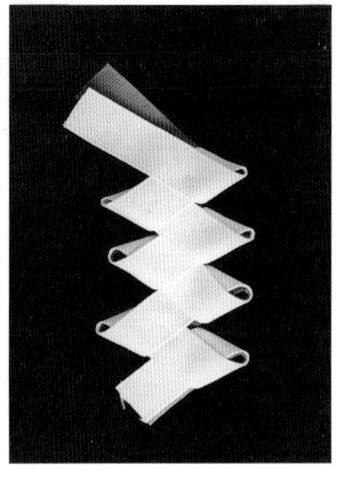
Fig. 14

Figs. 12–16. The simplest fold braid, worked with one set of two (flat) elements, has the semblance of an accordian bellows. Triangular and hexagonal 1SOE forms can also be worked with two and three elements. The angle of the fold determines the final configuration.

Fig. 15

Fig. 16

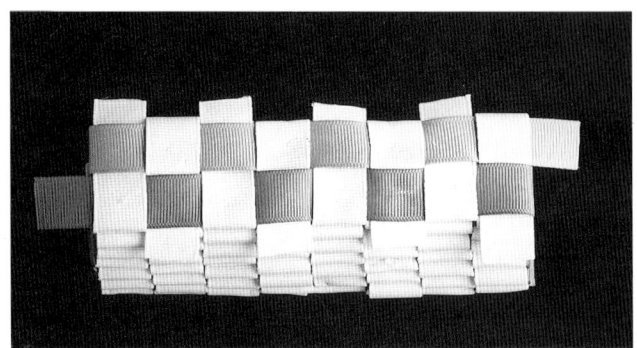
Fig. 17

Fig. 18

Fold braids worked with more than four elements can be extended into long rectangles (Fig. 17). Spirals occur when elements are folded diagonally across the center rather than at a right angle (Figs. 16, 18).

Figs. 19, 20. Flat fold braids have sawtooth selvages when the elements are worked in both horizontal and oblique directions.

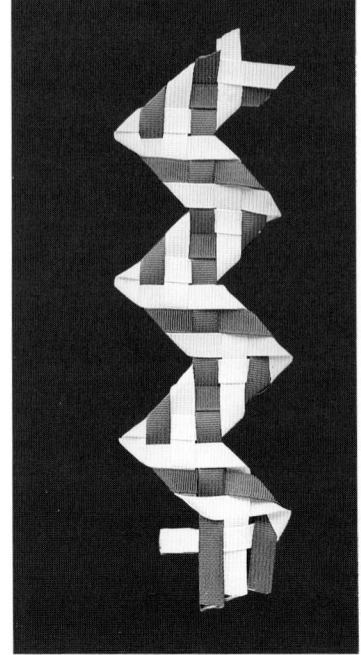
Fig. 19

Fig. 20

120 Interlacing

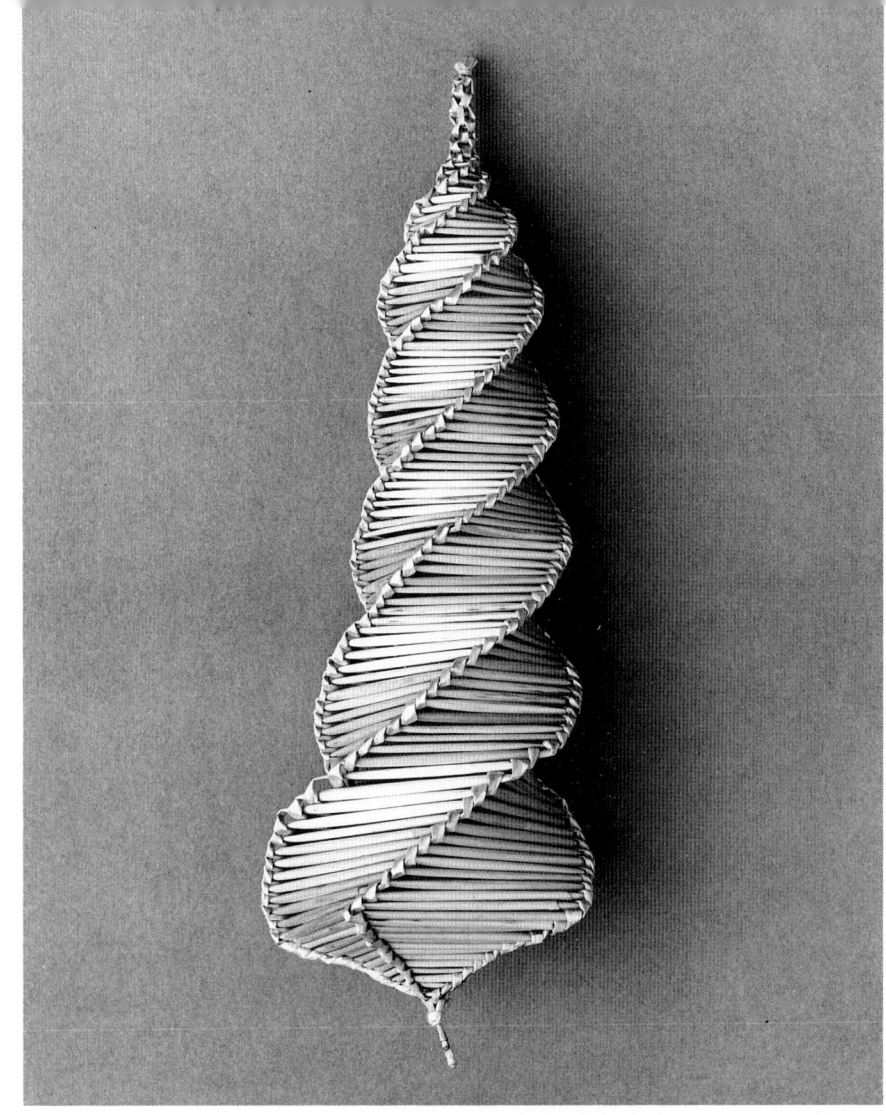

90–91. For millennia grain straw has been plaited to form the small harvesttime fetishes still found in many parts of the world. An extremely high ratio of strength to weight permits a minimum of interlacing. The spiralling ziggurat form, sometimes called a corn dolly, is achieved with fold braiding. The other form shows progressive crossings similar to rush seating. Note the braided hangers.

90 |
corn dolly (small idol)
fold braiding
5E, 1/1 oblique
straw
H. 6″
Guatemala

91 |
fetish
2SOE, 1/1 oblique
wheat straw
W. 8″
Afghanistan

Tubular Braids

While some form of woven tubes is common to most textile cultures, they tend to retain a flat cross-section. Frequently the creases on both sides reveal the increased tension of the warps at the margins. Tubular braids, on the other hand, are usually plaited in the round so their form is a perfect cylinder without variations in the circumference. Industrially produced shoelaces and lantern wicks typify flattened tubular braids.

Most often worked with eight or more elements, tubular braids may begin with strands looped over removable rings or two parallel bars. Others start and finish with solid braids that become the ties of a belt or the handles of a sling.

A unique property of tubular braiding is its ability to elongate and contract as the pitch is changed. The "Chinese finger torture," a child's toy, is a familiar example. An industrial application of this principle is the wire "grip." When tightened, this can be used to mechanically lift heavy pipes. A push toward the grip releases the burden.

Cassava bread serves as the staple diet for the Indians of the Amazon. However, the manioc root from which the flour is ground contains poisonous prussic acid, which must first be extracted. The contraction property of tubular braiding produces the necessary constrictive action. When the manioc squeezer, stuffed with bulbous roots, is suspended and counterweighted, toxic juices gradually exude until the tube regains its elongated form.

Because the side walls of obliquely interlaced baskets are the same structure as tubular braids, they, too, elongate or contract to accommodate weighty burdens.

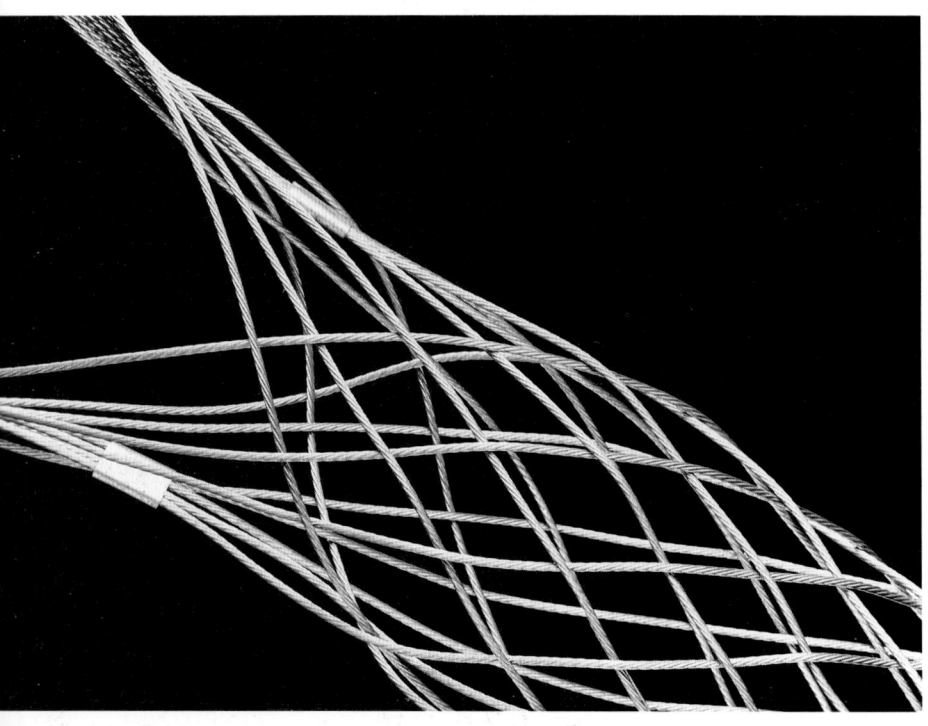

The pipe grip employs the elongation/contraction property of tubular braids to grasp and lift heavy metal pipes.

92 |

double eye parallel pipe grip
tubular braiding
1SOE, 1/1 oblique
steel
U.S.A.

To achieve a firm cylinder that will conform to the hand, this tubular braided handle was interlaced over a core of three leather braids, whose ends form the whip.

93 |
whip (quirt)
tubular braiding
1SOE + 1E, 1/1
leather thongs
L. c. 4'
Mexico, 1970s

A manioc squeezer from the Colombian Amazon relies on the elongation/contraction property particular to tubular braids. Observe the side-stepping twill that randomly admixes light and dark elements.

94 |
manioc squeezer (detail)
tubular braiding
1SOE, 4/2 twill oblique
bast
18" shown; total L. 4'
Colombia

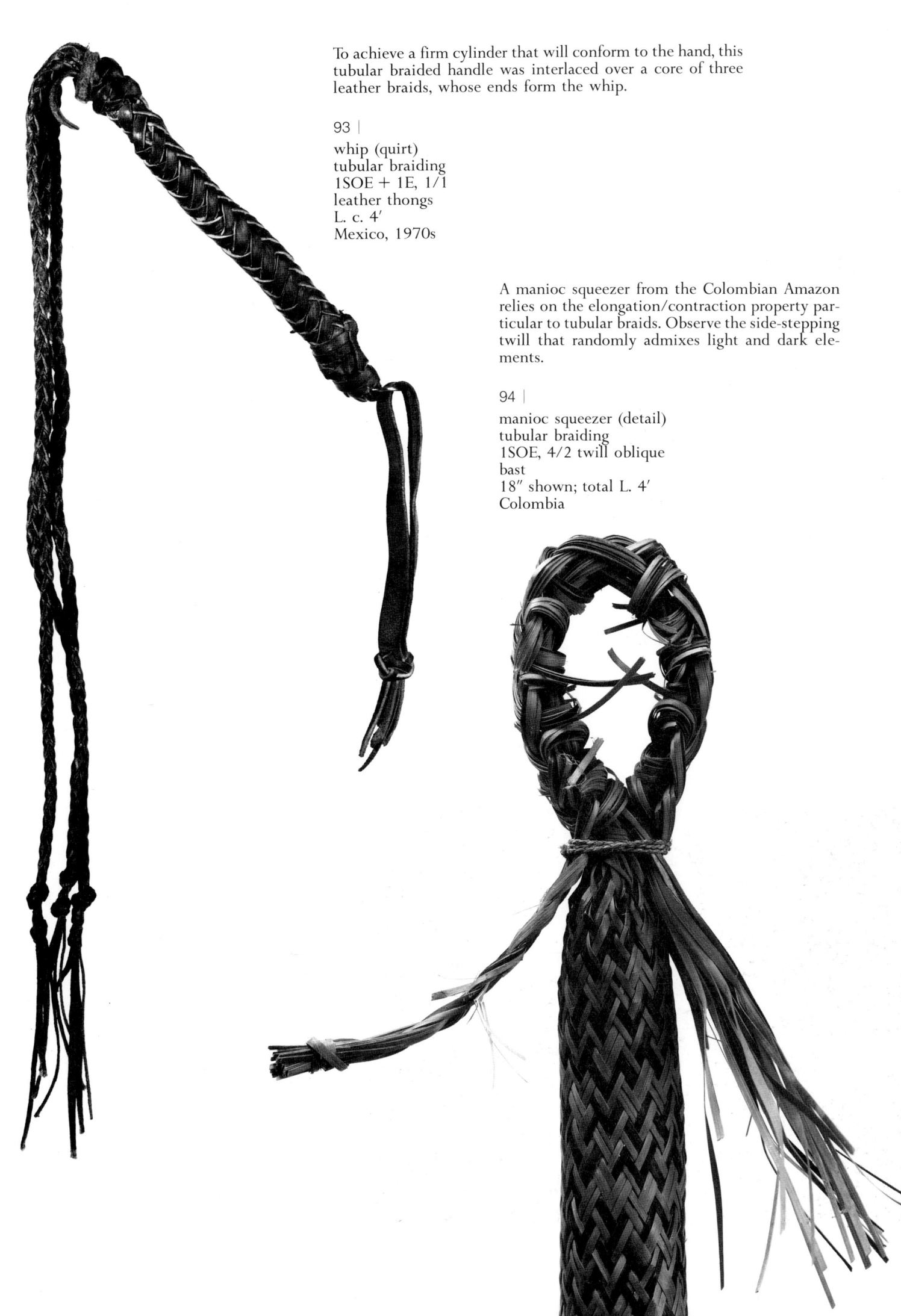

Core Braids

More often than not, tubular braids are formed over a cylindrical form that maintains a set diameter and assures even tension and pitch. Other times, a removable core element serves this purpose. If the core remains, it provides tensile strength, firmness, or even rigidity. Cowherds braid around the handles of whips and riding crops to achieve a solid grip. Welting cords and leashes, round laces, and soutache braids often retain their core elements.

Machine-made braids in particular are often interlaced around removable cores, then stuffed with a replacement core. Such are the casings for electrical cords. Reinforcements for garden hoses, tubes for synthetic arteries, and window sash cords are other examples of industrially produced tubular braiding.

The extremely delicate Victorian braided hair "jewelry" (p. 194) was sometimes worked over removable cores. Starched with sugar water, the braids still had sufficient flexibility to be manipulated into all the convolutions in vogue at the time.

There are rare instances of compound tubular braids, that is, a braid within a braid. More common are core braids in which strands of the core interlace through the tube to create a pattern. For these, the core is not a supplementary element, but a supplementary set of elements.

Traditional sling braids of the Andean altoplano are rich in examples of patterns created by exchanging the active face elements with the passive core elements.

95 |
With less than classic grace, Vermont girls "Dance the May" and so create a tubular cord braid of some size.
photo: Erik Long

More than anyone else, Lisa Rehsteiner has explored the possibilities of tubular braids. Hers open and close, increase in diameter, and change the number of working elements. Here, she enumerates possibilities for core elements, most of which are wrapped with a fine thread.

96 |
Palos de Lluvia II (detail), 1976/7
Lisa Rehsteiner, Spain
1SOE, 1/1 oblique, plus splicing, plying, and wrapping
hemp, cotton

For two decades Francoise Grossen has braided heavy ropes into large biomorphic forms. Here, the core of her typical wraparound braids are two braids worked "from one side only."

97 |
Anatid, 1981
Francoise Grossen, Switzerland
   (lives in New York)
braiding
hemp, cotton
56" × 18" × 24"
collection: Renwick Gallery,
   Washington, D.C.

Braiding 125

This long fish trap, both tubular and braided, is not a tubular braid. Rather, the four-strand braids across it position the vertical elements, producing amazing strength in relation to weight. The ends are the same braid, but compacted. Interlaced cones of wider, thinner bamboo form the "mouths."

98 |
fish trap
1SOE + 1SOE, 1/1, but 3/3 around verticals, oblique
2SOE, 1/1 ("mouths")
split bamboo
48" × 8"
Laos, c. 1970

A tubular braid and a grouped core with brushlike ends form this East African beer stirrer. Note the small, neat horizontal braid that binds the strands of the brush.

99 |
beer stirrer
1SOE, 1/1 oblique
bast
L. c. 9"
East Africa, 1970s

100–102. Minute braids by Guatemalan children (Pl. 100) demonstrate a potential for almost limitless color play. The precision of the repp braid bag (Pl. 102) is the more remarkable for its eccentric grain and "tapestry" joining. Its center panel includes a neat pattern of glass trade beads. The small bag (Pl. 101) was frame braided in Colombia.

100 |
four braids
1SOE
plied wool
Guatemala, c. 1980

101 |
coin bag with drawstring
frame braiding
1SOE, 1/1 oblique
handspun wool
Colombia, c. 1970

102 |
bag with drawstring
repp braiding
1SOE, 1/1 oblique
Germantown wool, beads
13″ × 9½″
Pawnee, early 20th century

Braiding 127

103–106. Africans have long used braids for all manner of headdresses, but the applied braids of the face mask of Plate 103 draw the contours of its entire surface. Doug Fuchs's braided dance mask (Pl. 104) is similarly contoured, but in an open filigree. The fold braided festival mask from Sri Lanka in Plate 106 is also amazingly expressive. Braided wrappings are often employed to cradle and cushion containers or to wrap a handle. Here brilliant braided plastic is wrapped and interlaced around a modern Italian bracelet (Pl. 105).

103
face mask
braiding
1SOE, 1/1 oblique
bast
H. 18″
West Africa, early 20th century
collection: Frank J. Thomas, Hollywood

104
dance mask, c. 1980
Douglas Fuchs, U.S.A.
braiding
1SOE, 1/1 oblique
plastic covered wire

105 |
bracelet
braiding
1SOE, 2/2 oblique
plastic film
Italy, 1980
collection: Gay Odmark, London

106 |
face mask
fold braid
1SOE, 1/1 H-V
Polwatta Village, Sri Lanka, 1970
photo: Yvonne Hanneman

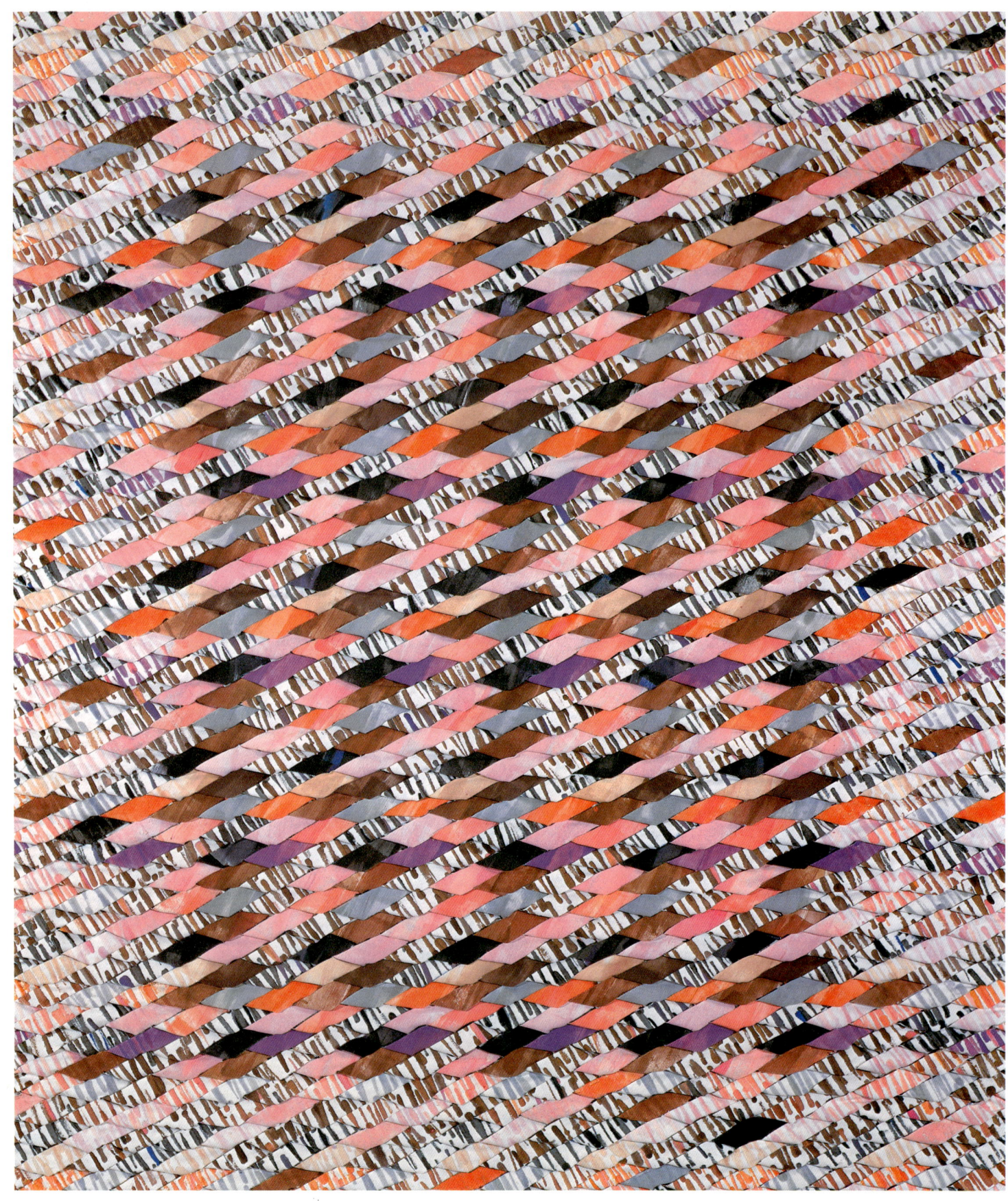

107–108. For several years, Karen Chapnick has produced sizeable wool hangings with a rare method of joining successive, parallel braids by engaging the turns of their selvages (see *The Art Fabric: Mainstream*, p. 83). Typically, these are worked with grouped strands of many colors, but in recent years she has also used larger, single strands of dye-patterned paper.

107

African Allusions, 1985
Karen Chapnick, U.S.A.
 (lives in Vancouver, Canada)
braided fabric, painting
1SOE, 2/2 oblique
54½" × 45"
photo: Henri Robideau

108 |
Nuclear Free Zone, 1984 (detail)
Karen Chapnick, U.S.A.
braiding, space dyed
1SOE, 3/3 oblique
sisal

Both Sheila Fox and Mark Pollack have explored the potentials of fold braiding in solid dimensional forms. While squared fold braids are usually worked in a linear progresion, Fox first "cubed" them to create simple geometry, then discovered the potentials of bending her rectangular walls into arched and vaulted segments. In *Aggregation*, these braided walls are worked more openly to roll into stackable cylinders.

109
Aggregation, 1985 (detail)
Sheila Fox, U.S.A.
fold braiding
1SOE, 1/1 H-V
cotton canvas strips
26″ × 53″ × 6″ (variable)

Mark Pollack's small piece playfully demonstrates three other potentials. Depending on the angle of the fold, his squared braid can have four, six, or eight sides; tapered elements expand or reduce its width. The possibilities for color effects are far greater here than in flat interlacing.

110 |
untitled, 1980
Mark C. Pollack, U.S.A.
fold braiding
1SOE, 1/1 H-V
paper strips
4″ × 6″ × 7″

Braiding

111–112. Rod Owen of Oxford has worked for several years in the tradition of American wide braids. Such is the shaded stripe of his extremely wide repp braid "worked from one side only." The earlier cross repp braid (Pl. 112) employs a grouped strand technique perfected in Peru 2,000 years ago.

111 |
Swimming Pool, 1984
Rod Owen, England
repp braiding
1SOE, 1/1 oblique
wool
54" × 31"

112 |
cross repp braid (detail)
Rod Owen
1SOE, 1/1 oblique
wool
c. 9" wide

Light motifs on a dark ground can be formed by exchanging two layers of compound plaiting—the equivalent of double plain weave. The mat is composed of wide braids in several patterns, joined at the selvages. The bottom of the photograph shows a myriad of loose strands on the reverse face.

113 |
mat (detail)
compound braids, joined at selvages
1SOE, 1/1 oblique
1SOE
bast
40" × 74"
East Africa, c. 1970

Joined Braids

Methods for joining braids during interworking were outlined in the classification. The braids that are joined with a supplementary element were omitted there because such joins are not integral to the structure. Among them are the familiar rag rugs composed of spiraling flat braids, stitched together through *adjacent* edges. Parallel braids can also be stitched through *overlapping* edges—a practice common in straw hats, but rare in baskets like the one on page 140. For the sturdy soles of espadrilles and sandals, flat braids are stitched *face to face*.

These three braids are ingeniously attached by interlinking the turns of successive strands as they extend beyond the selvage.

114 |

maquette for work in plaited aluuminum, 1981
Shereen La Plantz, U.S.A.
braiding
1SOE, 1/1 oblique
grosgrain ribbon

Karen Chapnick's long series of wall hangings employs attached braids comprised of elements grouped with varicolored strands. Each braid is attached to the previous one by mutually interlinking at the turns of the selvage. In most of Chapnick's work, the attaching strands are inserted *underneath* the turns of the adjacent braid. In this detail, the section above the wrapping follows this method, while the section below goes *over* at the turn (see Pls. 107, 108 and Virginia Harvey, *The Techniques of Basketry*, p. 79).

115 |

Grand Sparkle (detail), 1977
Karen Chapnick, Canada
braiding
1SOE, 1/1 oblique
sisal, polypropylene twine
photo: Tod Greenaway

136 Interlacing

A hammock of braided bast, from Vietnam, combines narrow four-strand braids with twisting and twine plaiting. The result is a lightweight, durable filigree with ventilating properties.

116 |
hammock (detail)
braiding, twisting, twine plaiting
1SOE, 1/1 oblique
bast
South Vietnam, 1960

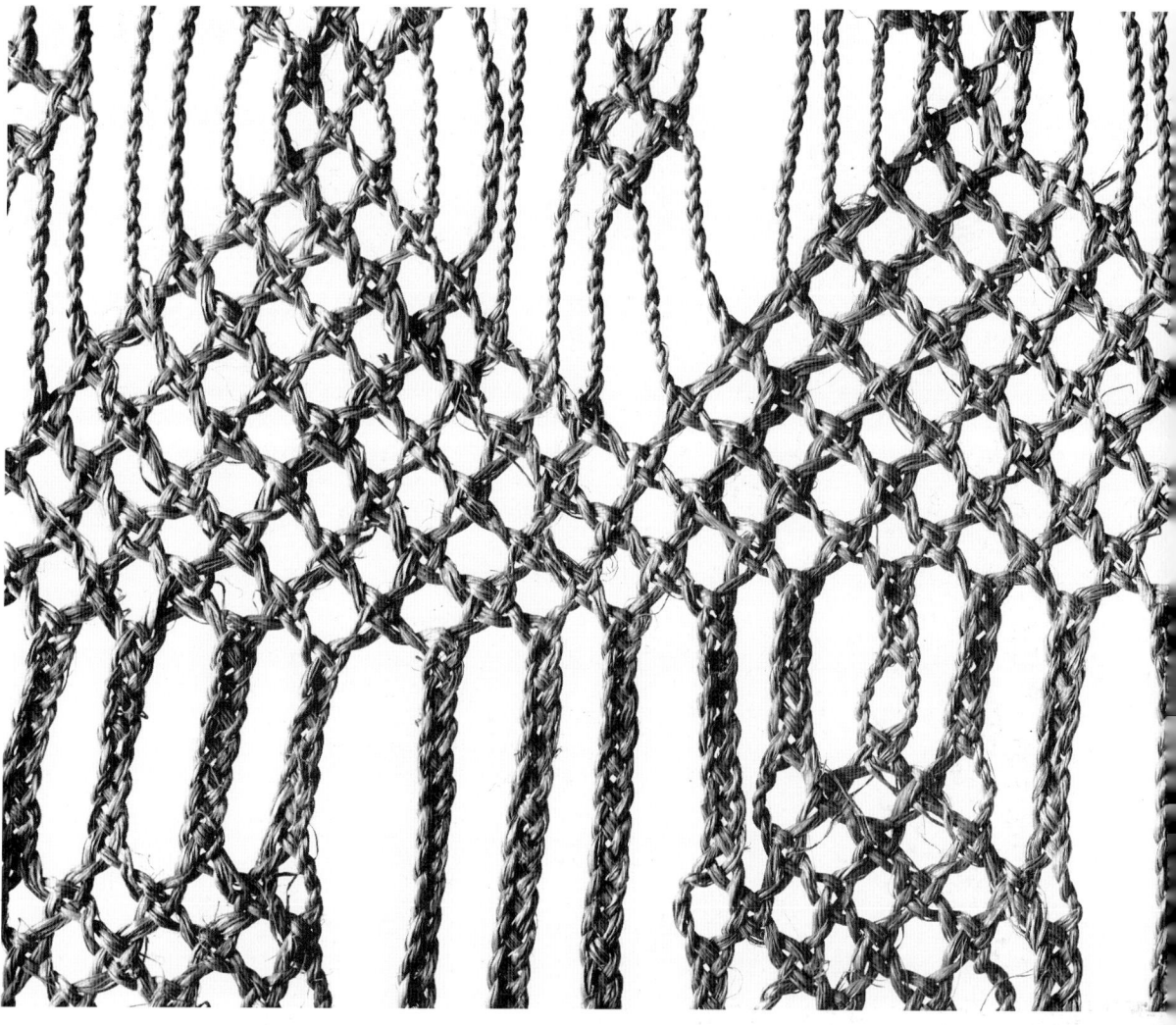

Silky fine braids interlace on a square grid to form an extremely open hammock that is smooth to the touch, lightweight, and sufficiently strong for two people. The loose fiber ends chase off bothersome insects.

117 |
hammock (detail)
braiding, joined
1SOE, 1/1 oblique
bast
Brazilian Amazon, c. 1970

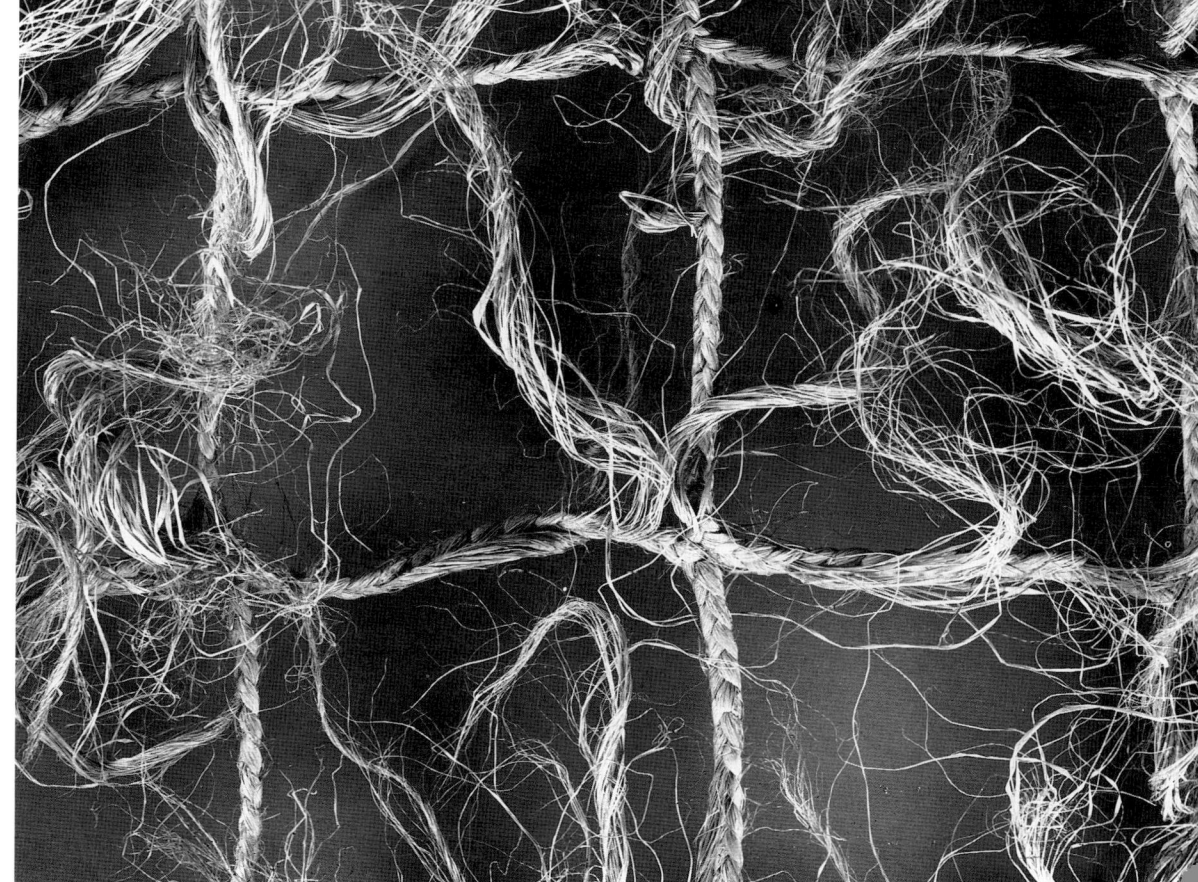

Braiding   137

118–119. The mats in Plates 118 and 119 were made by joining simple braids plaited with the loose ends dropped out to form a pile. In the door mat (Pl. 119), shown on its reverse side, corn husks were braided with a looped fringe, then stitched concentrically to form a deep pile rug. The process is similar to braiding onion or garlic tops.

In the Sardinian mat (Pl. 118), a deep pile was formed with raffia ends extended from the simple braids. The braids are joined by encircling an extra element at the turns of their selvages (see Fig. 23). Compare with the hammock in Plate 117.

118 |

mat (detail)
1SOE, 1/1 oblique, discontinuous
raffia
85" × 27"
Sardinia, 1950s

 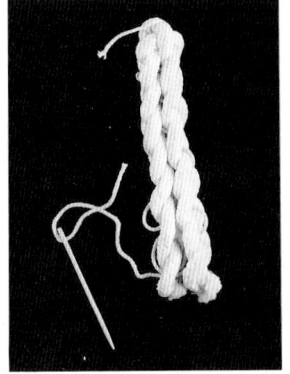 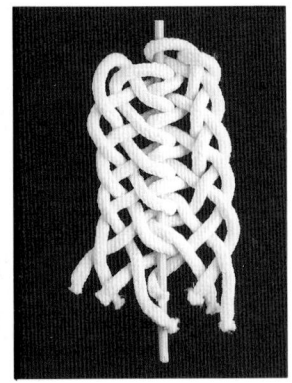

Fig. 21   Fig. 22   Fig. 23

Figs. 21–23. Typically, the braids of rag rugs are joined by stitching selvages (Fig. 21). Braids forming the soles of espadrilles are stitched face to face (Fig. 22). The technique of joining two braids by interlacing both around a common supplementary element is shown in Figure 23.

119 |

mat (detail)
1SOE, 1/1 oblique
concentric braids, attached by stitching
cornhusks
32" × 22" × 2"
Southern Appalachia, c. 1960

A modern rag rug is composed of four squares of parallel braids attached by lines of knotted cords. The shaded stripe emphasizes the alternation of horizontal and vertical squares with perimeters of alternating smooth selvages and shaggy fringe.

120 |
Goode Braids (detail), 1981
Anne McKenzie Nicholson, U.S.A.
braiding
1SOE, 1/1 oblique
cotton cloth strips, procion dyed; cotton string
64" × 64"
collection: Carolyn and Damon Goode, Indianapolis

Four African mats are composed of simple braids joined almost imperceptibly at their selvages. Bindings are also braided. The different interlacings and color effects distinguish them: starting at lower left, a 1/1 interlacing alternating dark and light; lower right, a 2/1 interlacing in a 2 dark, 1 light color sequence; upper right, a 2/2 interlacing in solid color bands sequenced to form stripes; upper left (and most intricate), 2/2 interlacing changes to 6/6 in the center of each braid. The color sequence of 11 light, 8 dark, 5 light, 8 dark produces a double check.

121 |
mats (detail)
braiding
1SOE, interlacings described above, oblique
bast
East Africa, 1970s

122 |
According to Iroquois legend, the other side of the world is inhabited by prophetic spirits who taught mankind the techniques of hunting and fishing. During the midwinter festival, the Life God's power, weakened by the Winter God, must be renewed. Wearing braided husk masks, members of the Corn Husk Society perform magical rites to announce the coming of the "three sisters": corn, beans, and squash.

This basket is formed by stitching one continuous narrow braid. Serrated edges of this braid are the result of an unusual combination of oblique and horizontal movements. Centered in each point, the pronounced pattern of the concentric stitching adds a staccato rhythm. As in a "boater" straw hat, the stitching of overlapped braids creates a rigid structure.

123 |
covered basket
fold braiding
1SOE, 1/1 oblique-horizontal
bast
6" × 4"
Colombia, 1970s

An extremely long Bedouin sash is composed of three major sections. At each end, the dark strands are plaited outward from the center, creating two bands of red chevrons on a black ground. Through the wide center section, the black strands continue as simple narrow braids. The light braids between them were inserted by interlinking the turns at the selvages.

124 |
sash
braiding
1SOE, 1/1 oblique
wool, cowrie shells, beads
Bedouin people, Sinai Peninsula, early 20th century?

While braids are added to widen the center section of this pre-Columbian headband, the fabrication differs from the Bedouin sash in Plate 124. Here, three narrow braids are joined regularly by a smaller, zigzagging braid. At the fold, the three braids become six; in the central section, three of the connecting braids become spirals. Outside edges are ornamented with bird's heads formed with two or more dark braids.

125 |
headband
attached braids
1SOE, 1/1 oblique
cotton and alpaca
39" × 4"
Peru, South Coast, 400 B.C.–A.D. 500
collection: Dallas Museum of Fine Arts, Texas, The Nora and John Wise Collection

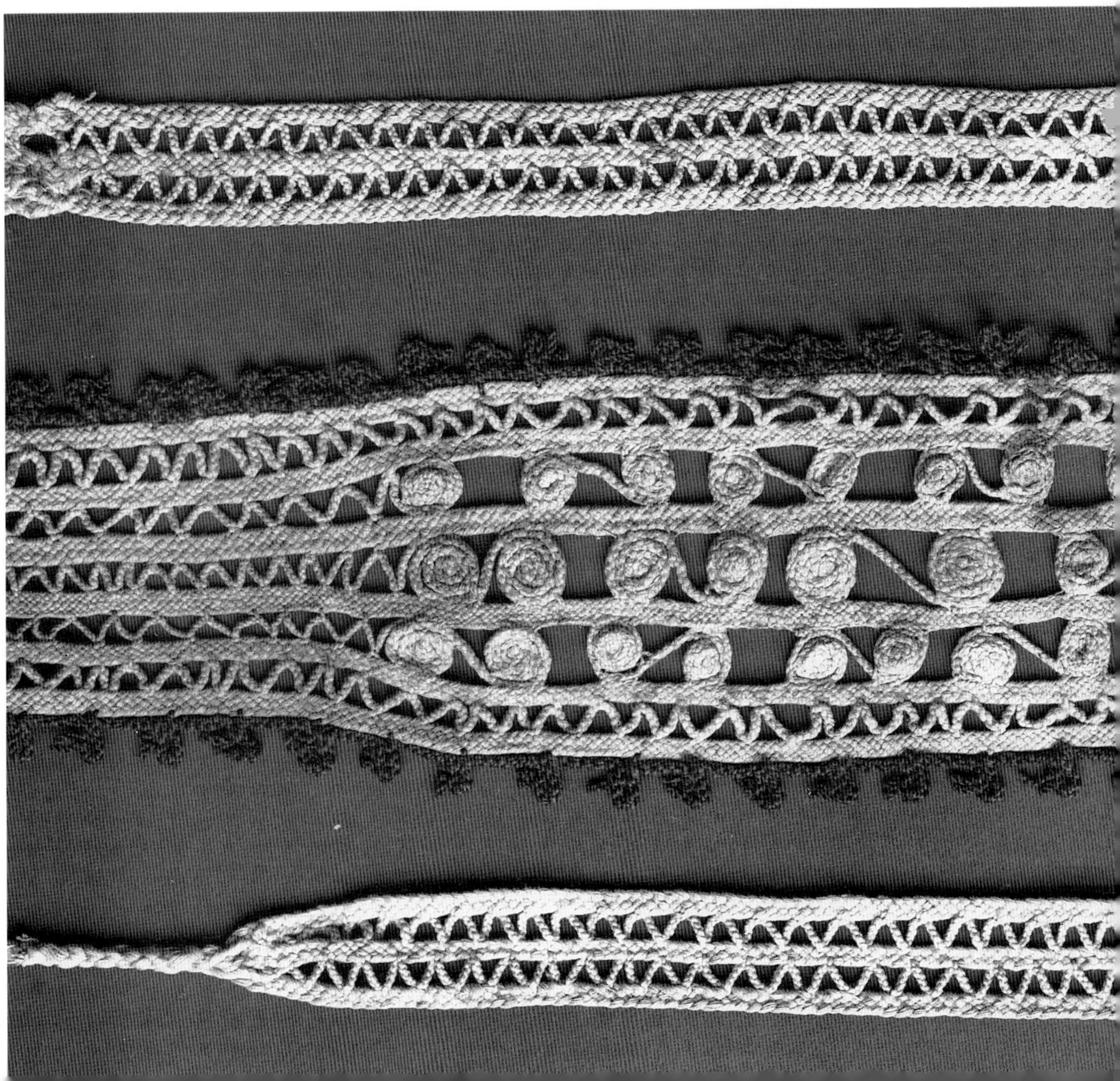

West African masks often include elaborate hair braids and beards. The polychromed Ibo helmet mask is richly ornamented with braids and wrapped raffia horns.

126 |
Mwo Society Maiden Spirit mask
braiding
1SOE
palm fiber, incised and polychromed wood
Ibo people, Nigeria
collection: Albert F. Gordon,
  New York

127 |
head covering, rabbit mask
1SOE, 1/1 oblique
bast fiber, polychromed soft wood
Senufu people, Ivory Coast,
  mid 20th century

127–129. Among decorated African masks, too many braids have been removed or lost. Almost all Dan masks had braided beards; few do today. In Plate 128, dozens of simple braids were stitched to a multiple braid heading, then attached through small holes in the wood.

The short, convoluted beard in Plate 129 graced another Dan mask. Note the two sizes of braids.

Ten braids were stitched together at their selvages to form the head covering of a rabbit mask. The alternation of rusty brown and dark natural bands forms stripes.

128
mask and beard
1SOE, 1/1 oblique
bast fiber
Dan people, Upper Volta, early 20th century
collection: Albert F. Gordon, New York
photo: Tribal Arts Gallery, New York

129
mask beard
1SOE, 1/1 oblique
bast fiber
Dan people, Liberia, early 20th century
collection: Albert F. Gordon, New York
photo: Tribal Arts Gallery, New York

Braiding 143

Braiding Without Loose Ends

Virtuoso braiding of leather by cattle herders led to bizarre forms that rarely occur in other materials. Some resulted from on-the-job requirements for extra strength and durability. Others derive from a spark of creativity struck by long periods of boredom.

One type is worked with elements created by lengthwise slits within a rectangle. An uncut end serves as the starting point (Figs. 24–26). If both ends remain intact, there are no loose ends and the interlacing involves astute maneuvering through twists and insertions of the unified ends into the course of the interlacing (Figs. 25, 26). Although the rectangles themselves might be viewed as single elements, this would not be valid when the "fragment test" described in Chapter 3 is applied. If the unslit end portion is missing, a slit braid is indistinguishable from the norm.

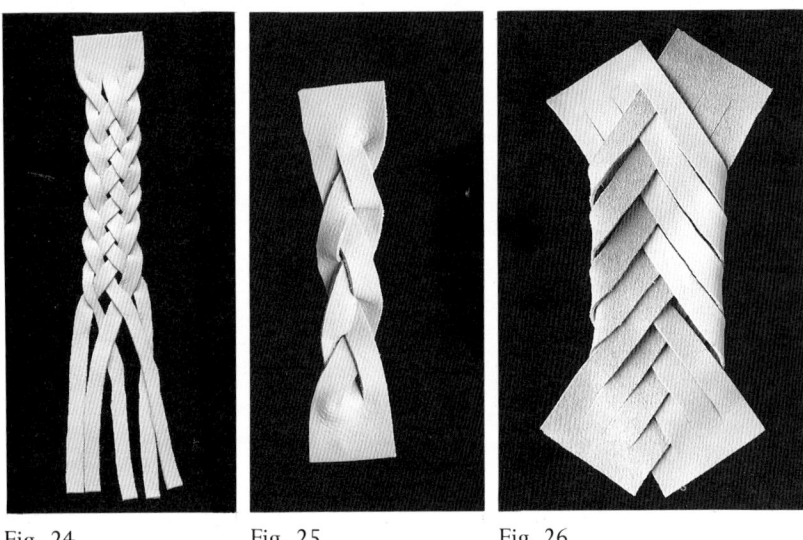

Fig. 24   Fig. 25   Fig. 26

Figs. 24, 25. When a long leather band is slit except for one uncut end, the braiding thongs have a unified strap for attaching a buckle or harness (Fig. 24). If neither end is cut, a "magic" braid results from an innovative method of twisting and inserting one end between the thongs (Fig. 25).

Fig. 26. To trap the bush spirit, the Indians of Guiana fashioned a puzzle interlaced with two flat elements. The spirit, while figuring how to take them apart, would be distracted from his usual mischief. Like the magic braid, the trick is to twist and inset one end.

Fig. 27. Defying all conventions, two rectangles partially cut into two suspended thongs interlace from opposite directions to simulate a four-element braid.

Fig. 28. Appreciated for bridles, this braid is worked as a compound structure with the two layers connected at the selvages. After completion, the selvages are pounded with a mallet to achieve a compact, rectangular cross-section.

Fig. 29. Worked in the manner of a frame braid, this mirror-image formation occurs within a leather rectangle centrally slit into multiple elements. Each set of three thongs is braided to the center and secured by a central tie. For saddle girths, gauchos work them with up to ten braids.

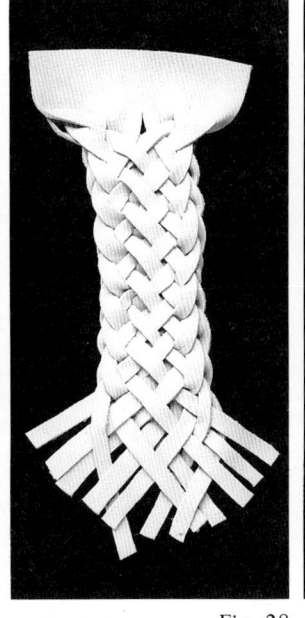

Fig. 27 Fig. 28 Fig. 29

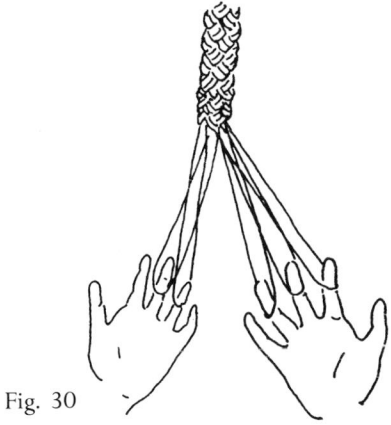

Fig. 30

Braids worked on fingers with looped elements have the special assets of eliminating tangles and achieving an even tension. This method also keeps the elements in position. The principle is simple: elements are folded in half and both cut ends are secured at a stationary point. This produces paired elements with a loop at the working end; each loop encircles a different finger (Fig. 30). Interworking takes place as an empty finger on one hand is inserted through the loop on the adjacent finger and then hooked into a loop on the opposite hand. It is finally brought back to the first side. The same process then takes place in the reverse direction. Loops are moved progressively from finger to finger and hand to hand. The braider's arms are regularly stretched apart to tighten the interlacing, pushing it forward and into position (Figs. 31–33).

Relics from medieval churches in Finland and Sweden include braids with looped elements. Similarly worked specimens are discussed in Roth's 1929 report on the Indians of British Guiana and in Cahlander's chapter on Bolivian braiding. The term *slentre* braids, derived from a Dutch verb meaning "to stroll," refers to the slow progression of the elements from finger to finger and hand to hand.

A major limitation is, *a priori*, the number of (paired) elements that can be worked, one to a finger. Three, five, and seven are the most frequent combinations. An old photograph from Dalarna, Sweden, demonstrates a method of increasing the width through communal braiding—the Scandinavian equivalent of a quilting party. Three women are pictured, each holding five elements on her fingers; a fourth pushes the braided "web" into place. As mentioned by Speiser, a handwritten seventeenth-century pattern book from the Victoria and Albert Museum gives instructions for braiding purse strings with up to seven people working the loops.

Speiser cites the same book as the basis for her explanations of several types of joined braids that also require the cooperation of several workers in order to manipulate the large number of looped elements. One example has the braid units joined by interlinking—similar to Karen Chapnick's piece on page 136. Another, called the "Katheren Wheele," produces parallel braids intermittently connected by a braid undulating between them. The lacelike effect is strikingly similar to the pre-Columbian braid on page 141.

In all of the above examples, looped elements, adapted for convenience, should not be confused with 1E looped structures such as knitting or crochet. Even those bands worked with looped elements are not necessarily interlaced; Speiser describes several twined and linked ones.

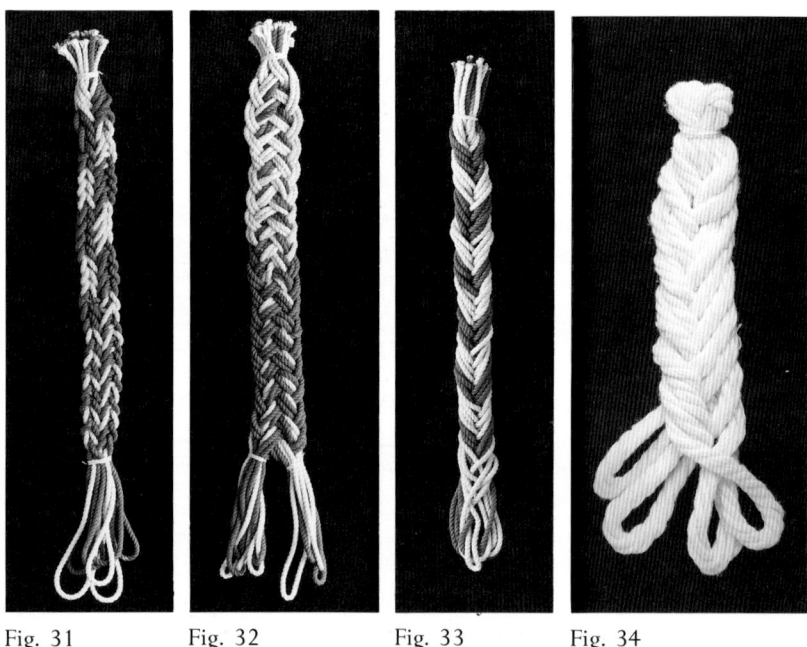

Fig. 31   Fig. 32   Fig. 33   Fig. 34

Figs. 31–33. Braids worked with looped elements, each encircling a finger, avoid the common problem of tangled loose ends. The interlacing is pushed into place by spreading the arms. Using the same tensioning principle as the backstrap loom, the Indians of Guiana anchored these braids on a big toe. As shown (Figs. 31–33), braiding with two looped ends of different colors creates special color effects.

Figs. 34, 35. Several looped elements can be grouped on a single finger. By bringing the rear loop forward, twisting and then slipping it back onto the front of the finger, a "wraparound" braid is effected (Figs. 34, 35).

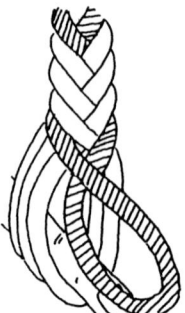

Fig. 35

Fig. 36

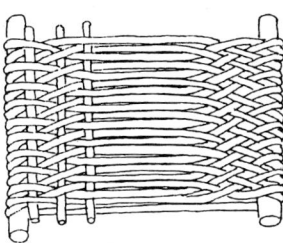

Fig. 37

Frame Braiding

The most obvious example of braiding without loose ends is frame braiding or interlaced *sprang*. In the classification, this was defined as a mirror interlacing of both ends of the web that terminates in the central region with a row of interlinking or a supplementary element (Fig. 36). If this holding feature is removed, the entire structure returns to its original parallel elements.

A variation, called "circular warp sprang" by Collingwood, is usually worked on a horizontal plane. Although elements have been continuously wound around two parallel beams, interlacing takes place only on the upper level, but again with the typical mirror-image interworking. As the work progresses, the rods that hold the interlacing are pushed back and around both beams, forcing the completed fabric to the lower level. This, in turn, clears the verticals on the upper tier for further working. Before chaining off and cutting, the final product is a circular band (Fig. 37). Kent's *Pueblo Indian Textiles* (pp. 82–84) explains this technique in greater detail. The traditional Hopi wedding belt on page 149 was interlaced in this manner.

A brilliant Bedouin sash is frame-braided in a stepped chevron pattern. The tab-fringes and pompoms are especially handsome.

130
sash
interlaced sprang
1SOE, 2/2 oblique
plied worsted yarns
54" × 2"
Sinai Peninsula, 20th century

Jan Janeiro's frame braided *Kimono Form* radiates a ritualistic presence. Its size and body are factors; more important is a consistent "rightness" in relying on structure to determine form. The kimono correctly uses the center line for the fold and the loops for a fringe; the side seams are equally architectonic. Knotted raffia ends are emphasized by wrapping them with copper wire; this metallic glint is repeated in the tabs of copper mesh attached to the sleeves.

131
Kimono Form #1, 1979
Jan Janeiro, U.S.A.
interlaced sprang, wrapping
1SOE, 1/1 oblique
raffia, copper wire, woven copper tabs
4′ × 3′6″
photo: Ted Macke

Although braids are even more frequently interlaced over one element and under one (1/1) than are baskets and textiles, many occur in other orders. That this frame-braided Hopi wedding sash is a 3/3 twill accounts for its heavy density. Note the transition to a fringe of narrow braids. The center just above the fold is typical of all sprang.

132 |
sash (detail)
interlaced sprang
1SOE, 3/3 obliquue
cotton
85" × 3½"
Hopi people, late 19th century

The oblique interlacing of this type of Colombian market bag influenced the large hangings of Olga de Amaral (see *Beyond Craft*, pp. 98–107, and *Mainstream* pp. 108, 216–17). The bag, as well as certain of the Amaral hangings, are interlaced sprang with diagonals emphasized by dark stripes. The ends—once looped over the frame—serve to connect the carrying cords, while two thick strands of the horizontal center line weight the bottom. Compare with the wool sprang bag on page 127.

133 |
market bag
interlaced sprang
1SOE, 2/2 oblique
maguey
20" × 18"
Colombia

The Influence of Materials and Modifiers

As will be demonstrated in Chapter 7, the characteristics of materials affect all types of interlacing. For braiding, the flexibility of the strands selected contributes to an intrinsic pliancy. Just as flat materials that can be bent 180 degrees are essential for the fold braids mentioned above, those special braids worked with uncut ends require a pliable flat material such as leather. While braiding with rigid elements is rare, an exception would be the braided splints of basket rims.

The impact of materials on resiliency was recently demonstrated by an examination of a large group of Amerindian sashes. Those braided with springy Germantown yarns were exceptionally supple, while those worked with wiry cords were relatively stiff. Density, of course, is a factor; so is pitch. Braiding is the most resilient of all fabric structures interlaced with sets of elements, but this characteristic can be increased or reduced by materials and modifiers as influenced by the order of interlacing. Stretchy yarns, openly worked, especially in a construction with floats, grouped elements, and a steep pitch, would produce the most compliant braid. One such sash was further exaggerated by the inclusion of hundreds of rather large bone beads and a long, weighty fringe. This braid would tie compactly and, in dances, the free-hanging ends would swing to exaggerate the movements of the wearer. In contrast, some East Asian braids of similar measure are closely worked with rigid elements in a nearly right-angle pitch, denying the potential resiliency of braids.

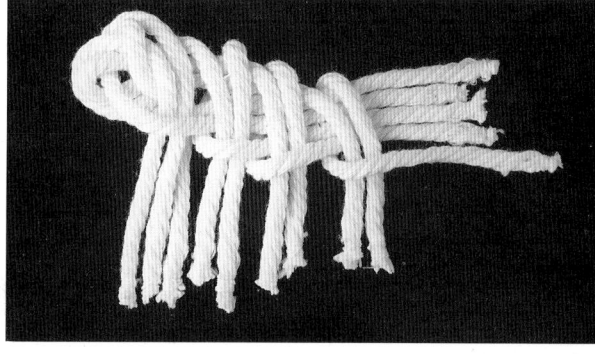

Fig. 38. The name "thrum" braids, contracting "thread" and "crumb," is derived from a weaving term for discarded warp ends. These braids are worked with discontinuous elements; new elements are added as previous ones become too short. Referring to the fringe of loose ends extending along the structure, these are called "Bag'o Wrinkles" by sailors who worked them over topping ropes to protect sails from chafing.

In Chapter 3 we illustrated how interworking elements of varied sizes can modify an appearance without changing the basic structure. For the few braids worked exclusively with short elements, new elements are added continuously as the work progresses (Fig. 38). A typical example is a braid of garlic bulbs. Additional tops are spliced in as the original ones taper off. The trim horizontal braid that finishes Navaho rugs and blankets is achieved with the same principle. So are the braided pile surfaces shown on page 138.

For most interlacings, grouping is a decorative device used to vary the elements, i.e., to give them additional colors and textures or a greater range of sizes. For instance, a basic three-element braid can be worked with six strands: three as one element, two as the next, and one alone. The greater the differential, the more the appearance is altered—but not the structure.

In repp braids the strands are alternately grouped and then interlaced as separate elements to produce a relief pattern that is often combined with color effects. In Alta Turner's instructions for Peruvian repp braids, in *Finger Weaving: Indian Braiding*, four or more strands are combined—first as a grouped element and then separately to singly interlace around other groups (Figs. 39–41). As grouped strands, they may be so hidden under the densely opposing elements as to be visible only at the selvages.

For a cross repp braid, the interworking is outward from the center to the two sides and then from the selvages back inward. The grouped strands can be seen as the focal point of the diamond-within-a-diamond patterning. One ancient Peruvian repp braid, a virtuoso example described by d'Harcourt (Plate 55-C), is so intricate as to defy description—or imitation.

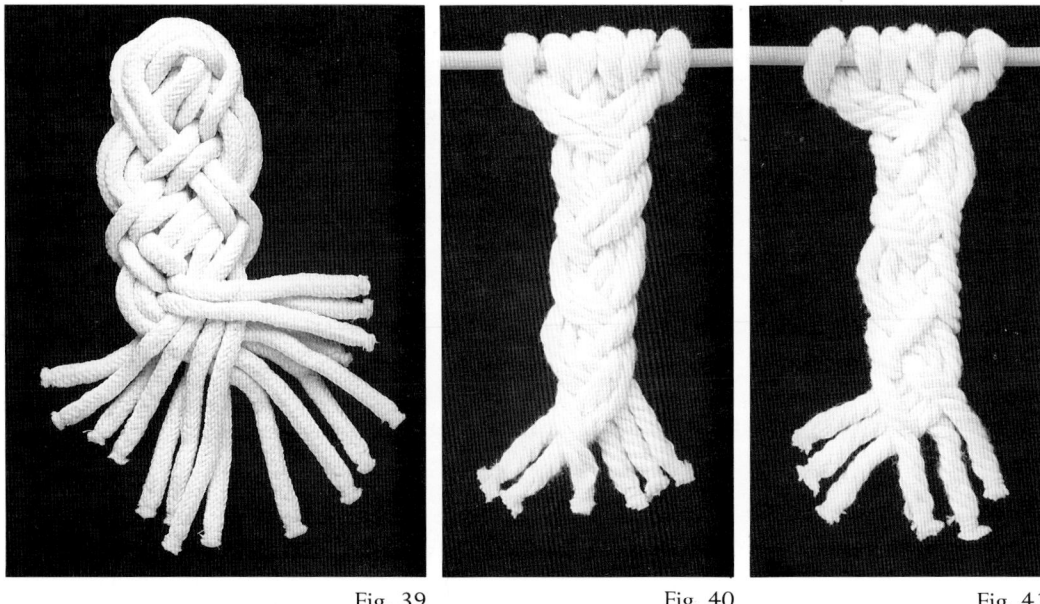

Fig. 39   Fig. 40   Fig. 41

Figs. 39–41. The strands of repp braids are alternately grouped and worked individually (Fig. 39). In cross repp braids, elements interlace to the center and then out to the selvage (Figs. 40, 41).

"Wraparound" braiding is the term the authors coined to describe a thick structure that is actually an exaggeration of a three-strand braid. Each element passes over a group of passive elements as it wraps around from the back and crosses at the center front. It then remains passive until all the other elements have made the same pass. Graumont and Hensel call them "running sennits"; others prefer the term "Chinese braids" (Fig. 42).

Twisting of elements subtly modifies the material used. In Japanese *kumihimo*, bobbins with grouped elements are often twisted just before interlacing. This effect is heightened when adjacent pairs are turned in opposite directions. Similarly, twisting leather thongs adds bulk to square braids intended for leashes and lanyards (Fig. 43).

Structural Modifiers

The tensile strength of braids is remarkably high, far greater than woven bands of the same size and material. Since there are no horizontals, all strands absorb the strain. This oblique structure also has more elasticity than woven structures. The manioc squeezer and the utility pipe grip on page 123 exemplify the special contraction/elongation property of tubular braids. The same property makes braided bindings so successful in turning a corner: the inside edge contracts, the outside elongates. Interestingly enough, woven bindings used for this purpose are cut on the bias so as to approximate the oblique interlacing of braids.

Density, a major factor in determining the character of braids, also impacts on color effects. The chevrons and diamonds typical of American Indian braiding would appear as oblique checks but for the considerable density of the covering elements (see p. 153).

Unlike weaving, braiding is usually worked without a mechanical tensioning device. With hand-held braids, all the strands may be held taut in a firm grasp. Counterweights attached to the bobbins perform this task in East Asian stool braiding. Tension is not necessarily the same for all elements within a braid. When some elements are relaxed and others taut, certain areas of the braid become compact, others more open. Such tension differentials may occur in all types of braiding (Figs. 44, 45).

Assymetrical braiding, produced by working from one side only, normally creates a shallow pitch (Pl. 134). When worked from one side for an interval and then from the other, the characteristic zigzag of rickrack occurs. The eccentric, nonlinear forms of assymetrical braiding shown in Speiser's book evolve from spasmodic changes in the direction of interlacing. Her drawings illustrate means of achieving several exotic profiles. She conjectures that this method could produce braided garments equivalent to those shaped on the loom.

The prehistoric White House shirt found in Canyon de Chelly, Arizona, has been minutely described by Kent. Its creators anticipated Speiser's concept of braided garments by more than seven hundred years. For this, Kent says, the yoke was braided from shoulder to shoulder with 480 strands suspended

Fig. 42. "Wraparound braid" is the term used here to describe structures in which each strand successively passes around several others, crosses over a strand at the center, and then rejoins the group.

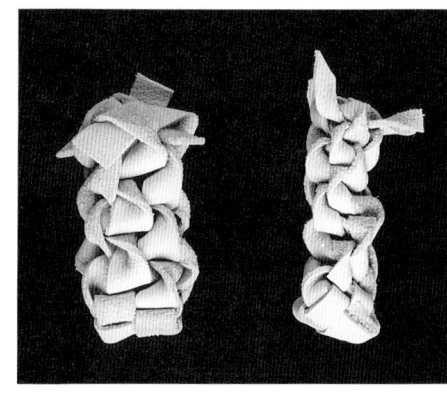

Fig. 43. Twisting the elements of fold braids as they are interlaced gives added strength and bulk to the structures. This is an asset for reins.

Figs. 44, 45. When tension varies within a braid, some areas become compact, others more open (Fig. 44). This may occur in square braiding as well (Fig. 45).

Braiding in which the active element is worked from only one side often forces all opposing strands to the surface, to affect an oblique rib.

134 |
belt
braiding
1SOE, 1/1 oblique
leather
Mexico, c. 1970

No fabric patterns are more colorful nor so intricate as the wide braids of North America. Outstanding examples were developed in the 18th and 19th centuries by the Eastern Woodland and Plains tribes. A controversy over the Assomption sashes (*ceintures fléchées*) worn by the Montreal fur traders, has never been resolved. The question is whether the prototypes originated in Northern Europe (Lapps and Norwegians have made garters with similar chevron patterning) or among the Iroquois and Huron Indians. The Southwest tradition and the Andean one are certainly indigenous, as well as ancient (see d'Harcourt, Chapter 10).

The three examples shown here are all Plains Indian, braided with commercial plied wools. Note the small white beads worked into the center one.

135 |
belt for cradle (left)
braiding, 1/1 oblique
wool
W. 7"
Osage people, Oklahoma

man's belt (center)
braiding, 1/1 oblique
wool, beads
W. 7"
Osage people, Oklahoma

sash (right)
braiding, 1/1 oblique
wool
W. 6⅜"
Winnebago people, Nebraska
collection: The Museum of the American Indian, New York

Braiding 153

from a bar. The braiding was then turned 90 degrees to allow the front and back to be braided downward from the center yoke. She believes that the sleeves were braided last.

The wide Amerindian sashes sometimes referred to as *ceintures fléchées*, or Assumption sashes, utilize "tapestry" joins to juxtapose areas of contrasting color. Many of the finest examples have repeats of arrowheads or lightning bolts as motifs. Because they are normally worked from the center to both ends, there is often a slight puckering at the center section.

In one rare braid, elements interlacing in both oblique and horizontal directions create saw-toothed selvages. Although this variant of braiding is considered unique wherever specialists encounter it, the structure recurs in widely separated cultures. Harvey describes it as a Maori braid; Parisians adopted it for straw hats of stitched overlapping braids. It is also known to Argentine gauchos and the Indians of British Guiana (Fig. 20).

Orders of Interlacing

Although most flat braiding is 1/1, cultural differences affect the orders of interlacing. Kent says that in her studies of prehistoric braiding from New Mexico, all Anasazi examples were 2/2, but eleven non-Anasazi specimens were 3/3. The Japanese favor 2/2 progressions for their silken *obi* ties. Gaucho leather braiding may be 1/1, 2/2, or 3/3, but Grant describes a flat braid of twenty-one thongs that is worked with 5/5 interlacing. And quirts, the short whips found hanging from Western saddle horns, often have handles covered in tubular braiding with 5/5 floats.

Orders of interlacing are not always consistent. Combinations of 2/1 and 1/1 are not uncommon. For some solid braids, the order of interlacing may be 1/4 from one side and 2/1 from the other. The variables are infinite.

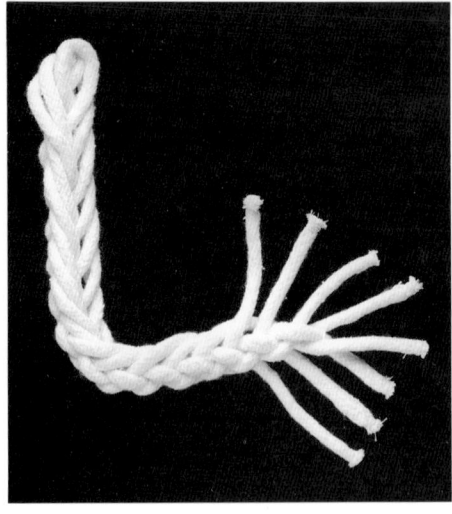

Fig. 46. Some braids appear completely different from front to back. This example is 1/1 on one face but has long floats on the other. Cowhands say these "oval" braids make good reins.

Gary Trentham's coiled basket is hidden by hundreds of braids. Their wiry crispness contrasts sharply with the outer fringe of brushed fiber. The braid yarns are attached to the structure by looping them around a coil before plaiting.

136 |
basket, 1980
Gary Trentham, U.S.A.
braiding, coiling
1SOE, 1/1 oblique
linen
6" × 22"
collection: Robert L. Pfannebecker, Pennsylvania

Machine Braids

Since machine-made braids are simply translations, their structures are intrinsically the same as those made by hand. The elements are usually wound on bobbins that move on discs controlled by gears. These follow circular crisscrossing paths as the braid, suspended above, is formed. Sometimes dozens of bobbins revolve in these intricate systems. The first machines, developed in the eighteenth century, were of wood and turned by hand. The *naikidai*, a Japanese braiding machine, was invented to produce special tubular braids for samurai armor. For this, weighted bobbins rotate in a large circle; each element is carried by a shuttlelike hook from one position to another.

In researching for this book, the author has acquired a new respect—or what might be better expressed as an awe—of braids and braiding. The diversity of applications is formidable, but not unexpected. It is the possibilities for variation within each structure, however, that astound. The narrow and broad flat braids, the round and solid ones discussed here are no more than basic examples of what is possible. Diversification through materials and modifiers, orders of interlacing, and specialized techniques broadens the scope a thousandfold.

As each culture developed braids to accommodate practical or decorative applications, new forms emerged. As in biology, some mutations were discarded or forgotten, others adopted and modified. The Industrial Revolution did not halt the progress but, as machines reproduced structures formerly worked by hand, led instead to a proliferation of nineteenth century passamenterie. Still, it is the simple braiding devices developed in East Asia that have most increased the range of structural possibilities. Unlike the elaborate braids favored by the Victorians, Oriental examples tend to conceal their complexity within an aesthetic of simplicity. Because these are too extensive to deal with in these few pages, we leave open the prospect of a major text in English.

137 | Machine braids need not be simplistic; some are far more intricate than these. The wide braided webbing on the right is vertically patterned with the turns and joins of discontinuous elements. Note its shallow pitch. Next is a solid braid of gimped cords. The third and fifth examples, with looped *picotee* selvages, are plaited with a fine matchstick rattan that requires occasional spliced joins. The fourth is a tubular braid of jute cordage.

6
Beginnings and endings

Particularly in the Western tradition, woven cloths are shaped by cutting and sewing—and discarding the residual fabric. Planned and executed as finished units, plaited forms are more economical. There is no waste and, as a rule, no subsequent joining. The original form is also the final one. In this sense, plaited forms are more akin to knit structures such as stockings. Weavings are, by comparison, most often used as raw material, unspecific as to end use.

The plaited start is not just a preliminary step but integral to the piece. Since the final form is also conceived before the work commences, both beginnings and endings are major, correlated aspects of the whole. The configuration of elements, the completed shape, and its dimensions are directly influenced by the initial and terminal modes.

Until now this writing has focused on structures reduced to general abstractions to point up their affinities. It is materials, plus beginnings and endings, that take the abstract to the concrete and so determine the diversity of interlaced forms. While materials greatly change appearances, they do not affect structure. Beginnings and endings, on the other hand, directly influence plaited forms—how they look, how they are made, and how well they will serve.

Since the potentials for beginnings and edge finishes are more limited than other variables, it is not unusual for such radial forms as mats, baskets, and hats to begin with an identical configuration. Endings such as selvages and simple returns are also common to many types of interlacing. Particularly in basketry, aptness of the method for starting and ending work testifies to human ingenuity. The varied demands of shape and material call forth inventive solutions, each potentially producing an intrinsic "rightness" similar to that found in nature.

A comparison of interlacings with architecture elicits striking parallels. Both rely upon horizontal and vertical structural systems. Both depend on materials for durability and appearance, and both utilize highlight and shadow to create surface interest. "Foundation," "supports," "skeletal structure"—words used to describe the initial stages of plaiting—bring forth associations with steel girders or wooden beams rising from a firm base to outline transparent boxes against the sky. From this framework, our imagination fills in the forms of finished buildings: a tower to be sheathed with a glossy skin of steel and glass or a compact house complete with peaked roof and fenestrated walls. Only color and surface are not predetermined by the initial steps of the construction process. The same terms and even the structural progressions are applicable to certain interlacings. Like buildings, classic baskets involve the correlation of a base, a containing form, and a reinforcing rim structurally and aesthetically not unlike a cornice or pediment.

However, a "building block" approach to architecture does not anticipate the final structure. From the beginning point, units are added block by block in a linear fashion. Lines of blocks extend gradually in the form of adjacent planes until the final dimensions are determined. This approach has parallels in such knotted fabrics as the basket on page 77.

Such similarities between architecture and interlaced structures seem coincidental but may not always have been so. Archaeological finds indicate that the more advanced fabric systems and permanent buildings developed in the same periods and, in some instances, of the same materials. Someday we may become aware of their common roots.

Forms

"Form follows function" has been the leitmotiv for the crafts of Japan, Shaker communities, and the Bauhaus. Focusing on the importance of ultimate use and elimination of the nonessential, these forms are not barren, but pure. From the time of the earliest plaited forms, other cultures discovered the same relationship between structure and use. Initially this was not a conscious philosophy—artisans simply continued to make, and improve upon, the forms that worked. A classic example is the framed interlacing of snowshoes—a minimal structure to evenly distribute weight. Their two materials, wood and animal gut, must withstand prolonged exposure to dampness and freezing. But it becomes evident that function alone does not determine the interlacing or the shape. The materials are so vital as to prescribe one method or shape over another. To achieve a functional form, materials must complement the manner of interlacing.

Weight is a consideration of people on the move. Their containers must be lightweight and resilient. If softer fibers flex and give, conforming to the body in motion, the rigid elements of a container can protect the contents and hold up in use. Bamboo, reeds, grasses, or yarns—customary components of interlacing—are frequently flexible and notably lightweight. The varied characteristics of fibers allow myriad contours— from pliable fabrics to curved baskets and rigid fish traps. Yet, archetypal basketry forms result when metal wires, plastic tapes, or strips of clay are interlaced (pp. 2, 14, 15).

Method

A given method of interlacing does not prescribe a certain shape. For example, virtually every method of interlacing will produce a disc. While a round mat may be formed by spiral interlacing over radiating spokes, the same shape occurs in braided rugs. There are round trays of 3SOE interlacing; even a 1E Turk's head can assume a disc form, albeit with a scalloped edge (p. 68). Although most rectangular planes result from 2SOE interlacing, the 1E Chinese and Turkish knots (p. 70) are also flat and square. 1SOE frame braiding forms a rectangle; so do 4 and 6SOE interlacings within a rectangular frame.

The position of a start, discussed above, strongly influences the ultimate form. While round and spherical shapes are likely to be worked from central starts, beginnings that occur on a point or line usually develop into rectangular or cubical forms. There are exceptions, of course. Tubular interlacing starts from a line, albeit a circular one. The familiar "melon" basket (opposite), worked over a hemispherical skeleton, proceeds from a point on the rim to the one diametrically opposite.

Style

Shapes are also strongly influenced by prevailing styles. Sometimes these evolve from the functional pragmatism of discovering what works, but they can also result from imitating forms that are successful in other media. For example, if many plaited vase shapes are carryovers from ceramics, the reverse is also true—*ollas* are baskets in clay. Religious or ceremonial practices may set a style with no relationship to practical use; ritual objects commonly have exaggerated forms in materials quite removed from the originals.

Specialized Forms

A form characteristic of many plaited containers is the square-based basket with a circular top. Modified by the flexibility of the materials, the shape changes as the encircling element rounds the four-sided base. The initial corners simply dissolve into curves. Along with the predictable interlaced forms regenerating themselves through the centuries, some aberrations have sprung up as specialized adaptations. Such is a tubular African basket with five consecutive chambers. When inverted, it works like an hourglass with interior seeds slowly decending from one chamber to the next, measuring the time a litigant may speak out in court.

Other forms express both function and ornament. A segment of a shape may be repeated like a musical motif, as in an East Indian nested basket. Here, pyramids project from both the base and lid. The six-fold plane chosen to create rigidity with a soft fiber becomes decorative; the twisted elements of the sidewalls repeat the formation. Shereen LaPlantz follows the same theme in her own manner (p. 107).

Asymmetrical Shapes

Shapes not conforming to conventional geometry also have predetermined requirements. Symbolism decides the asymmetrical form of such plaited toys and fetishes as the *bandolero* on page 16. The free-form basketry used by the Sogetsu school

138

138–141 |
Several current methods of interlacing hemispherical willow baskets in Poland are shown here. The traditional melon basket starts with two ovals laced to each other at right angles (Pl. 138). The ribs are added as interlacing progresses at each end. Note the cords that position the new ribs and the short temporary ribs, which will be replaced as the basket grows. As an alternative construction, the "eye of God" in Plate 139, first locks in the key oval hoops, then anchors the six midribs. An oval basket without a handle (Pl. 140) is started with a single hoop. The three center ribs that pierce it are spread and stabilized by the first interlacing. Successive rib splints are sharpened for insertion into the web. Those that show as doubled or tripled will divide as the melon form swells. A similar basket (Pl. 141) is being twined over paired verticals. Work is facilitated by temporarily tying down the spoke ends, by lacing them to a temporary cross rib, and by heavy interior braces.

photos courtesy of Jolanta Owidzka, Warsaw

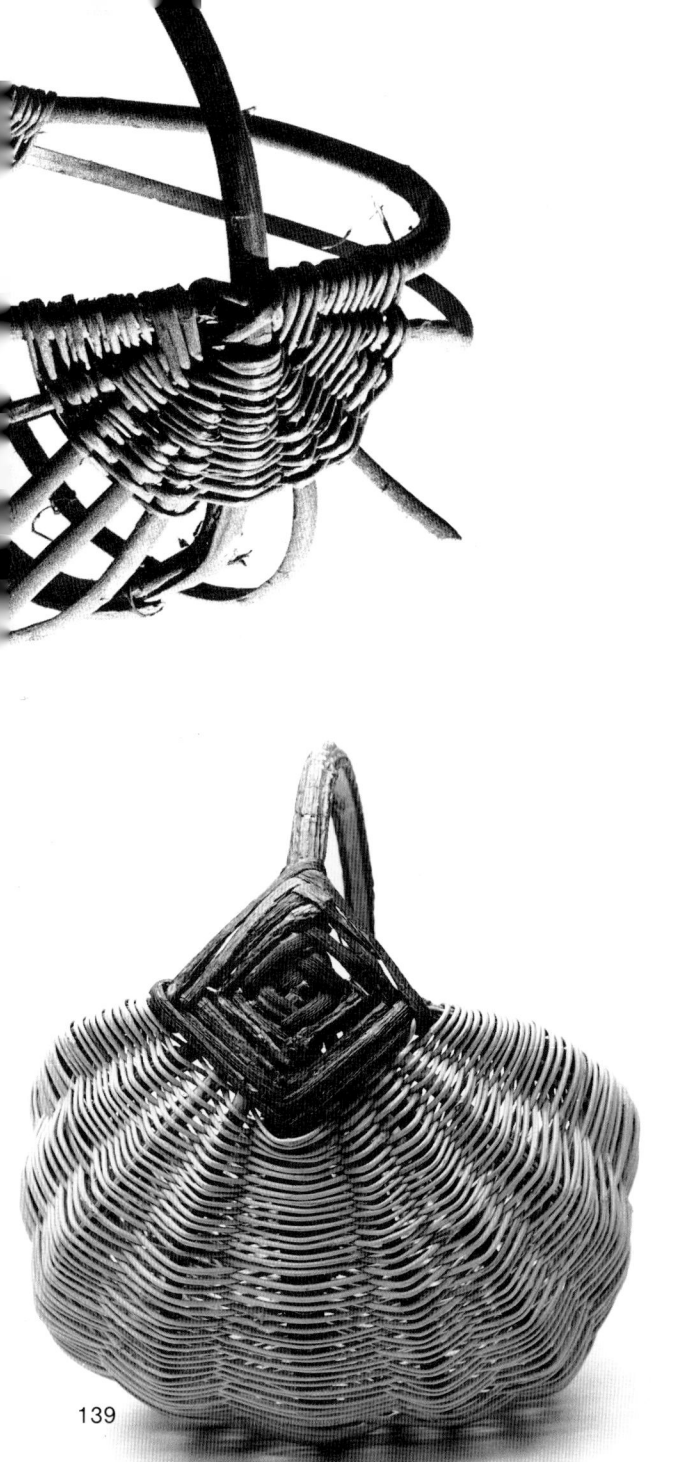

139
140
141

of Japanese ikebana has certain size and shape requirements to complement the lines of selected flowers and branches. These functional baskets are precursors of a highly individualized craft equivalent to abstract expressionism. Strands are interlaced, linked, or twisted according to intuition, without the controls of preplanning. Impulse dictates; the intentional accident results. Related to sculpture, many of these examples mask any useful purpose or inherent limitations (see pp. 7 and 257).

Lids, Handles, and Added Bases

Whether round or rectangular, flat or domed, lids conform to the contour of baskets. While some curve slightly over the rim, others telescope over the side walls. Another type fits inside the rim. A few basketry lids are hinged with stitches or other simple means. The technique used to produce the foot is frequently repeated in a lid. In many cases, because of its high visibility, a decorative cover is the primary focus, rich in pattern or distinguished by an exotic silhouette.

Handles can be an extension of a skeletal armature, with their elements extending down the sides of a basket. Such is the hen basket with curving spokes swirling upward to form a handle that completes the oval shape. Grips for wicker baskets are often an outgrowth of the rim. For the rug beater (p. 72), both beginning and ending of the interlacing are the handle.

Wood, bamboo, metal, or plaited handles may be added after interlacing has been completed. Semicircular handles are sometimes hinged so that they lie flat when not in use, allowing containers to be stacked. Dating back to prehistoric times, hang straps are still practical for freeing the hands; the Chinese use them to suspend a pair of containers from the ends of a shoulder pole. To prevent their loss, telescoping covers may slide up and down a cord that doubles as a handle.

Common to temporary baskets, the simplest and earliest handles were merely a looped strand of bast fiber sufficient to hang the empty basket. These were later supplanted by braided handles that are stronger and more flexible. Sometimes handles encircle a soft basket to cradle the heavy contents. In other cases they are attached to a major rib or reinforced rim, or are integrated into the web. For comfort and strength, handgrips are often wrapped or covered with a tubular braid: the handle proper becomes a core, the braid a sheath. Braided shoulder straps and tumplines often broaden at the carrying point.

Added base constructions such as feet or legs can lift a container from the ground, thereby aiding air movement and preventing mildew. This is essential for carrying and storage of clothing, tools, weapons, and grains in damp climates. The base armature may be added inside, outside, or simply stitched onto the bottom surface. In some cases corner braces extend to become feet.

142 |
A child's haversack from Sarawak, beautifully worked in a face reverse pattern, terminates in braided loops to hold a drawstring closure.

A classic carrying basket of a type dating from Colonial times is so thoughtfully conceived and executed that it becomes an object of enduring beauty. The vertical staves, which turn over a horizontal then interlace downward until secure, are reinforced by lashing on a double rim. Note the workmanship of the hinged bale and the reinforced feet.

143 |
basket with bale
staved plaiting
2SOE, 1/1 H-V
H. 23" × D. 22"
Nova Scotia, Canada, 1979

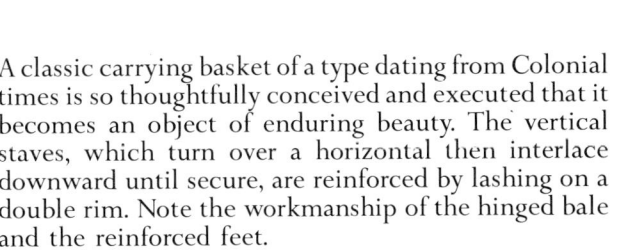

Starting Points

One-element structures, such as the knotwork trivet on page 72, present a conundrum because they meld the start and finish within the essential form—alpha and omega become one and undifferentiated (Fig. 1). Knots transcend mere function to broach the realms of symbolism and religion (see Chapter 9).

Generally, interlacing begins at one of three locations: 1) from an end point or edge; 2) in the center; 3) within a framework. Endings, on the other hand, occur at the point or line farthest from the starting point, or, in the case of a center start, at the outer rim. With the third category, both the beginning and termination of the interlacing is on a frame, as in tennis rackets.

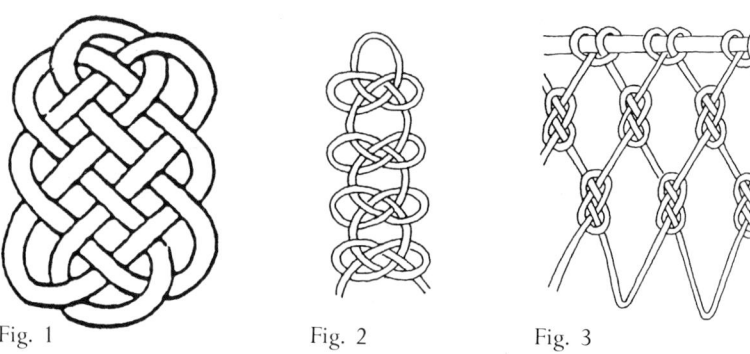

Fig. 1   Fig. 2   Fig. 3

A skirt made by African pigmies starts with the pair of braids that supports it. When bundles of wiry grass are hitched over it, these braids become a belt.

145 |
A dense palm leaf fan was started at its upper corner. At its center the strands begin to float over the mat to form a handle.

146 |
In many cultures braids are the consummate finish for both weaving and plaiting. In a Congolese bustle, the warp ends are reduced—first to thirteen braids, then to four—to terminate in a plied tying cord.

Beginnings, Endings   163

Starts and Endings at an End Point or Edge

Braids commence at either a point—for instance, a knot or head of hair—or with a series of knots or loops along a rod or cord (Figs. 4, 5). As mentioned earlier, to avoid entanglements typical of working with long elements, starts for braided belts sometimes take place at the middle of the strands; plaiting is worked first to one end and then to the other, but the principle is the same. Slit leather braids are worked from an uncut end (Fig. 6). Even tubular braids start from a circular top line or two parallel rods (Fig. 7).

Narrow braids are usually completed with a knot, while the ends of hair braids may be wrapped with another material (Fig. 8). The terminus of wide, flat braids may be subdivided and worked as narrow braids, or, narrow braids may be combined to form wider ones (Fig. 9; see the Tibetan hair braids on page 236).

That 1SOE maverick, frame braiding, begins simultaneously with loops encircling two parallel rods at the extremes and is worked in a mirror-image progression (Fig. 10). Frame braiding is unique in that the final working is done at the center. There, one or more supplementary elements are interworked through the verticals as a transverse binding cord (Fig. 11). If this cord is removed, the entire interworking unravels.

Fig. 4 Fig. 5 Fig. 6 Fig. 7

Fig. 8 Fig. 9 Fig. 10 Fig. 11

A row of looped elements, often secured with pins on a pillow, constitutes the beginning line of bobbin lace. As the bobbins crisscross, elements interlace or interlink. Before the ends are finally tied, the lace may take on the shape of a tape, a rectangle, or a free form (Fig. 12).

Such diversified interlacings as plaited bands, mats, and woven textiles can also progress from a line. They often start from knots or loops over a rod; elements may be positioned with one or more courses of twining (Fig. 13).

To start a mat from a point, one element is folded twice at 90 degrees, creating the first corner. As elements are added, the structure widens; decreasing takes place after the third corner has been reached. Work ends at the point diagonally opposite the beginning, but, since all corners are identical, it may be impossible to identify the start and finish (Fig. 14).

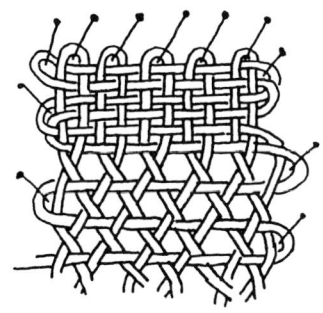

Fig. 12

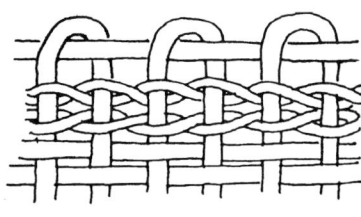

Fig. 13

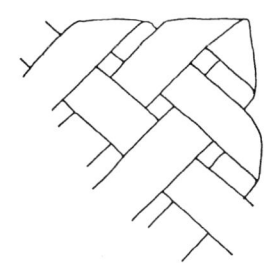

Fig. 14

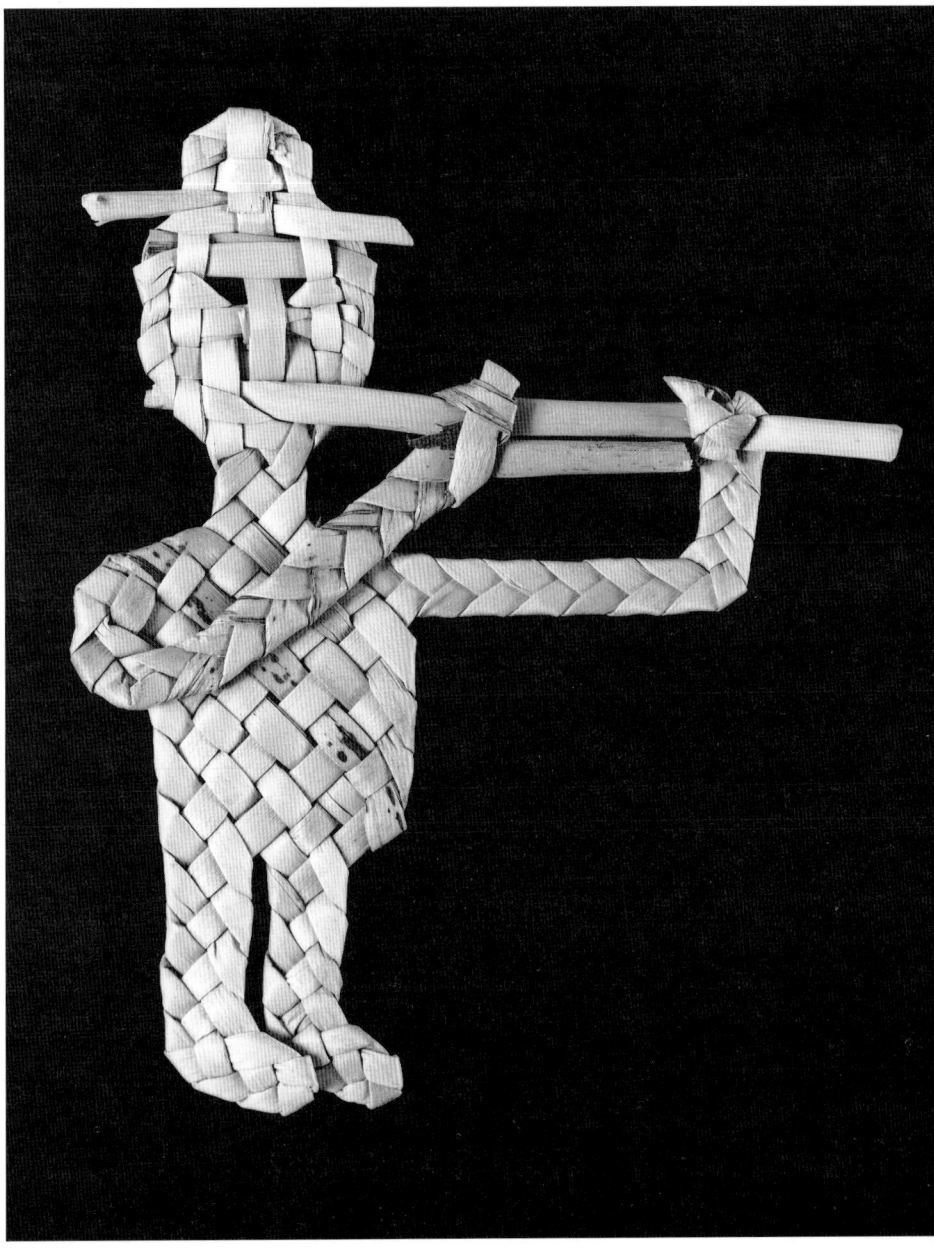

While geometry and symmetry determine the shapes of most interlaced objects, toys and festive objects do not fall within the same restrictions—here, imagination is freed from the conventions of function. This tiny plaited form is amazingly expressive. That each small distortion contributes to the imagery is the result of skills refined over generations.

147 |
piper
1SOE, 1/1 oblique
bast
H. 5″
Mexico

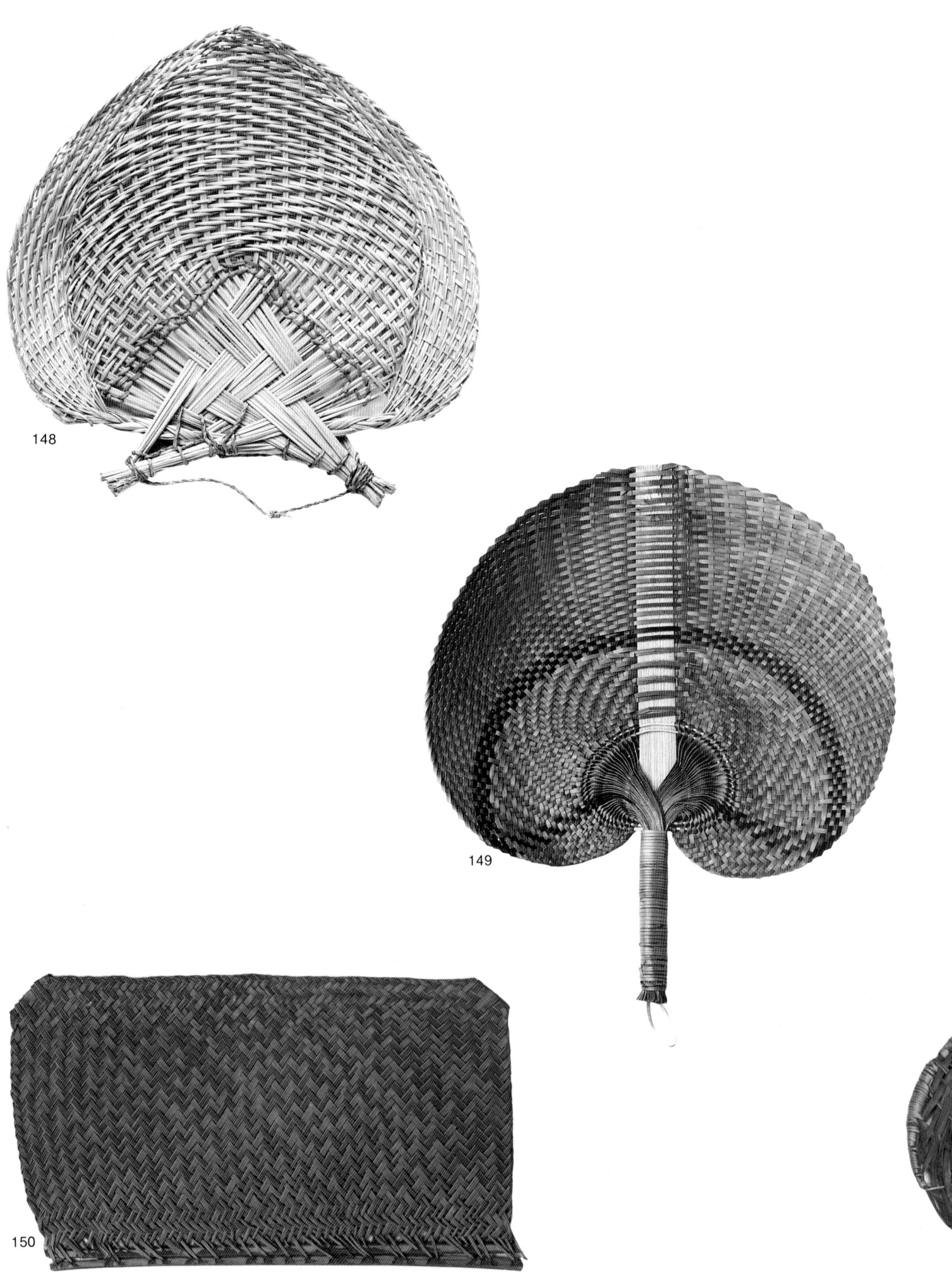

148

149

150

166　Interlacing

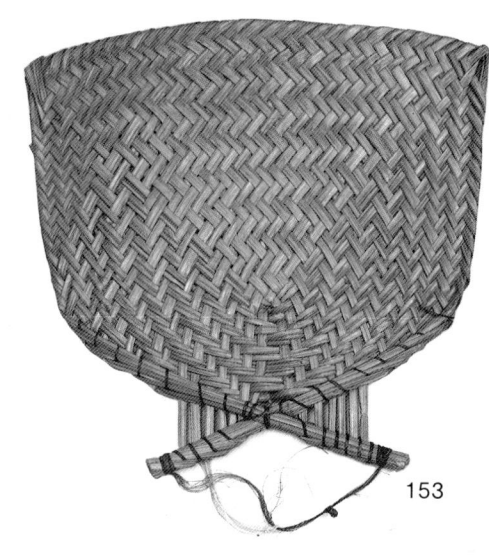

153

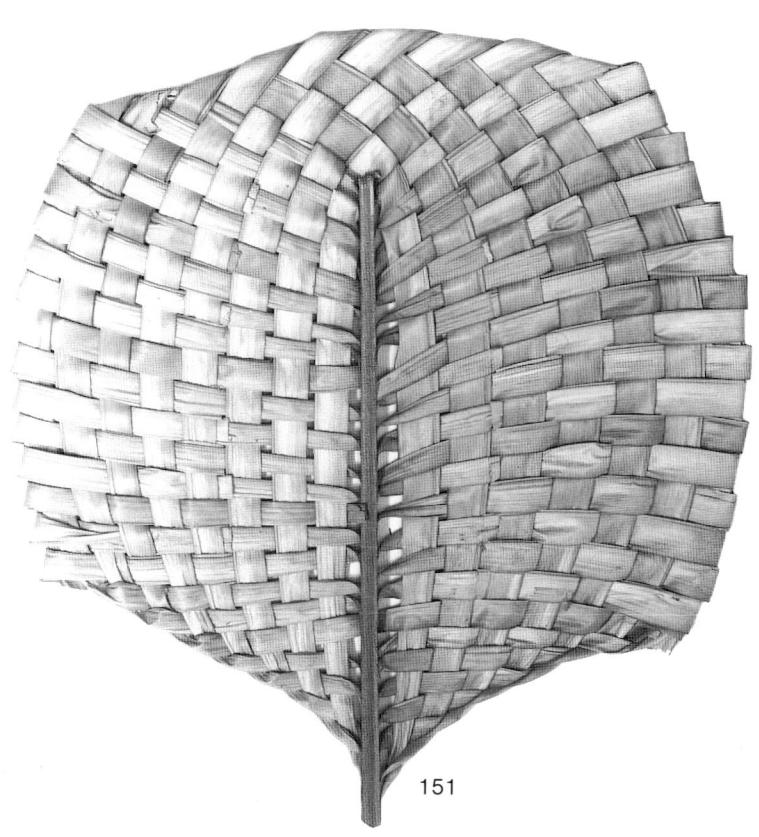

151

154

148–154

From all over the world, plaited fire fans present an amazing testimonial to human ingenuity. Often these same fans are used to cool people or food, as pot or basket covers, as food mats, spatulas, or even as ceramic glaze spreaders. Some of the simplest (Pls. 150–54) are worked from the mid-ribs of palm fronds. Sometimes (as in Pls. 152 and 150), two of these are overlayed so as to produce more working ends. Leaflets are also split for the same purpose. The opposite edge is finished by folding over the strands to interlace them back into mat. In the ceramic glazer (Pl. 153), two mid-ribs are crossed over and wrapped with rattan to form a handle.

Twill plaited with fine bast strips, the example in Plate 148 has a similar handle. But here the first (1/1) interlacing is with groups of four pairs of strands. These are separated with two courses of twining, then 2/2 plaited towards the top. A broadening frame at the sides supplies horizontal elements. So do the paired spoke ends, which turn about 90° to become single horizontals interlacing to the opposite edge.

In Plate 149, fine strips of palm leaf are lashed to a central support to form a handle. These are positioned by two matchstick bamboo rings, then interlaced. Following the movement of the dark stripe helps to read the progression. Within it, the plaiting is a dense 2/2 twill progression. Beyond it is a lighter weight 1/1 interlacing.

The examples in Plates 149, 150, 152–54 were collected by Boris Malkin from 1956 to 1963 in the Mato Grosso of Brazil. They belong to the Glenbow Museum, Calgary. The others, the author's, are without provenance.

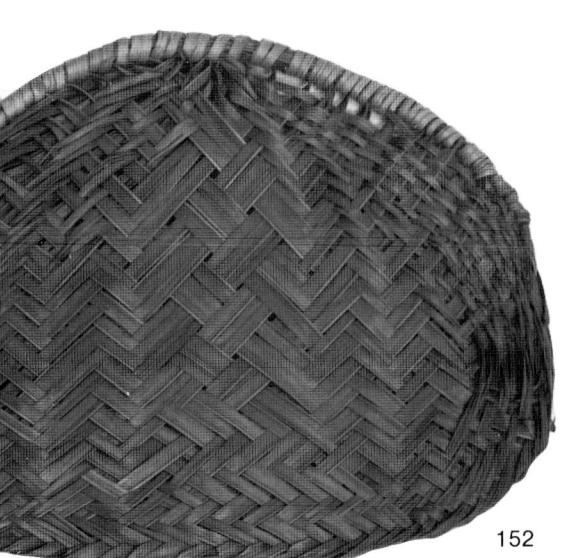

152

Beginnings, Endings

Central Starts

Interlacing that begins in the center, as in round mats, hats, and most baskets, is easy to identify. As it interlaces, an active element circles the radiating spokes. If a narrow element is used, the spiral of the outward progression may be almost imperceptible (Fig. 15).

Methods for central positioning of the initial radiating elements are universal; each basic method must have been "invented" many times. In a common example, the start is matlike with H-V interlacing of two opposing SOE; elements are bent upward, and all become parallel. One active element does the interworking around the four sides (Fig. 16). The most direct method is to lace elements together. Twining helps to keep the elements in their proper position before interlacing begins its spiral path (Fig. 17).

Sometimes four or more converging spokes are interlaced by a spiraling element; extra struts are added as the spiral circuit enlarges. Interlacing may also begin around spokes that are paired for the first courses and then separated to be interworked individually (Fig. 18). When there is an anchoring course, consisting of looping or twining, the twist between spokes serves not only to secure them but to separate them as well (Fig. 19).

A technique found primarily in willow baskets consists of cutting slots along the center of the spokes. Interpenetration of the elements secures the crossing and facilitates two-handed manipulation (Fig. 20). In the drawing, the elements are cut and paired then separated into individual elements for interlacing.

In a rarer practice, work starts from a disc of leather, wood, or other rigid material with holes pierced around the circumference. The spokes are bent 180 degrees at the outer edge, then reinserted into another hole (Fig. 21). For the double rattle made in this manner (opposite), the twin leather bases serve as sounding boards.

Because they avoid the impass of too many elements crossing at the center point, techniques for starting with a star shape are many. In Figure 22, the central elements form a pinwheel effect as they are folded before the initial interlacing. This serves as an anchor and a decorative center of a temporary basket. In Figure 23, multiple spokes form an intricate pattern with minimal interlacing.

Also working outward from a six-pointed center are the starts common to 3SOE matting and 4SOE caning. As interworking expands outward, parallel strands are added in three or more directions (Fig. 24). For shaping, some of these baskets are worked damp over oval or hemispherical forms.

From the compact geometry of a center star, the long elements of the baskets on pages 172 and 173 swirl into curvilinear finishes. In all three examples, the first six elements are 1/1 interlaced around a hexagonal opening. Floats lengthen as elements are added to enlarge the dimensions of the star. The strands of two of them are grouped for the final flourishes; the third star opens into a plaited mesh terminating with a neat braided edge.

Fig. 15

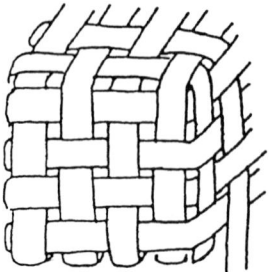
Fig. 16

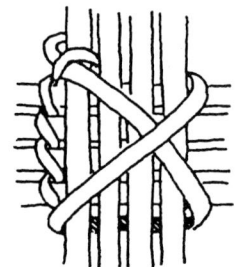
Fig. 17

Fig. 18

Fig. 19

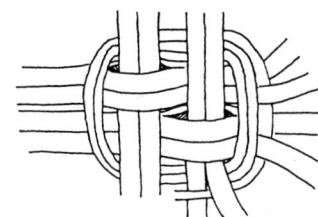
Fig. 20

For a grasshopper storage basket, a single willow branch has been slit into strips for the first verticals; others are added as diameter increases. Essential ventilation for the live fish bait is provided by the openings in 1/1 interlacing of rigid elements. A corncob forms the stopper.

155 |
bait basket
2SOE, 1/1 H-V
willow, bast
12" × 3"
Caraja, eastern Brazil
collection: Glenbow Museum, Calgary

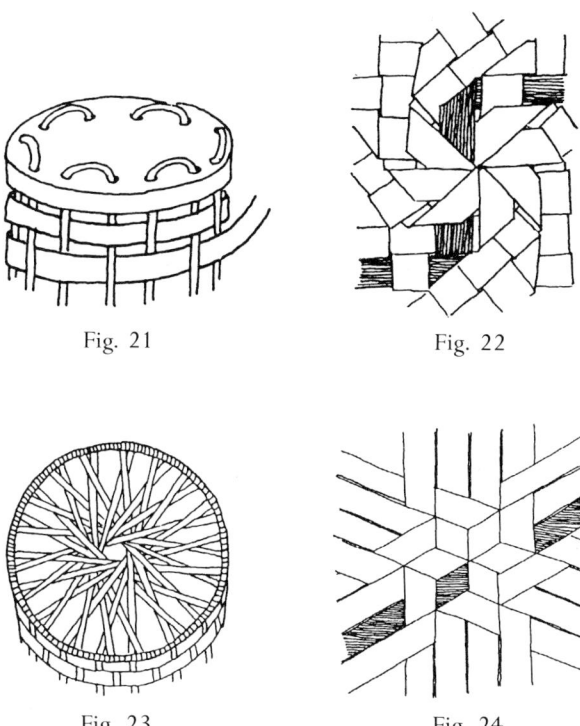

Fig. 21   Fig. 22

Fig. 23   Fig. 24

156 |
This African double rattle starts with a long continuous spoke laced back and forth between two pierced leather bases. The two rattles are then plaited as wickerwork, and the bare spokes between them simultaneously curved and wrapped to form a handle. The leather bases become sounding boards.

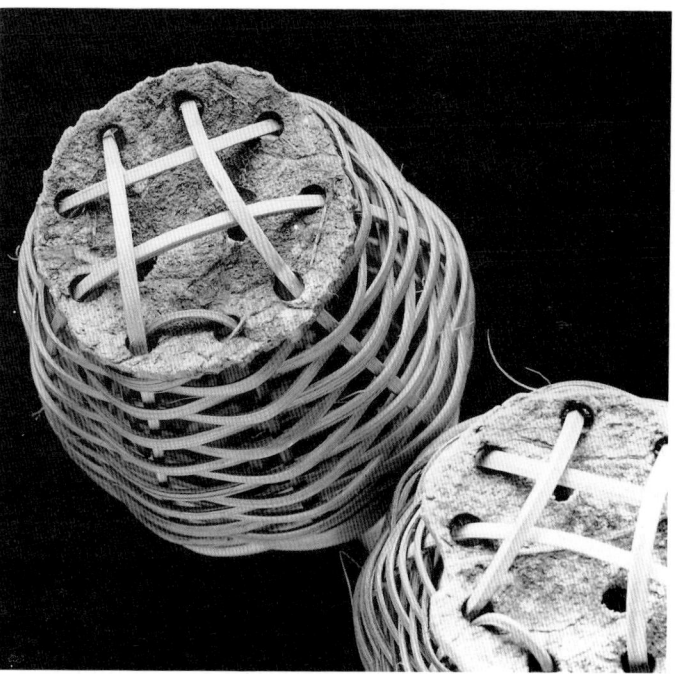

Beginnings, Endings 169

157

159

158

157 |
Double layers of wide palm strips are plaited as a rounded square then held in place with a thin strand. The layers then divide to increase the number of elements.

158 |
To achieve the rounded oval of a fine Panama hat, two central squares are interlaced together, then their elements manipulated into an elongated whorl as the plaiting proceeds outward in an imperceptable spiral. The two oval lines where new strands have been added are only faintly visible.

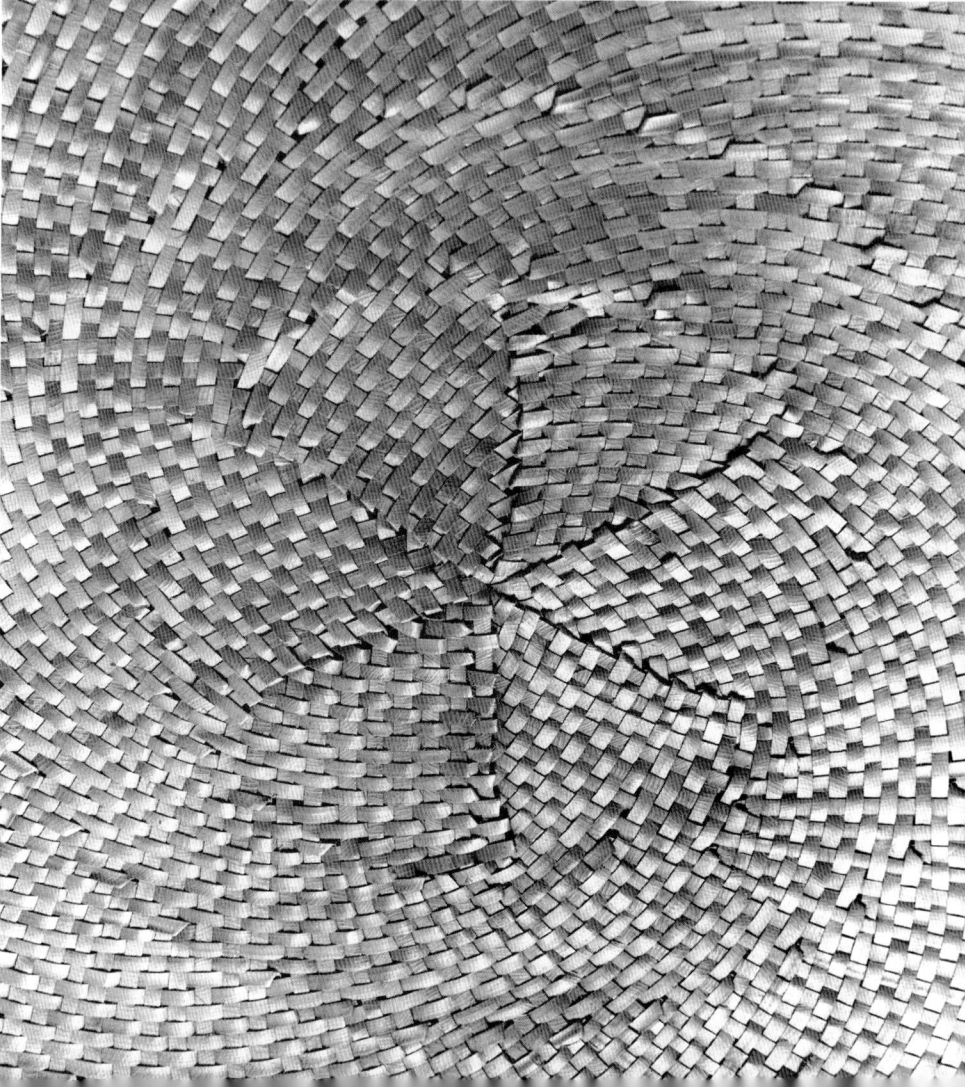

159 |
The whorl becomes a single spiral in a fanciful straw hat. The protruding seed heads of newly added strands add greatly to the effect.

160 |
The filigree of a hemispherical bowl is achieved with a spiral of neolithic braid. Radiating straws join the braid to interlace under, over, under and out to the next course.

161 |
The crisp folds requisite to increasing dimension result in a dynamic whorl radiating around a six-pointed star.

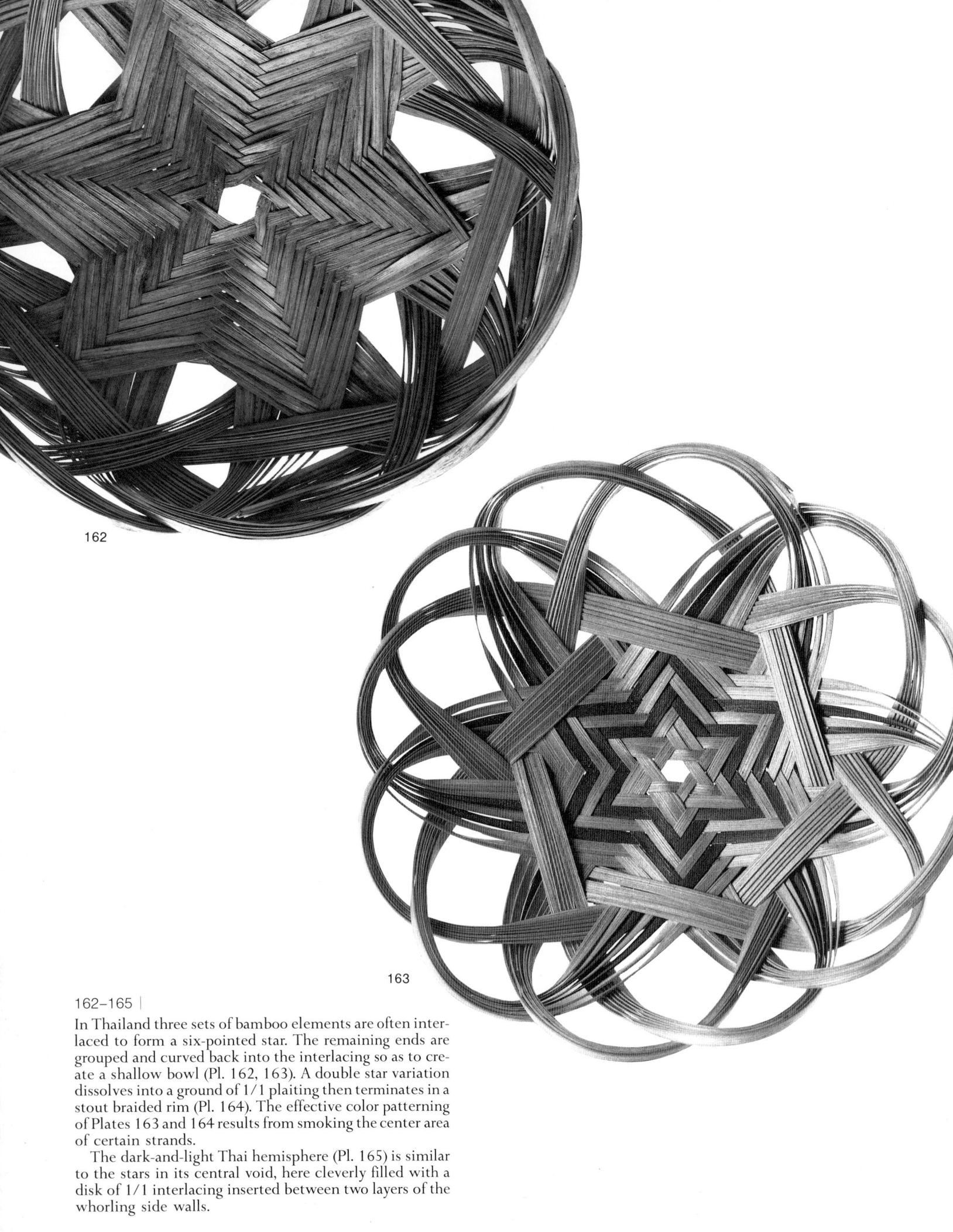

162–165 |
In Thailand three sets of bamboo elements are often interlaced to form a six-pointed star. The remaining ends are grouped and curved back into the interlacing so as to create a shallow bowl (Pl. 162, 163). A double star variation dissolves into a ground of 1/1 plaiting then terminates in a stout braided rim (Pl. 164). The effective color patterning of Plates 163 and 164 results from smoking the center area of certain strands.

The dark-and-light Thai hemisphere (Pl. 165) is similar to the stars in its central void, here cleverly filled with a disk of 1/1 interlacing inserted between two layers of the whorling side walls.

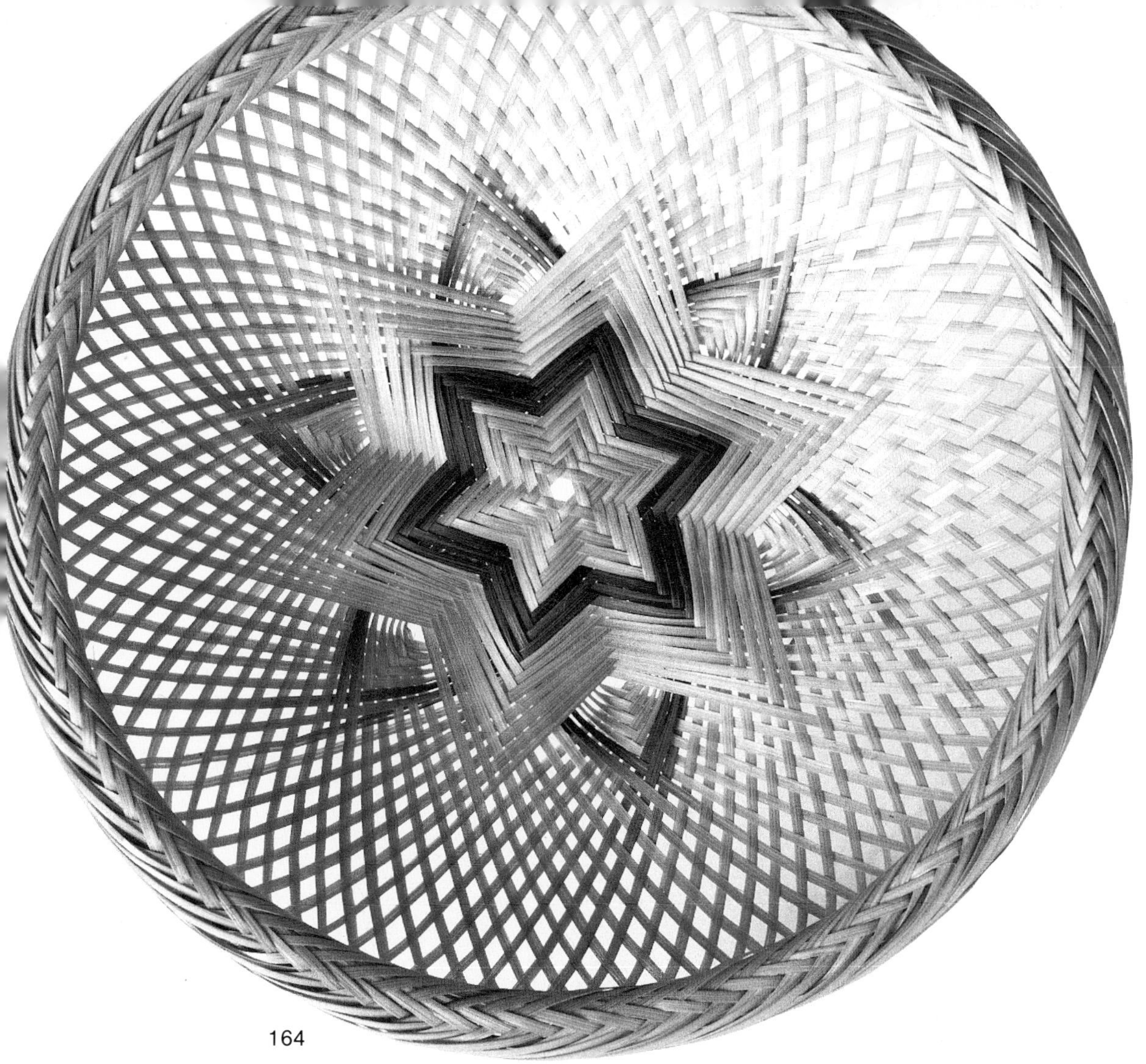

164

165

Edges, Endings, and Rims

The terms "edges" and "endings" are not synonymous. Endings, of course, are the means by which the interworking is terminated. We also speak of an outer edge of a basket as a rim. Selvages (*self edges*) are formed along the sides of the piece as the work progresses.

Interlacing that produces four selvages is often worked over pins stationed on at least two sides of a frame. Typically, cloths woven on backstrap looms also have four selvages. After the final element is spliced into place, weaving cannot unravel in any direction (Fig. 25). The same is true of obliquely worked mats. The raw ends of textiles and plaited bands may be hem stitched, knotted or braided, twisted into a fringe, or worked back into the web. Sometimes they are covered with a sewn-on tape or braid.

There are several means of decoratively interworking elements at the rim to enhance the beauty of a basket. Clipping the ends of protruding elements is the simplest method to form an edge, but this is practical only with materials rigid enough to hold without reinforcement. When the walls of baskets are merely folded over the top to form a secondary wall, the ends are usually cut at lower inside corners. More often, individual elements are folded back to interlace with several courses of the finished work before being discretely clipped. In either case, doubling over reinforces the edge.

Baskets worked with two palm fronds start with a central rib resembling the keel of a ship. The still-attached leaflets interlace to form the outer wall (Fig. 26). Braiding is the typical method for ending this work (Fig. 27).

Fig. 25

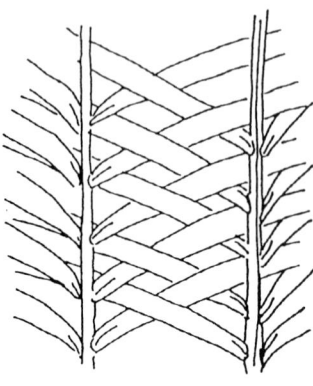

Fig. 26

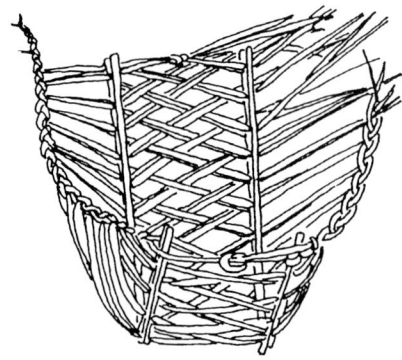

Fig. 27

166 |
A fine Japanese mat of bamboo slats strung together like very long beads is finished on both "selvages" with a braided edging worked over the notched ends.

A head ring for supporting a round-bottomed vessel is continuously interlaced around a core.

167 |
head ring
2SOE + 1E, 1/1 H-V
D. 8"
East Africa, c. 1980

Beginnings, Endings 175

168 |
Shown upside down, a small, double-walled Amerindian basket ends as neatly as it began. To start, 6 elements are placed across 6 elements and wrapped into position to form 12 paired spokes. As the form widens, additional spokes are added. To finish, the grouped spoke ends are braided, then hidden between the two walls.

169 |
With great finesse, a Thai bamboo basket worked in the old Chinese style employs a variety of braids to anchor the open hexagonal plaiting to a rattan frame.

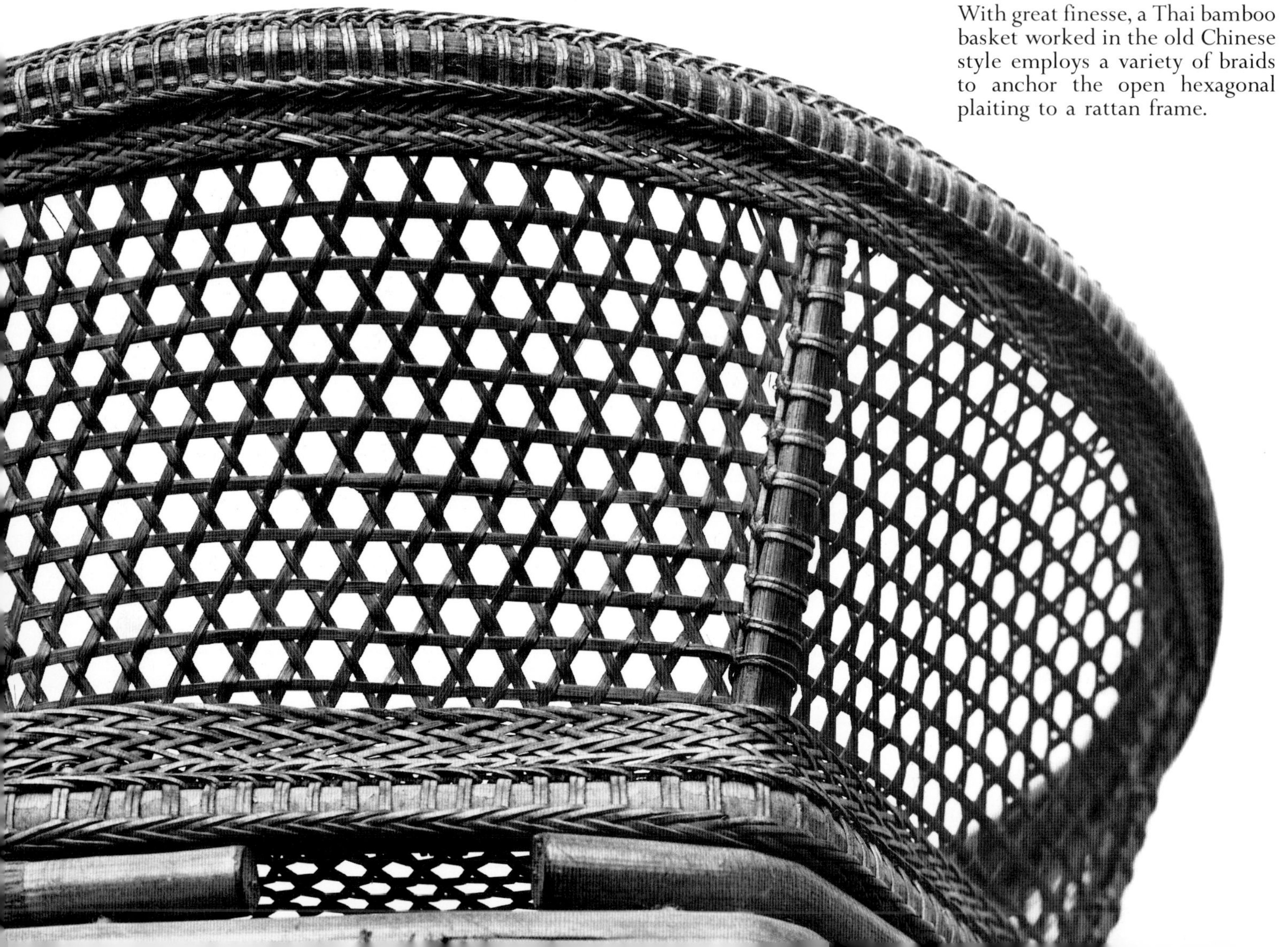

The methods for working basketry rims are even more numerous than for starts. While a simple return of elements into the structure unobtrusively strengthens the lip (Fig. 28), a sawtoothed edge may result from the right-angle fold and return of oblique plaiting (Fig. 29). Rims formed with elements bent into horizontals then twisted together resemble twining with short strands (Fig. 30). Methods involving arched spokes cannot be avoided when working with materials too rigid or brittle for folding or braiding, and the repeated arches may ornament an otherwise stolid form (Fig. 31).

To give laundry baskets a smooth, strong rim, two or three rows of twining are worked for the uppermost courses. This serves to "lock in" all the vertical and oblique ends. To form the solid rim, the spokes are then bent on a right angle, twisted, rolled, and finally clipped (Fig. 32).

Binding basketry edges with another material is comparable to using bias tape on hems of clothing. The most beautiful are braids worked directly over the edge (see page 173). Leather bindings have an added bonus of introducing a contrasting color and texture (see page 179). Raw ends can also be wrapped or enclosed in an overcasting technique resembling coiling.

The horizontal braiding used for the rims of so many baskets (Fig. 33) is comparable to the method used by Navaho weavers to end their rugs and blankets. The elements of these braids are never constant, but—after a few inches—are dropped out and clipped as new ones are added. "Corn row" braiding is an instance of the same technique worked in a radically different material.

The wide braid forming the side walls of a French bread basket is remarkably successful in that the turns of the lower selvage engage the plaited base, the upper selvage is itself a rim.

For the "false braid" edging (Fig. 34), double twining overlays the ends of the strands. The final row of tightly worked twining holds this structure in place.

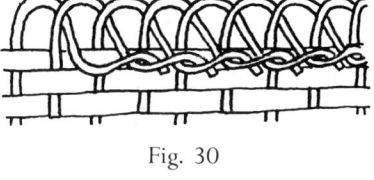

Fig. 30

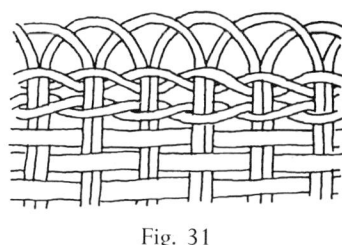

Fig. 31

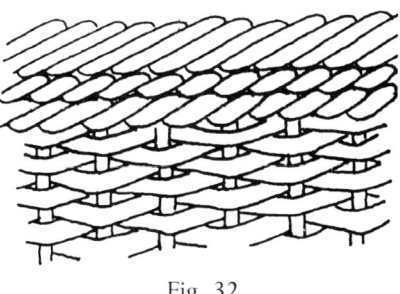

Fig. 32

Fig. 33

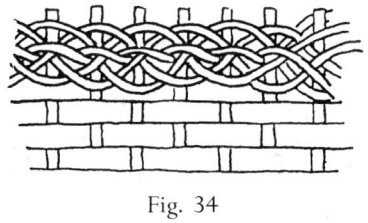

Fig. 34

Fig. 28

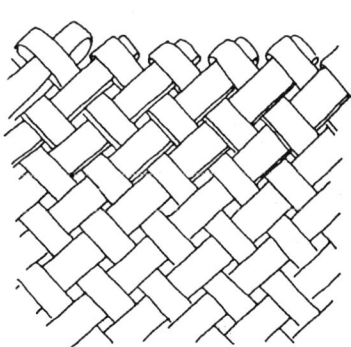

Fig. 29

Beginnings, Endings

Beginning and Ending on a Frame

Hand-caned chairs, snowshoes, and tennis rackets all represent interlacing worked into holes pierced at regular intervals along a framework. First one set of elements is laced into place; these are then interlaced with an opposing set. Additional sets of elements—as in 4SOE chair caning—usually penetrate the same holes.

In other cases, the elements are wrapped around the sides of a basic framework. This produces the 2SOE interlacing that is typical of the webbed chairs of the Shakers and garden furniture. The Indian bed and the ancient Egyptian bench (both on page 225) are forerunners of this method.

It is important to differentiate between interlacing actually worked into a frame from matting that has simply been enclosed within a frame. For the latter, the frame only performs a finishing role; it is not integrated in the initial or final stages of the working process (Fig. 35). In another method, a strand encircling an attached top frame secures the elements tucked into its course (Fig. 36).

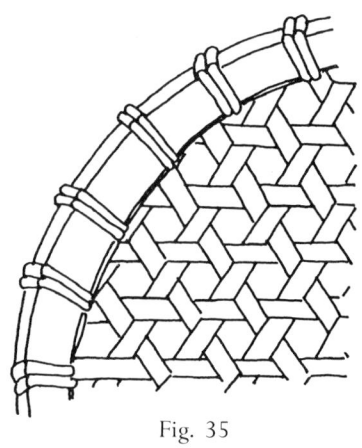

Fig. 35

Fig. 36

The intrinsic value of snowshoes lies in their ability to distribute weight over a considerable area. Although their interlacing-on-a frame structure is similar to a tennis racquet, it is often more intricate. Here the interlacing is hexagonal; thongs lace both through the frame and around it. The twisted lacings around the rungs facilitate tension adjustments.

170 |
snowshoes
3SOE, 2/1 oblique
leather, steam-bent wood
45" × 10½"
Cree people, Canada
collection: Glenbow Museum, Calgary

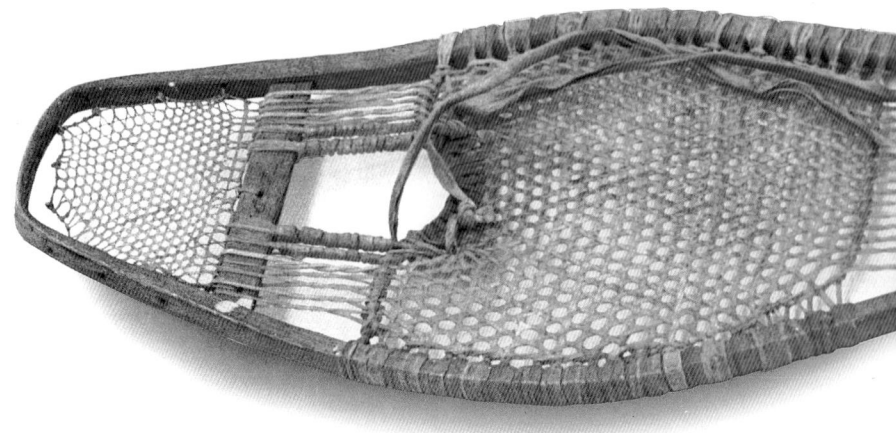

The nested wedding baskets of the Bobo people are remarkable for their meticulous size graduation and for their leather bindings and reinforcements. When given to the bride and groom, the set is filled with enough seeds to start a family garden.

171 |
nested baskets
2SOE, 1/1 oblique
palm fiber, leather
H. 7″
Bobo people, Burkina Faso
   (Upper Volta)

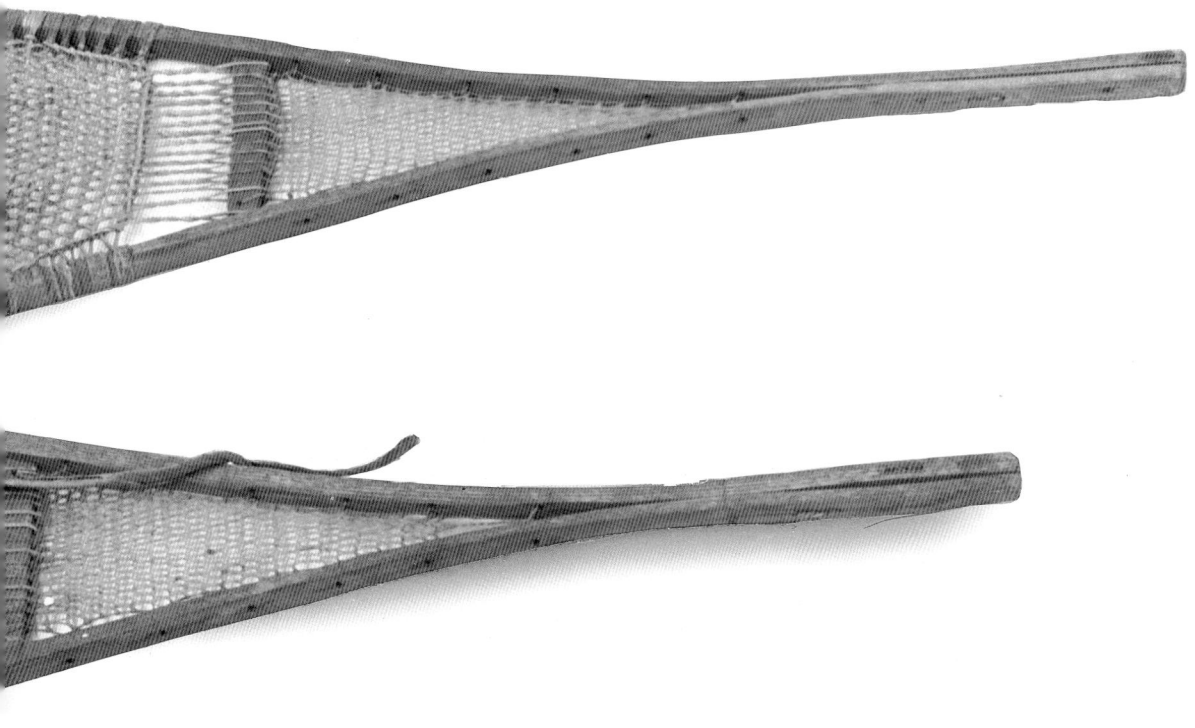

Beginnings, Endings 179

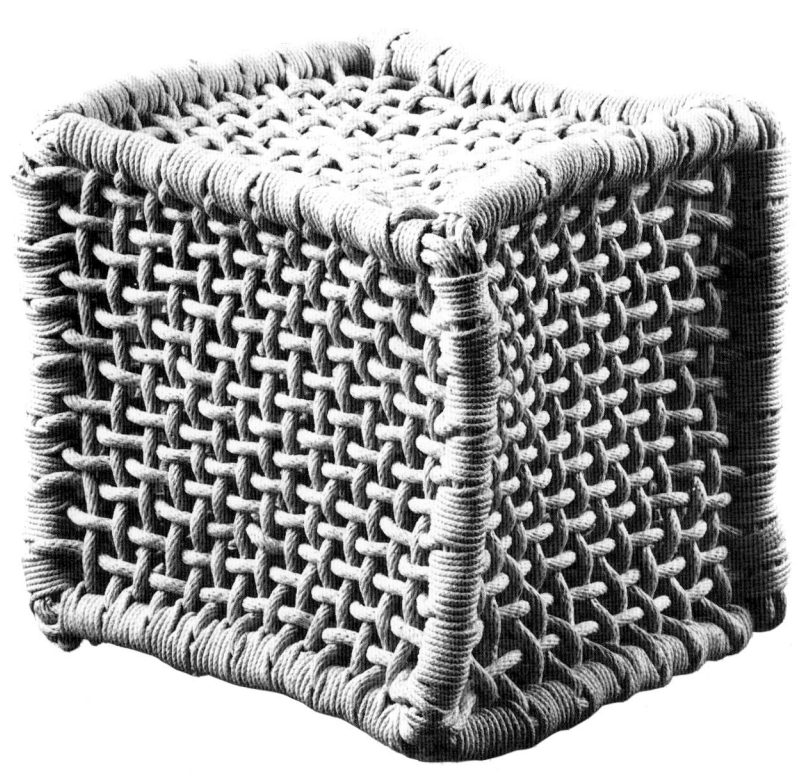

A "soft" cube, if less than perfect in its resolution of form, is nonetheless significant in avoiding a second material for the armature. The rigidity of the core-braided elements helps.

172 |
Cubic Expression IV, c. 1970
Mary Ashby, U.S.A.
2SOE, 1/1 H-V
core braided, cotton sash cord
12″ × 12″ × 12″

Shereen La Plantz often combines not only several techniques and materials in a single piece but several forms as well. Here the forms are stacked as decorously as the temple offerings of Southeast Asia.

173 |
untitled, 1983
Shereen La Plantz, U.S.A.
2SOE + 1SOE, 1/1 H-V
paper fiber strips, cord
c. 20″ × 16″

An Amazon tray for sifting cassava flour is both finished and supported with a double stick frame. Note the oblique plaiting used to secure the strand ends before they are pushed to the back and clipped.

174 |
tray
diamond twill plaiting
2SOE, 2/2 H-V
bast
7" × 7"
Colombia, c. 1970

175 |
Because of the crucial connection of sieves to their frames, many are interlaced directly onto the frame. Here the wide elements support the considerable weight of thick bean pastes.

7

Materials and color effects: the reality and the appearance

The range of materials used makes interlacing the most diverse of all craft processes. Its various methods and media accommodate vast differences in scale and weight of both elements and completed forms.

Availability and practicality have always determined material selection. Certain fibers, popular in one era, were unknown in another; even neighboring cultures have used different materials when sources or needs were not the same. Recent experiments with new media have extended the gamut. When appearance becomes the primary criterion, function may take a secondary or nonexistent position—for many of today's artists, anything goes!

The properties of materials are diverse, from fine to coarse, pliable to rigid, and ephemeral (think bread) to durable. Contrast the thick posts of wattle walls with the slender strands of a Panama hat. The latter may be slit into elements so fine that nearly one hundred are required to interlace one inch. Of course, differences in color and surface multiply the variations in weight and appearance.

The method of interlacing is not the determinant of material selection; all techniques can be accomplished in various materials. Braids, for instance, have been plaited in nearly every material represented in this book: grasses for sandals, cloth strips for rugs, leather for bridles, silk for *obi* ties, and wool for Amerindian sashes. One of the oldest known braid fragments, found near the famous paintings in the caves of Lascaux, is made from hair. Machine braids reproduce traditional techniques in synthetic fibers.

The inverse is also true: a single material can be interlaced in many different structures. While yarns are commonly recognized as versatile, the range of bamboo is far greater. The convolutions of a 1E wicker rug beater, as it twists in a ballet of curves, seems to belie a kinship with the formal rigidity of the more solid forms of wicker furniture and carriages. However, young willows soaked for days before interworking have a tender flexibility that permits bending into a dense interlacing. Clay, dough, and wire have similar flexibility.

Bread dough is amazingly similar to clay in that it can be rolled into linear elements, interlaced, and "fired." The loaf of *challah* (Jewish sabbath bread, right) combines small and large braids. The loaf on the left, braided with rye, pumpernickle, and wheat flour doughs, produces tricolored slices.

It is not true, however, that the majority of materials used in interlacing can be applied ubiquitously. Selection cannot be, and never has been, random. Each material must be considered in terms of limitations as well as potentials. Brittle rigidity or soft pliability can be drawbacks for one product but assets for another.

Motivation for selecting a particular material may not be entirely pragmatic. Beyond the utilitarian aspects of each medium, beyond aesthetic qualities, lie psychological, sometimes esoteric, associations. A commonplace basket interlaced with silver elements takes on an aura of luxury; the modest form and the valued substance coalesce into simple elegance. Ritual objects are frequently functional forms worked in impractical but symbolic materials. Conversely, clothesline or sailor's ropes, braided into majestic art forms, still serve as reminders of their humble origin. Incorporating gentle lace into a plastic mesh presents a startling contrast in time frames. Sliced newspapers, photos, and painted canvases convey messages in the choice of material. The associations of modern technology with film strips or the primeval with dried leaves bring gratuitous attributes. In cultures where sackcloth is worn in mourning ceremonies, hempen fibers serve to commemorate sorrow.

Artisans often had limited options in their selection of supplies. In the beginning there was no problem of choice.

177–178 |
Three Mexican baskets demonstrate the transposition of materials. The one on the right in Plate 177 is in the traditional form of obliquely plaited split reeds. The transition from a square base to a round top is typical; so is the double wall and serrated rim. The coin silver example (Pl. 177, left) is similar except for a smooth rim derived from folding a more malleable material on the bias to effect a right-angle turn. Outside walls of both are banded with long floats. The tinned hamper form in Plate 178 echoes its wicker original.

184 Interlacing

Chapter 1 discussed how, for millennia, gatherers had to make containers out of available materials—the instant basket from the readily accessible medium. Long grasses, vines, palm leaves—whatever was at hand had to serve. Any selectivity was pragmatic, answering the basic question: what works? Other considerations would have been secondary, if not irrelevant.

With the beginnings of agriculture and animal husbandry came demands for new tools and the materials to make them. We have been taught the importance of bronze and iron for early tool- and weapon-making, but less durable fibers also had value. Besides the obvious advantage, locating communities near water supplies increased the likelihood of accessible reeds and grasses for mats and storage baskets. Domesticated animals provided wool and hair for spinning. In Scandinavia, nettle fibers were spun during the late Bronze Age, while hemp, flax, hop vines, leather strips, and sheep wool had widespread use for fabrics of the European Iron Age. The origins of sericulture in the Orient are believed to date back to 3000 B.C. In ancient Peru, agave fiber, cotton, and the fleece of the llama and alpaca were used for various fabrics. Yucca leaves and conifer roots were basic to much of the early basketry in the Americas.

Permanent dwellings meant that life-sustaining activity no longer had to be focused on immediate needs. Long-term schedules encompassed not only planting and harvesting, but

Materials, Colors

also the processing of materials for tools. Plant materials were dried over periods of weeks, even months. Interworking of elements could be slow, deliberate, and intricate.

In areas where animistic beliefs still prevail, craft materials and finished objects are often considered the abode of the living spirit that inhabited the leaves, roots, or vines before they were cut. Imagine the care with which cutting, scorching, soaking, and interlacing must be done in order to appease maleficent spirits. Alfred Bühler wrote that knowledge of secret rituals may be valued as highly as craft skills. These artisans, often endowed with awesome powers, have such titles as shaman or magician. Their practices inhibit technological progress, he said, because methods and materials change only if, and when, religion changes.

In the first decades of the twentieth century only archaeological journals and genteel ladies' magazines showed any interest in basketry techniques. By the post-World War II years, a phenomenal interest in baskets had evolved. Recently attitudes and approaches toward the materials of interlacing have progressed in two quite contrary directions. One group of basket makers has been attracted by traditional methods of processing materials. They researched age-old procedures for preparing plant fibers, just as many weavers turned to old manuals on natural dyes and ikat to color their hand-spun yarns.

But, like the young rebels of any generation, the other group eschewed tradition, choosing instead the ready-made products of the postindustrial world. Foraging through hardware and office supply stores, or industrial catalogs, they found such "new" materials for plaiting as plastic tapes, Mylar, aluminum flashing, and nylon netting.

Rare individuals like Ed Rossbach straddle both camps. As his research recognizes affinities in the crisscross of history, he sets up humorous juxtapositions containing digs at pedantic purists. At the same time, Rossbach points out that the preferred technology for preparing each fiber is the one that has evolved through the centuries. Information passed from father to son, master to novice.

"My baskets still have the tree in them," said John McQueen. "The bark, the bug marks—all those things that show they were alive." This meticulous craftsman cuts, strips, dries, or otherwise prepares the plant materials himself. Similarly, the late Shounsai Shono, a Japanese artist who was given the title of "Living National Treasure," personally selected his bamboo—limiting harvesting to specific periods of the full moon. He also supervised every step of its processing. Both men exemplify a long tradition linking the actual collection and preparation of basketry materials with the final working of the strands. Just as a potter moistens and kneads his clay to attain the proper pliancy, the basket maker soaks and then dries his strands, often hanging them under tension to reach the proper pliancy.

Throughout the world, the plant life available to basket makers has determined the nature of the objects they create. Bamboo is cultivated and interworked in China and Japan, palm leaves in the West Indies, rattan in Indonesia. Palm leaves that have been dried and slit provide the raffia used in Madagascar and Zaire. American Indians used over one hundred differ-

Reversing tradition and the natural inclination of basketry materials, John McQueen has terminated a flattened sphere with a rectangular opening. The steep pitch of the oblique interlacing produces an elongated diamond, proportionate to the piece itself.

179

basket, 1976
John McQueen, U.S.A.
2SOE, 1/1 oblique
birch bark
8″ × 14″ × 14″
collection: Milton Sonday, New York

ent wild and cultivated materials, including wood splints, stems, branches, roots, bark, grasses, and corn husks.

Peruvian natives of the Piura region plait Panama hats from *paja toquilla* straw. Because it is collected under highly limited conditions of growth, temperature, and weather, the material for one choice hat may take months to collect. The hairlike strands must be worked only during night hours, when the air is humid. From Hawaii to New Zealand, Polynesians strip the thorns from the margins of tough pandanus leaves, then, in preparation for mat-making, smoke them in shallow pits. The Maupiti of the Society Islands pull coconut palm leaves through a blazing fire to toughen them.

Yarns for braiding are often animal fibers spun from wool or human or horse hair. Dog-hair apron braids of the prehistoric Basket Makers were found in Danger Cave, Utah. The mummy cap from pre-Columbian Peru (p. 237) has a dense fringe of human hair braids with striped wrappings of alpaca. Spun cotton is the usual medium of early Amerindian braids. Materials derived from animal sources are leather, sinews, and the gut used for snowshoes. The first is soaked, scraped, and tanned for weeks before being sliced into strips.

Recently the art of paper making has experienced a renaissance, not just for fine books and framed artworks, but also for plaiting. As shown in *The Art Fabric* and *Mainstream*, the Californians Neda Al-Hilali, Dominic Di Mare, and Ed Rossbach were among the first to experiment with plaited paper; now there are many. Felting, a somewhat similar process for meshing wool or fur fibers, is often incorporated in plaited works. Sometimes elements are felted; others are cut from felt. Less often wool yarns or rovings are plaited, then felted.

Artists working with less conventional materials may not always use ready-made products. They often have inventive, intricate methods for preparing their elements. Several of Arturo Sandoval's wall hangings are plaited with eight layers of material including paper strips overlaid with bands of netting. Each is enclosed in Mylar before the layers are machine-stitched in place. He has also plaited large hangings with flat Mylar films and more dimensional ones with wide strips cut from the tin roofs of Kentucky tobacco barns. A singular example is twill plaited with braided copper battery cable—plaited plaiting!

180–181. Because of its potential for shaping, felt making approximates ceramics, and, like clay, felt can be formed into linear elements for interlacing. Van Derpool's small basket in Plate 181 is plaited from felted strips. Kacillas (Pl. 180) uses doubled strips cut from industrial felt.

180 |
JoAnne Kacillas, U.S.A.
(base) 3SOE, 1/1 horizontal-oblique
reprocessed felt
D. 18″
photo: John Perry

181 |
Karen Van Derpool, U.S.A.
felting, plaiting
2SOE, 1/1 H-V
3¾″ × 6″ × 5″
photo: John Wesley

Materials, Colors **189**

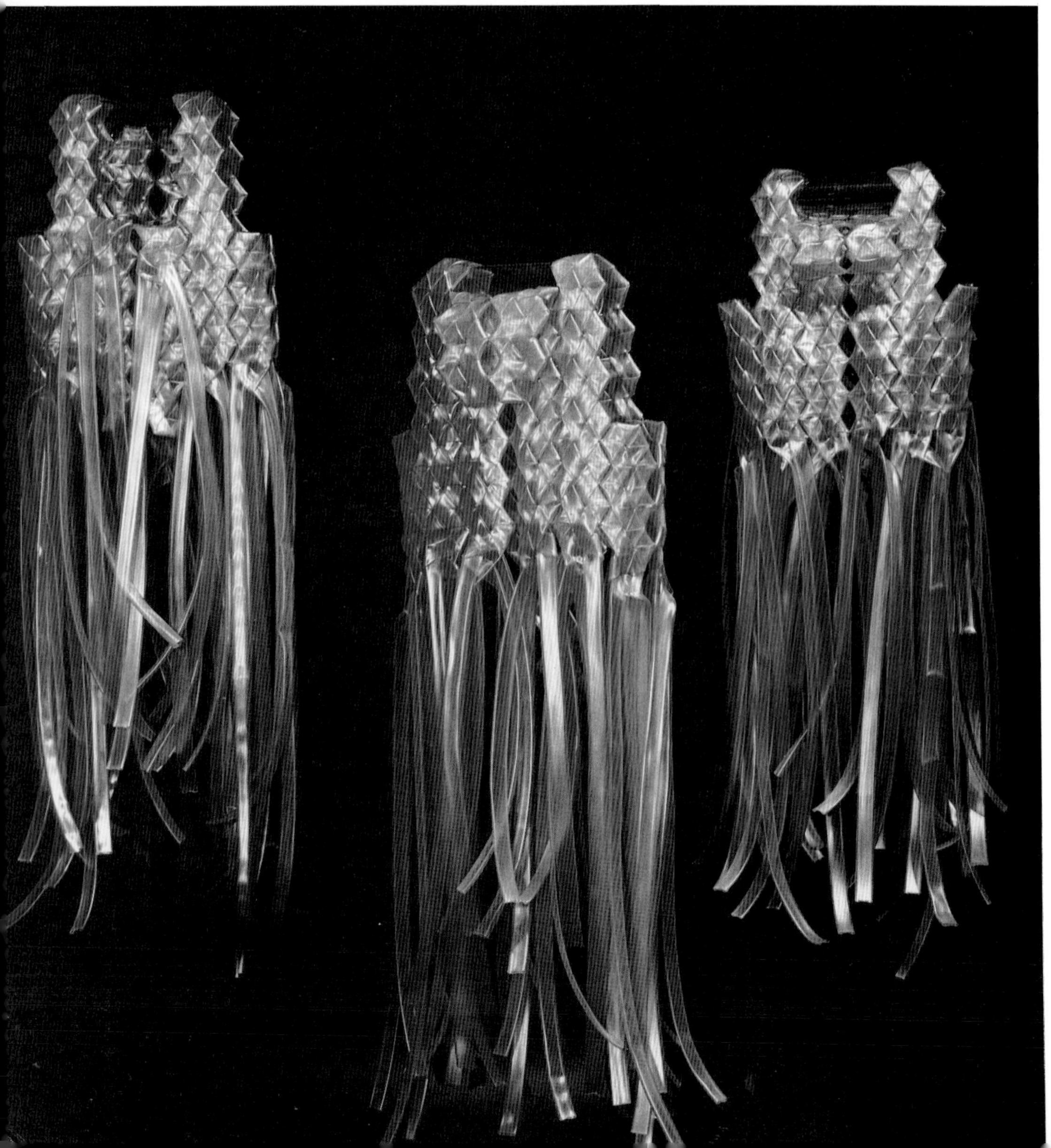

182–183. Plaiting accommodates a variety of materials—here are a miniature basket plaited with varicolored braids and mythic vests of vinyl tubing.

182 |
Baby Basket, 1978
Betsy Blumenthal, U.S.A.
mad weave
3SOE, 1/3 horizontal-oblique
rayon braid
1" × 8" × 8"
courtesy British Crafts Centre, London

183 |
The Knights, 1976
Glen Kaufman, U.S.A.
attached fold braids
1SOE, 2/1 horizontal-oblique
vinyl tubing
68" × 70" × 8"

Dorothy Gill Barnes is most concerned with the integrity of natural materials worked in many-layered structures. Here the layers are single, the telescoping nest of baskets are separate and removable.

184 |
nest of baskets, c. 1981
Dorothy Gill Barnes, U.S.A.
2SOE, 1/1 H-V
mulberry bark
10" × 5"

Materials, Colors 191

Processing of an Element

CHARACTERISTIC: METHOD

whole: Many grasses, bast fibers, roots and stems require no processing.

divided: Palm leaves, leather, cloth, films, etc. are slit before interworking.

formed: Wire is drawn; clay and dough are rolled or extruded.

Extruded filaments include natural silk and all of the man-made fibers.

combined: Elements may be composed of grouped or spun strands or meshed fibers. These strands or fibers may be homogeneous or varied.

interlaced strands: Braids, woven tapes, and ribbons are typical examples.

185

Flat elements, even narrow ones, may be colored on only one side to produce a dramatic change from face to face. The front of a Papuan waist band is shown right. The back, at left, clearly reveals a 3/3 reverse twill structure with an inordinate number of the rattan strands paired as they are spliced. On the front, two out of three strands are painted black to effect a negative chevron motif.

186–189. Though the materials of interlacing are usually humble, they need not be. Fine silks and precious metals have been plaited since earliest times. Through her own work, her writings, and demonstrations, Arline Fisch has spearheaded a revival of fine metals worked in fabric techniques. Her own pieces tend toward lightweight flexibility. Stuart Golder's are framed or backed with solid metal to achieve a classic solidity.

186 |
brooch, woven ribbon, 1980
Arline Fisch, U.S.A.
2SOE, 1/1 H-V
22K gold, silver

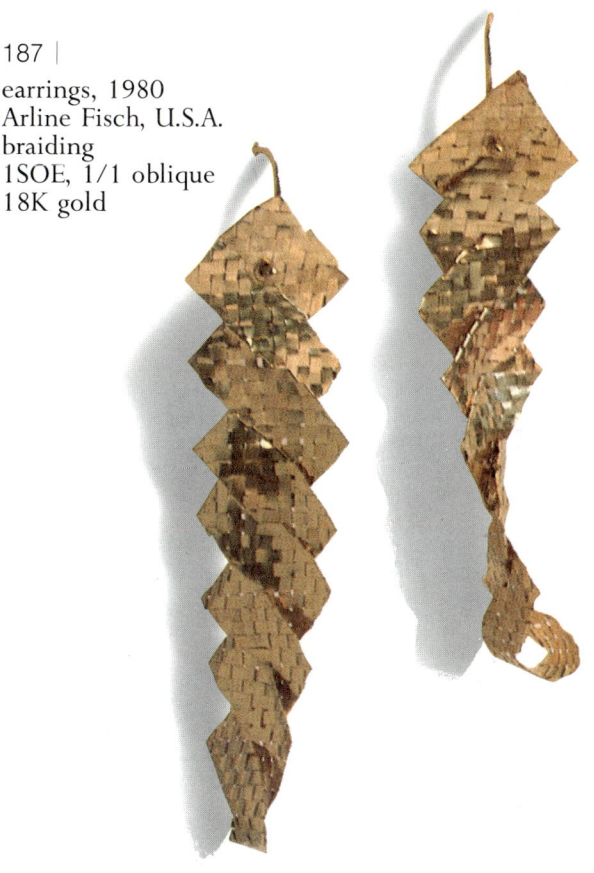

187 |
earrings, 1980
Arline Fisch, U.S.A.
braiding
1SOE, 1/1 oblique
18K gold

188 |
earrings, 1983
Stuart Golder, U.S.A.
2SOE, 3/3 H-V
silver, copper, *kuromi-do, shakudo*

189 |
cuff links, 1984
Stuart Golder, U.S.A.
2SOE, 1/1 H-V
silver, gold, *shakudo*

Materials, Colors

Jewelry plaited with human hair was prized by Victorians for its light weight and heavy sentiment. The bracelet is braided with pairs of twilled tubular elements; the delicacy of the locket frame is achieved by braiding over a removable core.

190 |
bracelet
tubular braiding
1SOE, 2/2 oblique
hair, gold, seed pearls, etc.
England, 19th century
Cooper-Hewitt Museum, New York

191 |
Like its bamboo mentor, this old bronze tray from China has a base of twilled matting inserted into a ring of radial interlacing. This is topped by twining and a wrapped rim. The craftsmanship is meticulous, the weight of the bronze surprising.

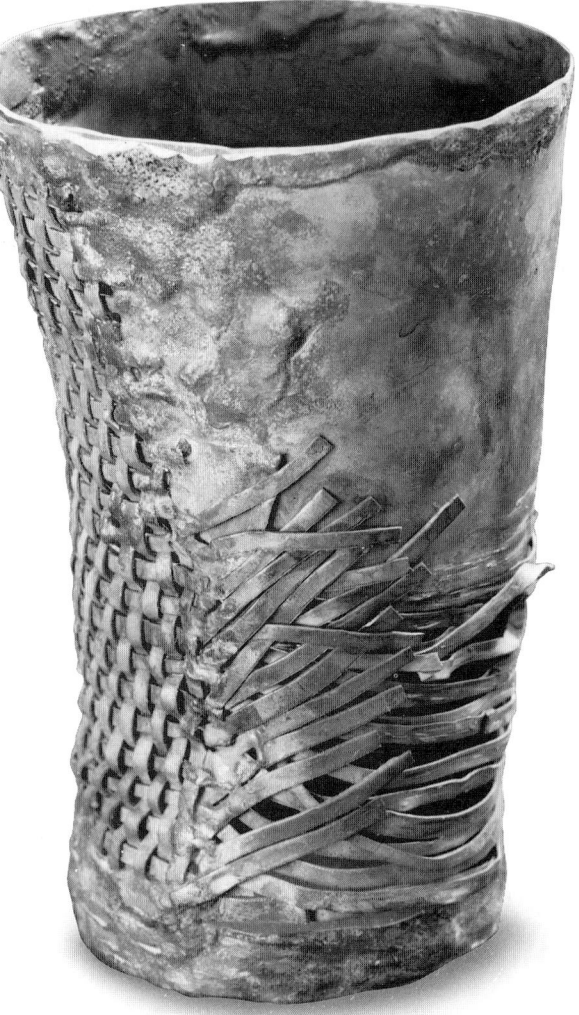

192–193. Interlaced copper ornaments the walls of two vase forms. Bacharach's is raised, then pierced to allow interpenetration of the copper elements. Du Grenier has sandwiched a mesh of high luster copper wire between layers of blown crystal.

192 |
vase, 1979
Robert Du Grenier, U.S.A.
braiding
1SOE, 1/1 oblique
copper, glass
12″ × 7″

193 |
vase 1981
David Paul Bacharach, U.S.A.
2SOE, 1/1 H-V
copper, pigments, lacquer
9″ × 3½″

194–197. More than other fabric techniques, plaiting accepts the use of metals. The author has long advocated metals for Art Fabric in public spaces because such work is resistant to the ravages of time, fire, and children. The Sandoval series interlaced with strips of rusted tin roofs from Kentucky tobacco barns is weatherprooof as well (Pl. 194). Barbara MacCallum (Pl. 195) combines tradition with innovation in plaited aluminum "quilts"; the ground is supplied by their supporting walls. The sensuous shallow reliefs of Joyce Crain are interlaced twice. As shown in Plate 196, tubular braided copper plaited through a cast plastic grid is testimonial to the expansion/contraction property of braids. The same braid is combined with colored iridescent film in the commissioned hanging (Pl. 197).

194
Spatial Grid No. 9, 1981 (detail)
Arturo Sandoval, U.S.A.
2SOE, 1/1 horizontal-oblique
weathered barn metal (leaded tin)

195
Moonlit Border Quilt, 1984 (detail)
Barbara MacCallum, U.S.A.
2SOE, 1/1 oblique
aluminum, plastic, acrylic paint
photo: Louis Saunders

196
Core Memory:
  Vienna Succession, 1984 (detail)
Joyce Crain, U.S.A.
interlaced braids
1SOE, 2/1 vertical
copper with tubular braid,
  plastic grid

197
Charles Residence commission,
  1985 (detail)
Joyce Crain, U.S.A.
2SOE over cast plastic grid
copper wire, tubular braid,
  computer tape, iridescent film
60″ × 60″ × 6″

For three millennia, East Asians have applied lacquer over interlaced structures to make them stronger than wooden ones and less given to expansion and contraction. The example shown is of mulberry paper stretched over hexagonal plaiting, then lacquered.

198 |
tray
2SOE, 1/1 horizontal-oblique
bamboo, paper, lacquer
D. c. 10″
Japan, c. 1970

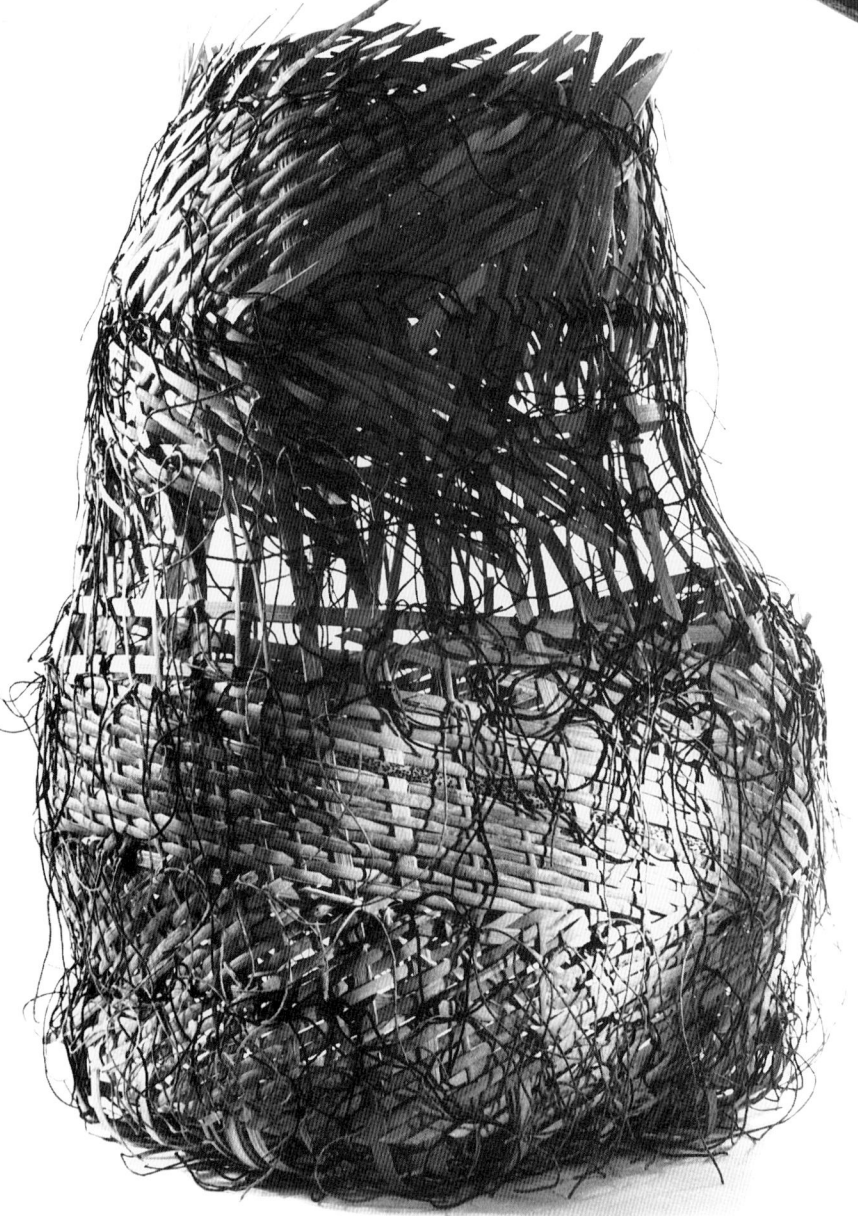

The San Francisco Bay artist Lillian Elliot has long worked on the leading edge of basketry. This basket is typical of her spontaneous expression. Later work is often coated with paper and lacquered.

199 |
Tag-Ends, 1980
Lillian Elliot, U.S.A.
3SOE + 1SOE, 1/1 oblique
bamboo, linen
22″ × 16″
photo: Musée des Arts Décoratifs, Lausanne

John McQueen's strong color is the more powerful for its patterning of opaque black paint. The stepped relief at top is rare, even in his work.

200
basket, 1977
John McQueen, U.S.A.
plaiting, painting
2SOE, 1/1 oblique
white pine bark
30″ × 11″ × 11″
collection: H.F. and Glenna McQueen

Materials, Colors

201–204. When, in the 1970s, American artists worked in plaiting and paper making, several combined the two. Best known is Nance O'Banion, who for a decade has fabricated featherweight structures with deckled paper strips, split bamboo, paste, and cord. To achieve strength without weight, Susan Lyman sandwiches interlacings between layers of translucent paper. Louis Marciante is more typical, in that he simply interlaces dye patterned elements to achieve nonobjective imagery. While paper baskets and vessel forms are less common than flat planes, Lisa Martin's, of unfurled, still-pleated paper cord, possesses a quiet beauty.

201
Paper Plait Kite,
  1978 (detail)
Nance O'Banion, U.S.A.
2SOE + 3SOE, 1/1 oblique
paper, split bamboo, cord,
  paste
3' × 4'
courtesy: Louise Allrich Gallery,
  San Francisco

202
Confectionary Box,
  1980 (detail)
Susan Lyman, U.S.A.
4SOE, various
wood, reed, palm fronds,
  Nepalese paper

203
Dekooning Smile Deposit, 1980 (detail)
Louis Marciante, U.S.A.
2SOE, 1/1 H-V
paper

204
White Corn Husks, 1985
Lisa Martin, U.S.A.
2SOE, 1/1 oblique
paper

Materials, Colors 201

205 |
Simple twilled interlacing can be spectacular for the effectiveness of alternating dark and light bamboo slats. The magic here, in the stepped ziggurats at the corners, is enhanced by the minimal rim and handles. The same pattern occurs in alternate bands of the place mat in Plate 208.

Interlaced through slits, the Fiji satchel has an intricate composition of three color values with two sizes of elements. The two twills of fine white elements interlacing through dark and medium slats create vibrant staccato rhythms.

206 |
satchel
2SOE, various, H-V
bast
Fiji Islands, 1880
collection: Peabody Museum of
 Salem, Massachusetts
photo: Mark Sexton

Color Effects

"Color effects" is a textile term describing large and small patterns derived from the sequencing of colors within a set of elements or with an opposing set of elements. The contrast is usually light and dark, but may be of differing hues or intensities or even matte and glossy textures. The result is most often the universe of stripes—that most ubiquitous of all patterns. Of course stripes over stripes produce checks and plaids. Color effects may also result in small texture patterns.

Color effects apply to all types of interlacing. Even 2E knots can be worked with different colors, and braids make use of them in a variety of ways. The twills of oblique interlacing are often remarkable for the strength of their dark and light patterning, while color effects applied to 3SOE and 6SOE structures emphasize their varied hexagonal patterns.

Color effects usually stand on their own, but may be used to reinforce an order of interlacing. Houndstooth checks and glen plaids create a perennial magic because of the perfect fit of color effect to their structure. For a weaver the wealth of plaited face-reversal patterns anticipates, and—in their blown-up scale—dramatizes the pattern potentials of woven damasks. It is not uncommon in plaiting, however, for stripes and checks to be worked over intricate twills without relating to the patterning involved. Instead, the broad color bands may conform to the overall form of the piece, as in the Mexican baskets on page 205.

The drama of color effects on plaited surfaces lies in the perfect marriage of structure and ornament. Its impact derives from three factors: 1) the broader elements allow clarity and scale unattainable in yarns, 2) fiber rigidity permits long floats, 3) admixtures of wide and narrow strips of dark/light elements are much more effective than combinations of thick and thin yarns.

Since flat elements tend to fill the interstices of the interlacing, they produce purer geometric patterns than do round reeds, yarns, or cords. The inverse is also true. Plaiting with rigid elements—particularly three or more sets of them—creates open meshes with considerable stability, providing options for combining dark and light contrasts with transparent voids. Further, the opacity of materials common to plaiting allows them to completely cover the elements passing underneath. This is particularly effective when working with high contrasts of dark and light, and so different from the silhouette of a sheer cloth in which both light and dark yarns appear as identical. This effective combination of opacity and rigidity is clearly demonstrated in the openly worked bamboo baskets on pages 214–15.

Modifiers such as density and balance influence color effects. The size of elements and textural variations within them may also vary the patterning. Wide, flat elements may be colored on only one side or colored differently on each side. Occasionally these bicolored elements are twisted within the plaiting or reversed at the selvage. Combining the grain and suede faces of leather strips is more common; so is a combination of outside and inside peel bamboo. In Burma, twilled panels for house

207 |

mat (detail)
2SOE, 1/1 oblique
bast
c. 20″ × 32″
Mindanao, Philippines, 1980

208 |

mat (detail)
2SOE, 2/2 oblique
bast
Mexico, 1970

207–209. In two simple mats and a clutch of baskets, the wide flat elements of plaited mats magnify the magic of crossing color bands. For the mat in Plate 207, high contrasts produce a salt-and-pepper tweed. The mat in Plate 208 alternates dark and light strands in a staccato rhythm.

A group of new baskets from Oaxaca illustrates the potential for color effects on obliquely plaited forms. Some depend on a set of dark elements countering a light set. Others have bands of light and dark elements in both directions, as in woven checks. In the right-hand example, both occur, rather irreverently. At center, both high and low contrasts coexist as red and natural splints interlace with green and natural ones. Note the discontinuous dark strands on the sides of the two lids at left.

204   Interlacing

209
baskets
2SOE, 2/2 oblique
bast
Oaxaca, Mexico, 1980

Materials, Colors

210–211. Two Amazon baskets illustrate color effects applied to oblique interlacing. Alike in size and material, both center a single band on the square base interlaced as a 3/3 diamond twill. Because the walls of the piece in Plate 211 example are the 4/1 structure of satin weave, with one SOE dominant, four different color areas appear. The basket in Plate 210 is a balanced 3/3 interlacing; the right and left sides are identical, as are the two faces. Observe how the twill pattern tends to disappear in the solid color areas.

210 |
basket
2SOE, 3/3 oblique
bast
11" × 13"
Colombia, 1970s

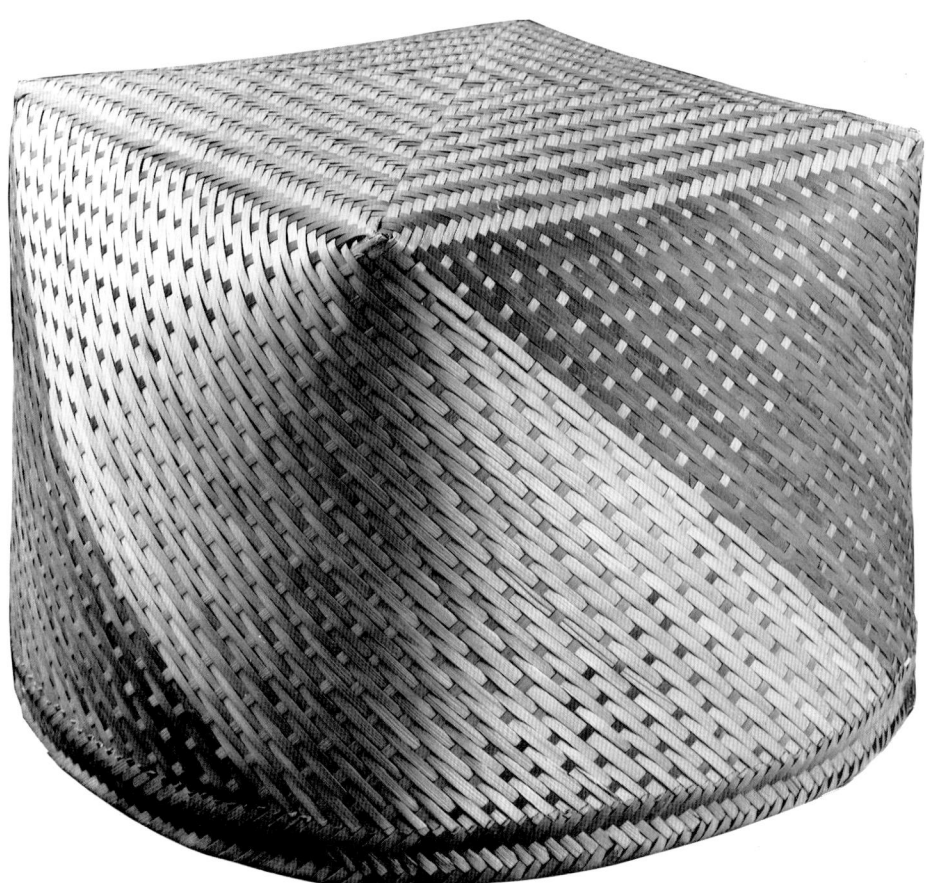

211 |
basket
2SOE, 4/1 oblique
bast
10" × 12"
Colombia, 1970s

A centered counterpane of natural reed discloses the diamond twill interlacing of this two-layered, lidded box from Tibet. The deep green verticals and violet horizontals are so close in value that they do not affect the patterning.

212 |
lidded basket
2SOE, 2/2 H-V
bast
D. 8″
Tibet

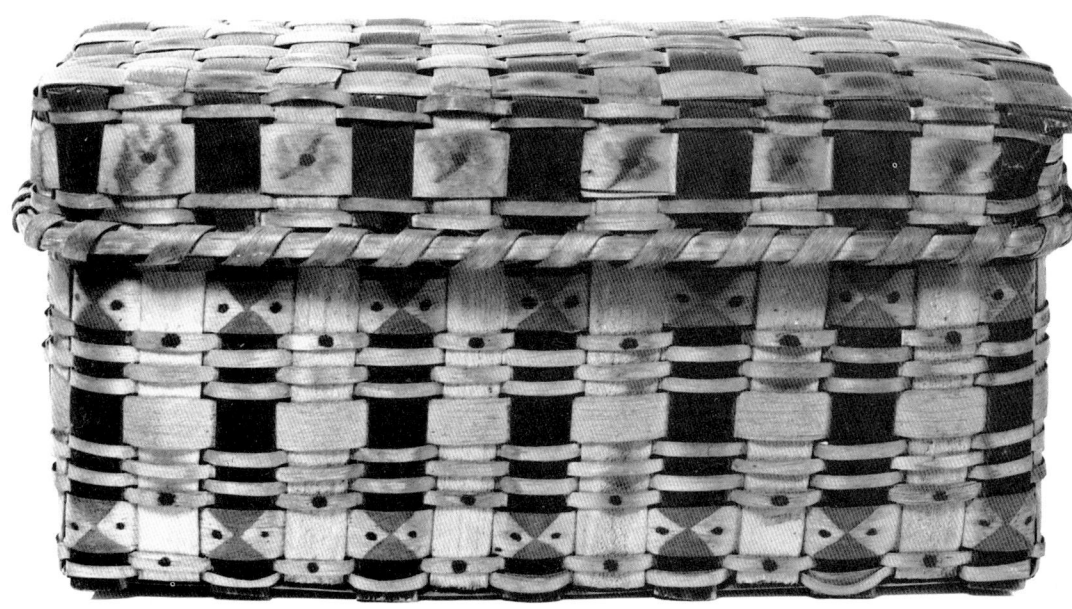

The Indian trade baskets of the Middle Atlantic seaboard (now associated with Americana) were often interlaced with colored splints then stamped or painted. The lidded rectangular form is typical. So is the combination of thick and thin elements.

213 |
lidded basket
plaiting, painting
2SOE, 1/1 H-V
wood splints
5″ × 10″
Mohegan people, Connecticut, 19th century
Museum of the American Indian, Heye Foundation, New York

Materials, Colors 207

Plaited leather has great antiquity and very wide distribution, particularly among herders with time on their hands and needs for whips, lassoes, and horse trappings. None has more finesse than the work of Ken Carlson. This vase-shaped piece combines panels of 10-strand flat braid engaging a bottom piece, then fastened with a simulated 8-strand round braid edge band.

214 |
cylinder form, 1985
Ken Carlson, U.S.A.
plaiting, braiding
2SOE, 1/1 H-V; 1SOE, 2/2 oblique
leather
11½" × 5"

walls are plaited with alternating outside and inside bamboo splints. Although both faces are nearly the same shade, the inside peel soon blackens with mildew. Like invisible writing immersed in a solution, a large-scale geometry is revealed.

Plaited color effects are also affected by dimensional forms. Modulations are caused by the foreshortening of perspective as well as by highlights and shadows on their contours. On flat textiles, color effects—especially stripes—only assume a special magic when the material is draped, pleated, or cut and sewn.

Dark and light patterning on plaited work probably developed in several ways. First, because basketry materials resist most vegetable dyes, combining different tonalities of natural materials was expedient. Early on, dark tones were attained by fuming strands with smoke or by soaking them in mud containing iron oxide. For preliterate peoples the desire to communicate through symbolism played a large role in developing the patterns. Even the simplest form conveyed meaning. Each dark/light pattern was achieved with the color effects that would read best. To determine where colors should pass over and under, the craftsman learned to measure and count. George Wharton James states in his book *Indian Basketry* that this need for a reliable number system brought about the dawn of mathematics.

Patterned Elements

Wide, flat elements lend themselves to surface patterning in a way that no yarn can. In traditional mats and baskets, this is less common than one would expect. Rag rugs braided with patterned fabrics are a notable—if fairly recent—exception. When braids are used as an element, there are many examples of patterns achieved by admixing varicolored strands. Dye patterning wide strips after interlacing is more common. Perhaps the best known are Amerindian baskets of the Eastern Woodlands, shown on page 207.

In the last decade, a number of artists have worked with wide, boldly patterned elements. Among them are the layered and stitched elements of Arturo Sandoval, the plaited card-"woven" stripes of Mark C. Pollack (p. 212), the bleached and dye patterned tapes of Sherri Smith (p. 13), and the painted bark splints of John McQueen (p. 199). Guy Houdouin, on page 9, also dye-patterns the strips for his plaiting, but in gradual transitions of close-valued colors that read as a fused modulation.

Finally, there is another aspect of dye patterning in relation to plaiting. This involves resists and particularly plangi (tie and dye); the rarest and least exploited is what Alfred Bühler would term a simple resist. As shown on page 18 of *The Dyer's Art*, the Wolof people of Senegal braid strips of cotton sheeting, dye it in indigo, unbraid it, and sew the strips together to achieve wide cloths with reptilian patterns. Plangi on plaited work occurs in a number of cultures. Perhaps the best known are the tubular plaited garments of the Dida of the Ivory Coast. As shown in *The Dyer's Art* (p. 27), these are tie-dyed in bold patterns. A more recent discovery is the resist patterned plaiting of the Solomon Islanders.

Coloring of an Element

CHARACTERISTIC	METHOD	EXAMPLES

monochrome	natural
	treated
	   bleached
	   smoked
	   dyed
	   painted
		too numerous to list

multicolored	natural
	
	treated
	   locally bleached
	   space dyed
	   printed
	
	painted
	scorched or
	smoked over resist
		nodes
		buds
		natural shadings
		
		stamped
		stenciled, etc.

front/back color differences	natural treated (color applied to one side)	peels (bamboo) leather
combined	grouped spun plied wrapped layered interlaced	heather yarns Moresque, jaspé yarns

215 |
A Somali braid, stitched to form a disk, is extraordinary for its powerful pattern achieved solely through color effects. Only three colors are used and, except for the outer band, a 1/1 interlacing. Space dyeing (dye patterning) the strands allows for three solid colors and three areas of admixed colors. Strands have been added to widen the outer band with its whirling chevron of long floats at both selvages.
collection: Musée de l'Homme, Paris

Summary of Color Effects

2E two elements of different colors

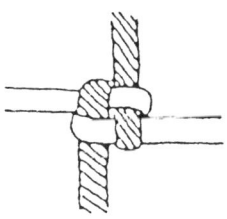 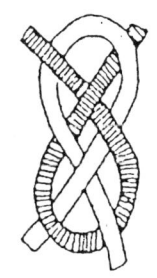 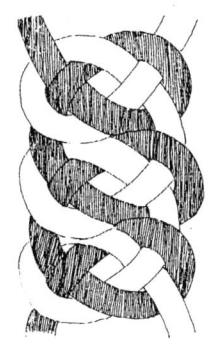

1SOE sequencing of two or more colors
  in elements
  in bands
  in elements + bands

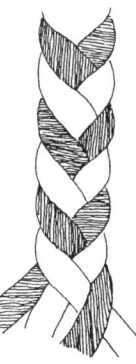 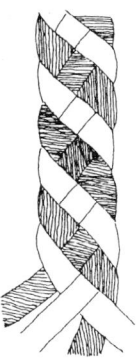 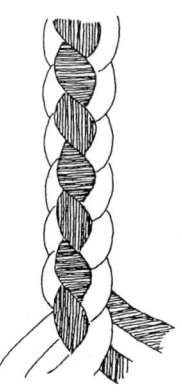

2SOE color effects achieved by contrasting one SOE against another
  by alternating colors within one or both SOE
  by exchanging colors from layer to layer in compound structures

3 or more SOE color effect possibilities multiply, and the differences in effect between constant and varied colors within an SOE increase

Materials, Colors 211

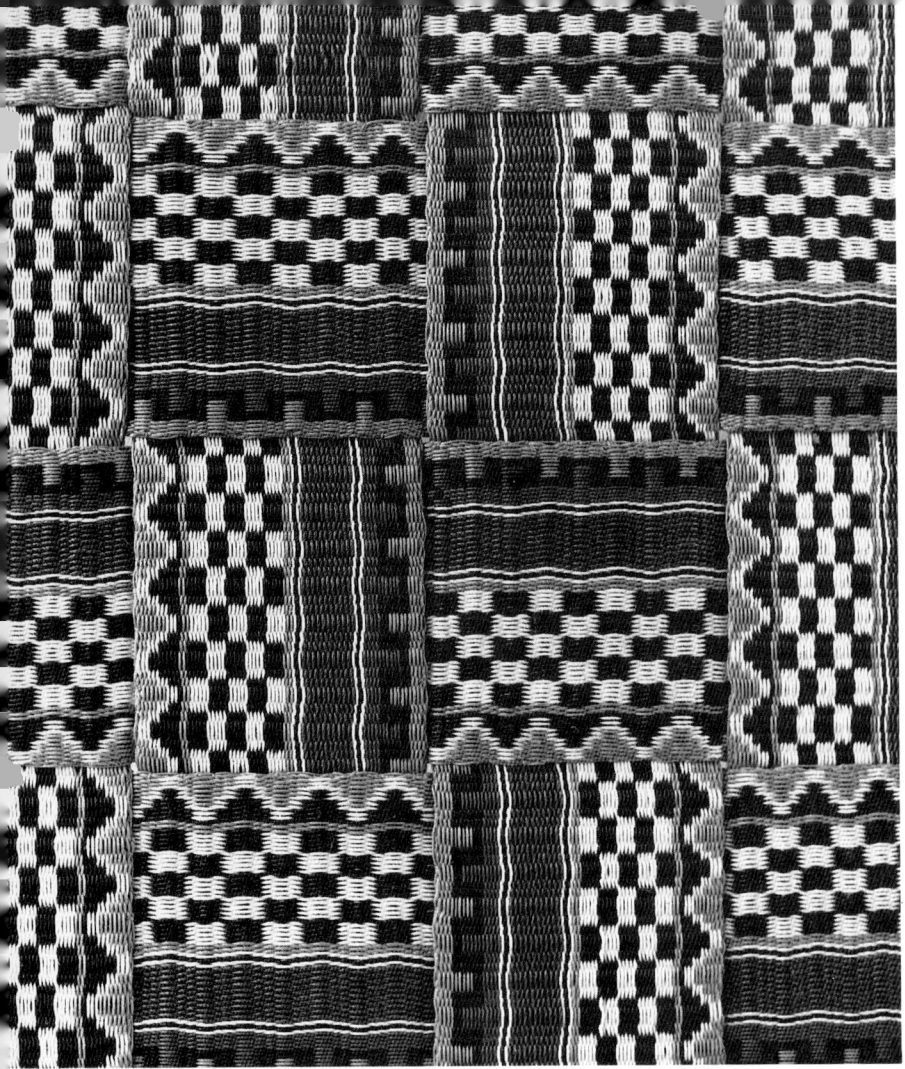

Here the "material," bands of richly patterned Egyptian card weaving, dominates the simple interlacing. By reversing alternative bands to form a mirror-image, the designer has achieved four different crossings.

216 |
sample, 1975 (detail)
Mark Pollack, U.S.A.
2SOE, 1/1 H-V
twined cotton bands

217 and 219. More frequently than in woven plaids, stripes and checks are arbitrarily superimposed over a plaited structure. Because the patterns are revealed only in areas of high contrast, some liken them to night and day. The two Borneo mats in these plates illustrate this; so do the Mexican baskets on page 205.

217 |
mat (*punan*) detail
2SOE, oblique
rattan peel
67" × 34"
Kalimantan, Indonesia

In Susan Jamart's *Soft Cubes*, the alternation of black and white ribbons is so powerful that it dominates over the fabric structure. The four cubes enumerate only some of the patterning possibilities. As in weaving, the negative pattern of the light against dark cube, upper left, "reads" best.

218 |
Soft Cubes, 1973
Susan Jamart, U.S.A.
2SOE, 1/1 oblique
woven belting
6″ × 6″ × 6″ (each)

219 |
seat mat (*tikat burit*)
2SOE, 2/2 oblique
rattan peel
25″ × 13″
Sarawak, mid 20th century

Materials, Colors

220
221

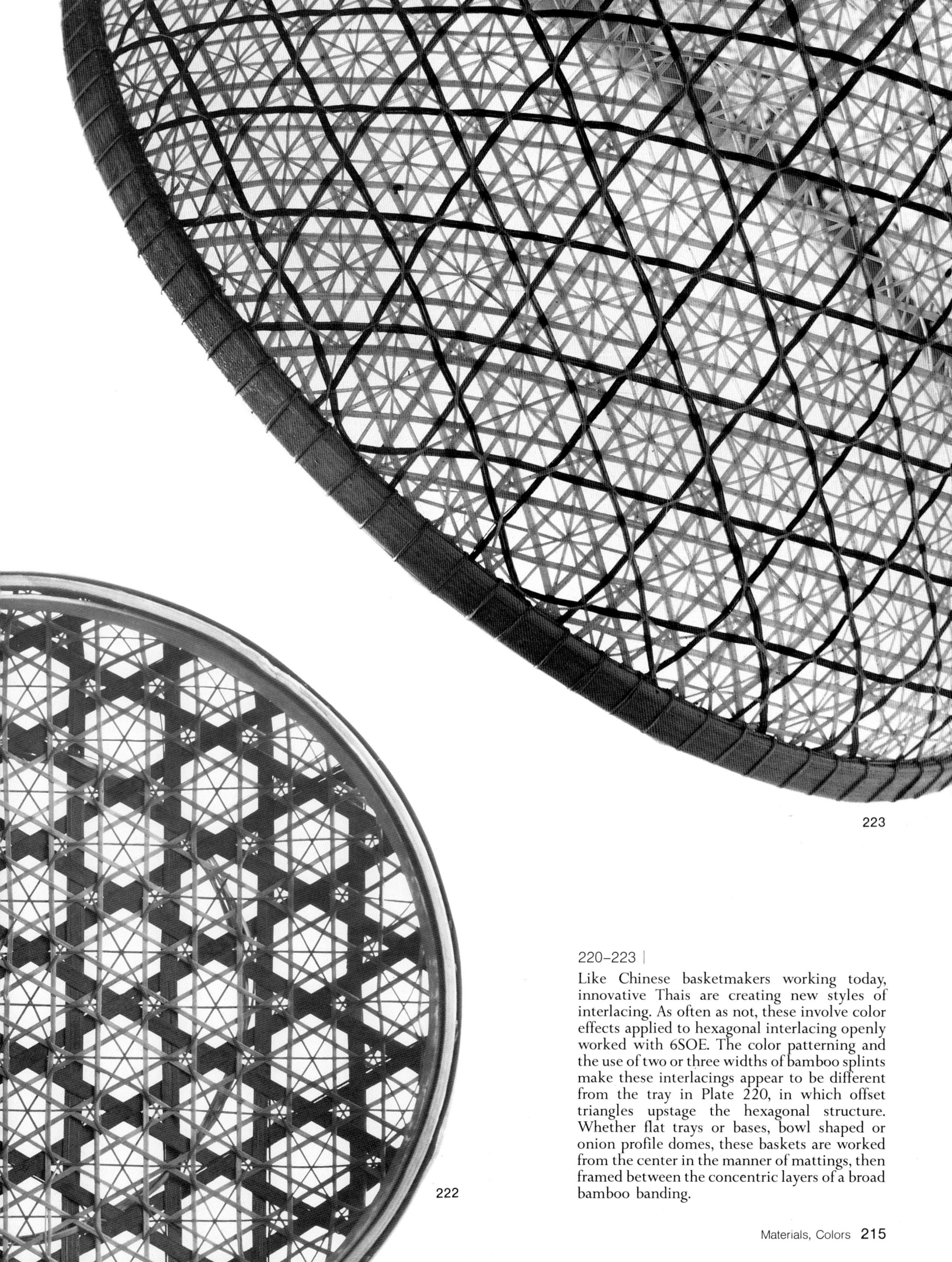

223

222

220–223 |
Like Chinese basketmakers working today, innovative Thais are creating new styles of interlacing. As often as not, these involve color effects applied to hexagonal interlacing openly worked with 6SOE. The color patterning and the use of two or three widths of bamboo splints make these interlacings appear to be different from the tray in Plate 220, in which offset triangles upstage the hexagonal structure. Whether flat trays or bases, bowl shaped or onion profile domes, these baskets are worked from the center in the manner of mattings, then framed between the concentric layers of a broad bamboo banding.

8
Applications

Today interlacing is so taken for granted that its prevalence is scarcely noticed; neither is the amazing variety of its applications. From the moment we tie our braided shoelaces in the morning, perhaps play a game of tennis with a plaited racquet, select fruit from a plaited basket, until we toss our soiled clothing into a wicker hamper and sleep between woven sheets, we are using interlacings. Familiarity causes us to accept, without notice, these ingenious solutions to our needs. We are unaware of their evolution, their many uses, spread through the millennia.

As communal living in Neolithic times brought specialization, skilled artisans were able to give full time to their trades; bartering gave opportunities for exchange of products and craft materials. Increased trading improved economic opportunities, hastening transfer of skills and raw materials of competitors. Occasionally innovations were acquired through artisans taken as prisoners—a practice that continued into the nineteenth century with Indians of the northwest coast of North America, who placed great value on craftsmen as slaves.

In classical Rome, Pliny the Elder (A.D. 23–79), pointed out the versatility of wickerwork in his *Natural History*: "Other willows throw out osiers of remarkable thinness adapted by their suppleness and graceful slenderness for the manufacture of wickerwork. Others again, of stouter make, are for weaving paniers and other utensils employed in agriculture; while from whiter willow the bark is peeled off and, being remarkably tractable, admits of various utensils being made of it which require a softer and more pliable material than leather, this last is also found useful in the construction of those articles of luxury, reclining chairs!" (BK xvi, Chapter 68).

Baskets were important exchange items in the early trade fairs established by the Romans in Britain, France, and elsewhere. During the Middle Ages, guilds brought refinements in the processing of materials and higher standards for craft production. New markets and new products arrived with the Age of Exploration. From the sixteenth century, trade embargoes were enacted to protect local production and vested interests.

Tales of fantastic contraband maneuvers enliven most histories of lace. In Holland, even imports of wicker materials were forbidden. One enterprising Dutchman, returning from London, packed his goods in a basket worked from newly cut green willows. He watered it every day of the crossing and, on arrival, dismantled the basket and planted the cuttings.

Mats

Apart from woven textiles, plaited mats are the simplest and most ubiquitous 2SOE interlacings. However, familiarity should not mask their merit; mats have been slept upon by peasants and mandarins, walked upon by priests, and formed into the thrones of kings.

As discussed in Chapter 1, clay impressions indicate that large mats were used to cover damp floors of Neolithic houses. Attached to stakes, they also became walls and roofing. What other man-made architectural component can boast a tradition that has persisted from prehistoric times up to the mat-walled houses still being constructed in many parts of the world? The Innuit of western Alaska hang them as room dividers. Wall paintings found in ancient Egypt depict colored mats arranged on a pulley system. It has been assumed that this permitted movable walls—a concept considered as "modern" in the twentieth century. The universality of mats can be attributed to their relative resistance to the ravages of moisture, dust, and mud.

The size of mats is almost unlimited. In South Vietnam, the author once designed seagrass mattings that were interlaced on poles in an open courtyard. As the horizontal elements could

224

Protecting the banks of one of the great rivers of China, this sinuous interlacing traverses an entire vista. Bamboo splints, openly worked in the hexagonal plaiting typical of East Asia, retain a bulwark of boulders against the onslaught of spring floods.

photo: National Geographic Society, Washington, D.C.

be terminated at any point by tapestry joins, the dimensions were virtually boundless. Working ballroom-size rugs just outside the building eliminated the difficulties of transporting long, heavy rolls.

Another mat form, plaiting with a long pile of loose fiber ends, sheds water so successfully that it is used for rain cloaks around the world. A simple one from Guiana is shown on page 21. The durable version on the facing page protects the contents of a Nagaland haversack. Examples from Japan, Mindanao, and Polynesia are well known, as are the cedar bark capes of the Alaskan panhandle. Rainhats and thatched roofs plaited with palm fronds employ the same principle.

The word "mat" implies a flat surface—we are accustomed to their use primarily for table settings or wiping muddy shoes, but mats are also curved into tubular shapes, folded into boxes and envelopes, or even interlaced into compound curves. Because large mats can be rolled for storage, they have often been used for bedding. Wealthy Chinese have long prized fine, twilled mattings as the coolest of sleeping surfaces. Lightweight, rollable mats make efficient sails. The ancient ones unfurled on the Nile differ little from those still employed on the upper Irrawaddy of Burma. Adventurous Polynesians knew them, so did the Innuit of Alaska.

Rather than listing the applications of all the basic interlacings, there is a greater value in analyzing their properties. This explains why certain structures have been effectively assigned to particular tasks.

226 |

The haversack (opposite) from Nagaland protects not the wearer but its contents from monsoon rains. Three layers of long bast fibers cascade from braided and twined headings.

225 |

Melanesian plaiting includes a small canoe of twilled bamboo to hold netted fish, also the walls and ceilings of houses.

photo: Musée de l'Homme, Paris

227 |
In the deserts of Mali these plaited sleeping bags provide a modicum of insulation and, once closed, protection from insects.
photos: Griaule, Musée de l'Homme, Paris

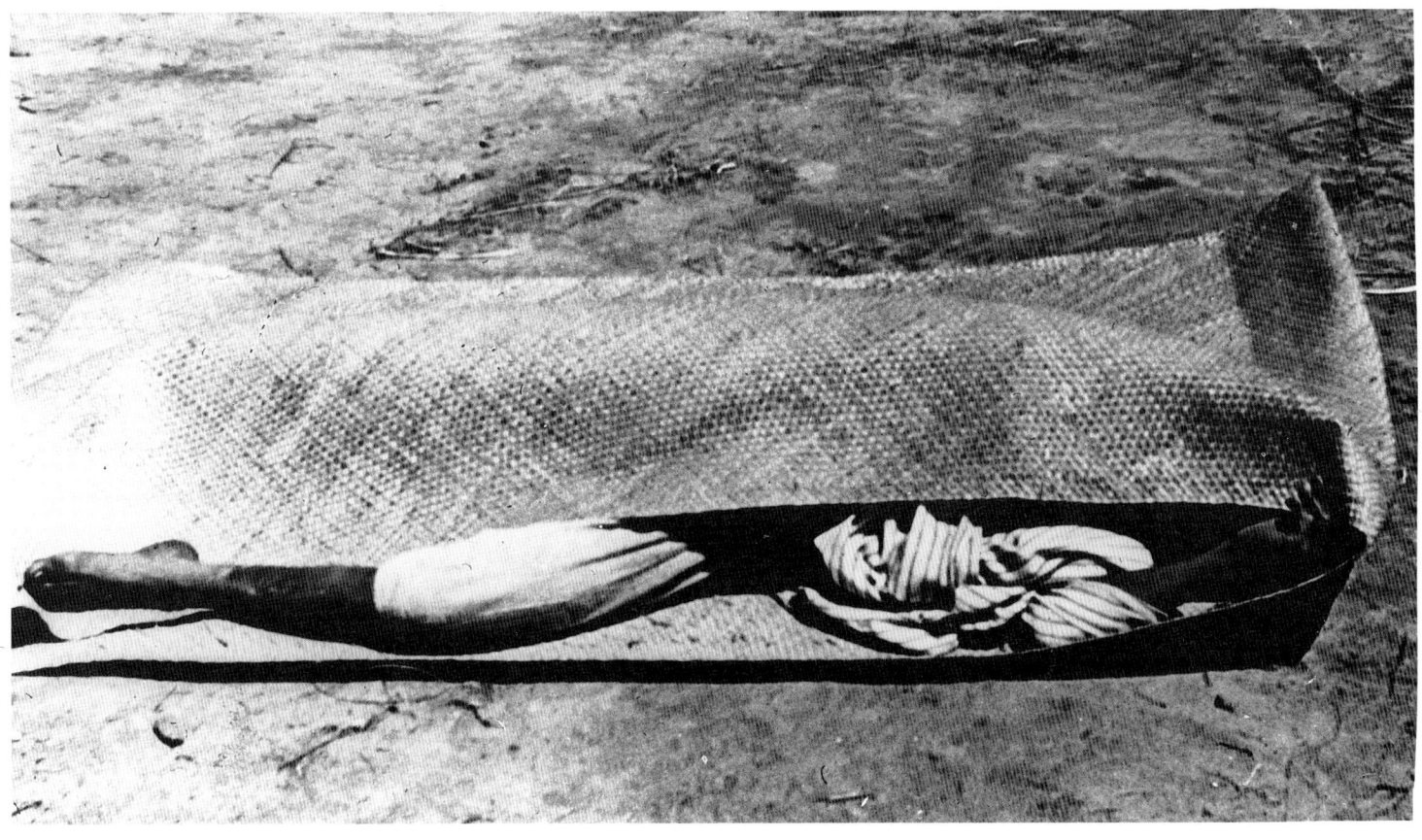

Applications 219

Tensile Strength

In elementary textile courses, one of the first lessons is the measurement for tensile or tear strength by the grab test. This test has been going on for so long that today few fabrics are too tender to pass muster. In the beginning, when there were no standards, tensile strength must have been sought for ropes, nets, traps, and burden baskets. It would have been valued in raw materials as well as finished products. Leather thongs, sinews, and bundles of animal hair created exacting standards to measure the endurance of plant fibers. One alternative solution, grouped strands, proved the old adage that there is safety in numbers.

Braiding also multiplies the resistance of individual elements, producing sturdy "ropes" from fragile grasses or silken strands. Since the elements are positioned close to the direction of the pull, braids possess an unusual longitudinal strength: they are less likely to tear at the selvages than woven bands. With agriculture, and particularly herding, came braided tethers, bridles, girths, whips, and lariats.

Tubular braiding, which doubles the surface area, also augments tensile strength. The mechanized braiders of the United States and Europe have long produced a broad spectrum of tubular products from shoelaces to high-pressure hoses. Recent developments include industrially plaited synthetic arteries. Core braids so successfully combine tensile strength with flexibility that they are the favored lifeline used by mountain climbers. Elastic cores add another dimension. Because of its strength, flexibility, and elongation, braiding is the fabric construction most often combined with elastic bands and cords.

228

Plaiting is probably as old as transportation—first sandals and burden baskets, then fittings for domesticated animals, chariots and sails, carriages, trunks, and gondolas for lighter-than-air craft. Sikorsky Aircraft has learned that plaiting filaments of icevlar/graphite epoxy for air frame structures creates a stronger, lighter plane than those of riveted aluminum.

photo: Sikorsky Aircraft Co., Stratford, Conn.

229–230. An East African beer stirrer (right) is interlaced with 2SOE, one of which is also the core and the brush (compare with the braided stirrer on page 126). On the left is the end detail of a long rattle called a "devil's walking stick" by people of Guiana. Like a tambourine, it produces two sounds—a tingle from the wood splints within and a deeper resonance when the tube is tapped. Its powerful twilled patterning varies over the entire length.

229 |
rattle
2SOE, various twills, H-V
rattan
c. 30" × 2"
Guiana, 1970s

230 |
beer stirrer
2SOE, 1/1 H-V
grass, cotton
L. c. 8"
East Africa, 1970s

231 |
Of the many knotted and plaited casings used to protect glass containers, those of Sardinia and the Aleutian Islands compete for finesse. The Sardinian one shown is typical in its attached cap and variety of interlacings. The author has never seen two alike.

Expansion/Contraction

While most weaves elongate when pulled on the diagonal—the squared mesh becoming diamond—oblique interlacings elongate and contract longitudinally. This property is useful for braided edgings, which, unlike woven tapes, make turns without puckers. The outer edge elongates as the inside becomes more compact. Concentrically stitched braided rugs demonstrate this advantage.

The author's appreciation of interlaced and looped structures was heightened when he served as consultant to Dupont on a nonwoven project. No matter how thin and filmy, these cloths did not elongate under tension because their fiber mesh was based on a triangular structure. A triangle is an immovable constant, producing a boardy fabric. Because hexagonal plaiting and caning have triangulated structures, they tend not to elongate and contract. In contrast, the rounded loops of knitting are extremely accommodating: observe a sweater elbow as the arm crooks.

Rigidity/Flexibility

The undulation (ability to go over and under) requisite of individual elements of interlacing is difficult to achieve with stiff materials; the common solution is an openly worked structure. Sometimes elements are hardened after the interlacing process—with less effect on the structure. For instance, baskets are often worked with supple young softwood branches that dry after interworking. A more radical change results from the baking process, which gives clay or bread dough a rigidity it did not possess during the interlacing. Bobbin lace loses some of its fragility when starch is applied as an after-treatment.

Similarly, the willows and reeds of wickerwork are transformed by soaking for hours or days to attain a proper flexibility before interworking. Compact construction followed by slow drying imparts an absolute rigidity. Sturdy, lightweight, capable of withstanding dampness, wickerwork has been utilized for laundry baskets, porch furniture, fishing creels, and burial caskets. Julius Caesar praised the wicker-sided chariots of the early Britons, envying their speed and maneuverability over rough terrain.

Overlapping braids that are stitched into place establish a form and rigidity not common to single braided units. This advantage is applied in hat making and basketry boxes. Normally, braids are so flexible that they can be knotted. Glowing works of art in their own right, Japanese tubular braids are used as ties for the *obi* sash.

Durability

Resistance to abrasion contributes to the durability of all fabrics. Of major importance is the thickness and density of the strands. Their resilience is another consideration, determining whether the surface will recoil when given a blow or remain firm and suffer a beating. Flexing relates to this aspect.

The elements commonly used in interlacing are peculiarly suited to the purpose. Whether grasses, willows, or slit bamboo, their fiber bundles run the length of the strand, thereby increasing flexibility, tensile strength, and resistance to abrasion. Fibers spun into yarns are usually carded and combed to achieve the same properties.

For resistance to abrasion and soil, the smoothness of the elements is a factor. They are often scraped and polished before interlacing or smoothed and honed afterward.

The brittleness of dried-out bast materials affects their durability. In our modern world the great destroyer of interlaced basts is the heated interior—low in humidity and flooded with sunlight. In contrast, the traditional Japanese home, despite cold, dim interiors, had small water jars placed near bast fibers to "feed their thirst."

Densely worked, asymmetrically balanced plaiting is particularly durable. The compacted floats of wickerwork fend off all kinds of abuse—whether blows on trunks and hampers or a body moving over the surface of a wicker chair. Baskets and other containers often employ the same principle: compacted floats running in the direction of maximum wear.

The tensile strength of braided whips, bridles, harnesses, and slings has already been mentioned; their longitudinal pull and smooth surface are also advantageous for durability. A specialized quality of braids to be long lasting shows up in candlewicks—braided ones burn slowly.

This enormous Wickerworks chair will be more valuable and about as sturdy in the 21st century. The East Indian cane is resistant to dry heat, and the canes are large and long. The asymmetrically balanced interlacing typical of wicker permits the closely crammed horizontals to take the brunt of abuse.

232
Tonda Chair, 1979
Peter Rocchia, U.S.A.
Indian cane
W. 48" × D. 38" × H. 34"
photo: Stone & Steccati, San Francisco

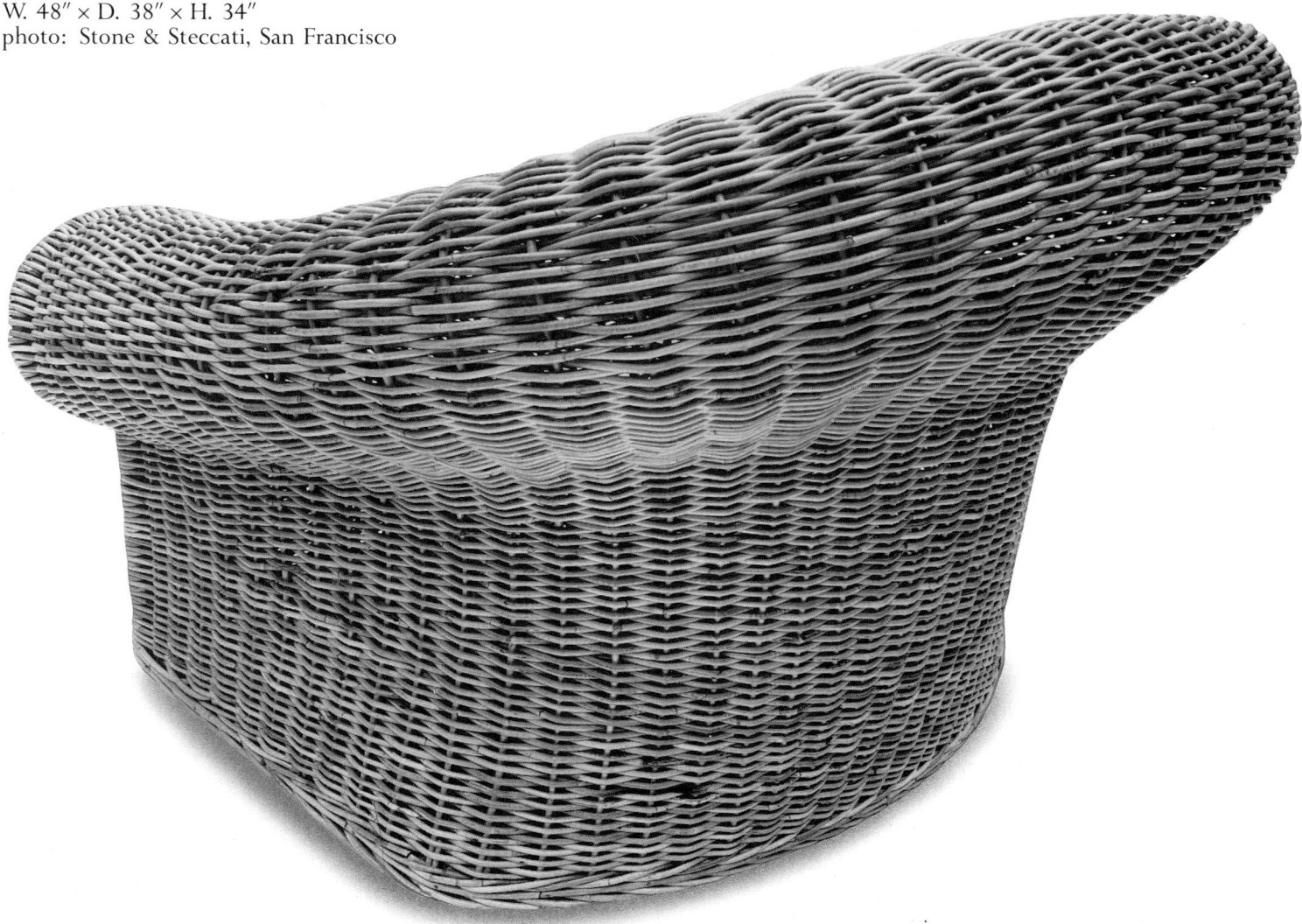

233–234

This serene portrayal of four ladies imparts a sensation of déjà-vu: the wicker chair and braided hair remain unchanged from Roman times to the present. The wicker chair (below) is still made today in the suburbs of Rome. Note its braided top rail.

Gallo-Roman marble found at Trèves, courtesy
  Photographie Giraudon
Chair, courtesy The Wickerworks

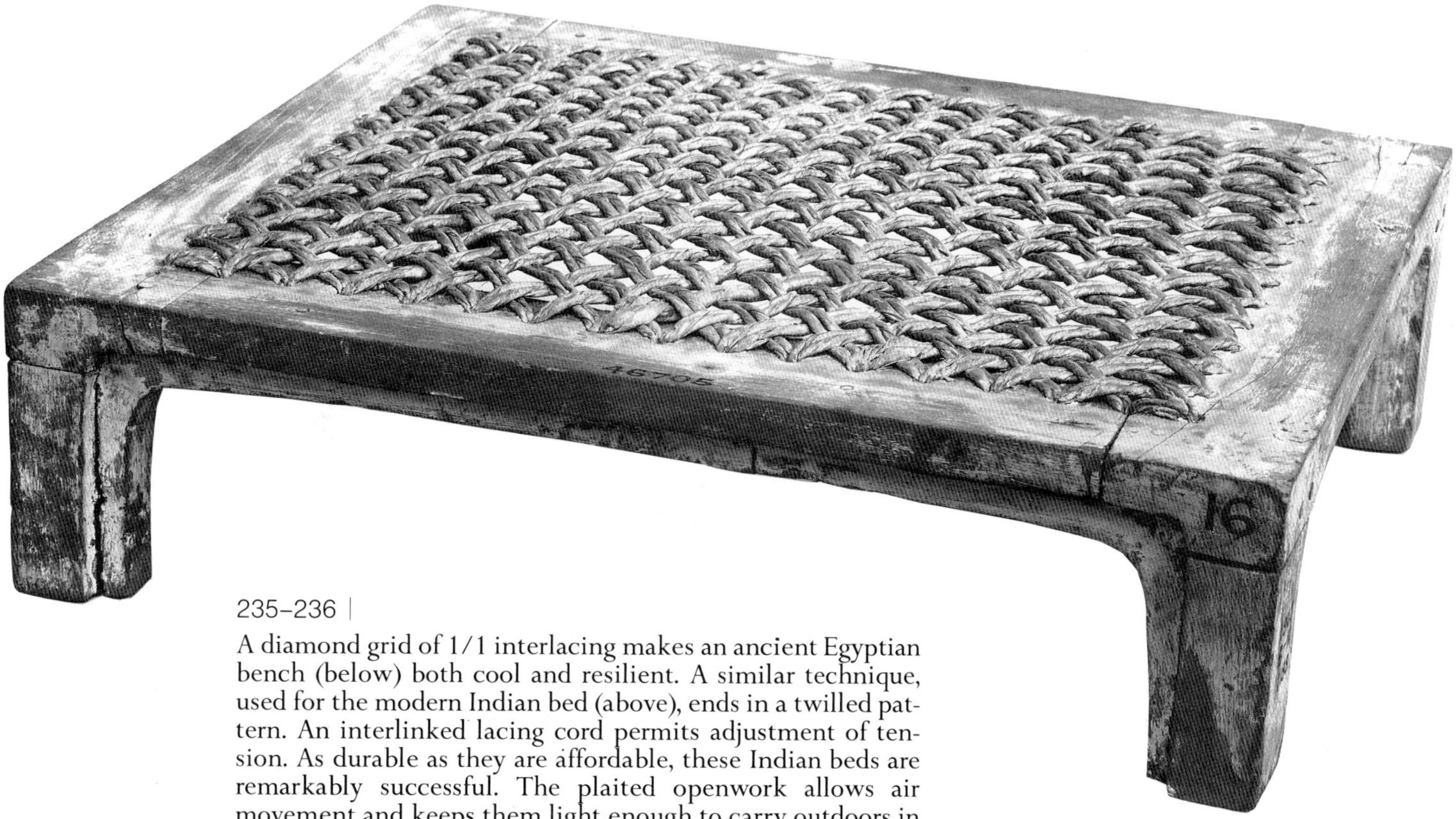

235–236 |
A diamond grid of 1/1 interlacing makes an ancient Egyptian bench (below) both cool and resilient. A similar technique, used for the modern Indian bed (above), ends in a twilled pattern. An interlinked lacing cord permits adjustment of tension. As durable as they are affordable, these Indian beds are remarkably successful. The plaited openwork allows air movement and keeps them light enough to carry outdoors in hot weather. A palatial version is similar but with finely turned, lacquered supports and a horizontal/vertical interlacing of cotton tapes.

photos: Ancient Egyptian bench, British Museum, London
       Indian bed, Susan Jamart

Applications 225

237 |
Observe how neatly the interlaced verticals tighten the horizontal straps that hold the double drumheads. When the hides have shrunk in dry weather, tension can be eased by spreading the verticals.

photo: Colorphoto Hinz, Allshwil-Basel

226 Interlacing

238–239. Two modern chairs use interlacing to achieve a durable surface conducive to air movement. The one in Plate 238—perhaps the first wicker chair designed after World War II—is interlaced directly into perforations in the wide frame. Dominant horizontals classify the structure as wicker. The detail (Pl. 239) shows two layers of machine caning pulled over an inner frame, then set into the exposed frame that forms the back. A spline of rattan closes the gap.

238 |
Basket Chair, 1950
Nana and Jorgen Ditzel (designers),
 Denmark
2SOE, 1/1
rattan, teak,
Larsen Furniture, New York

239 |
Ritz Chair, 1978
Ben Baldwin (designer), U.S.A.
4SOE, H-V, oblique
rattan peel, maple frame
Larsen Furniture, New York

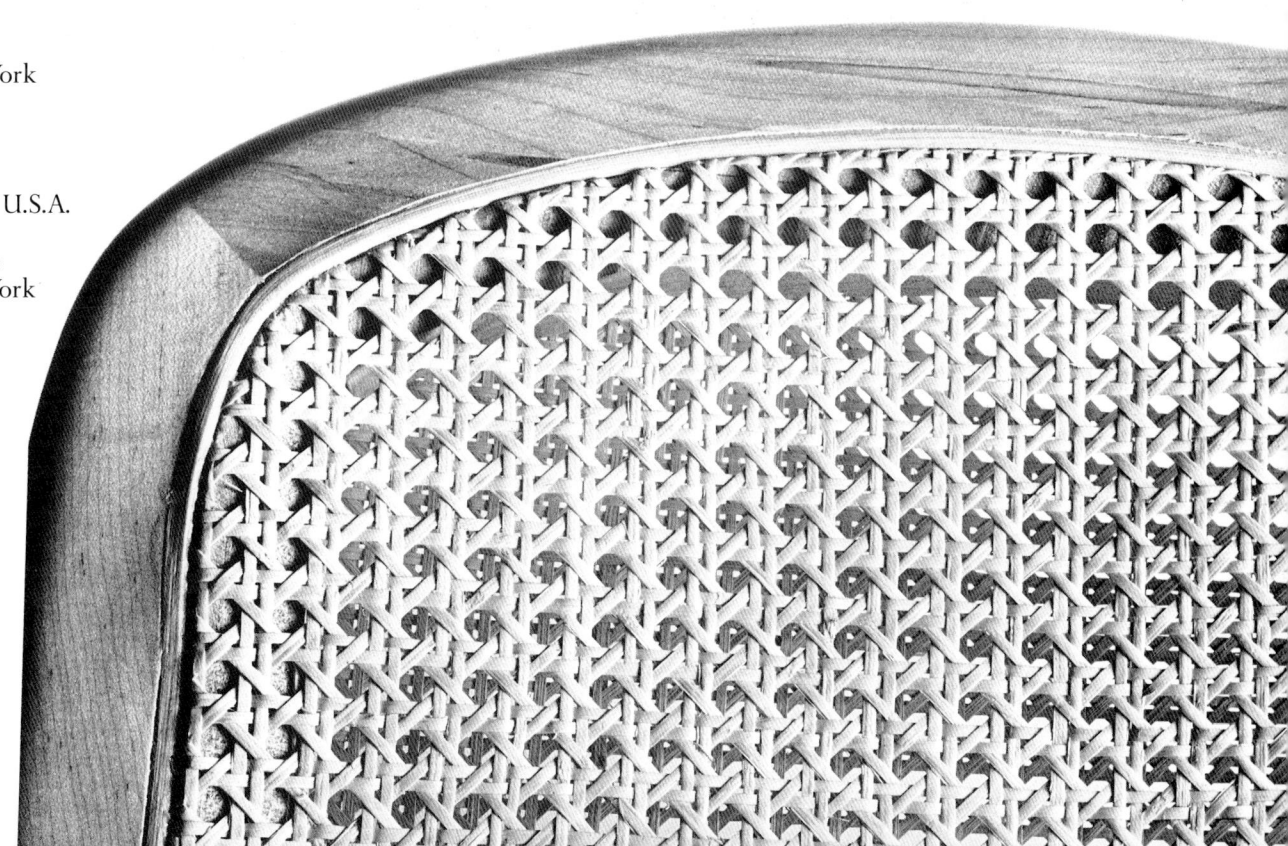

240

241

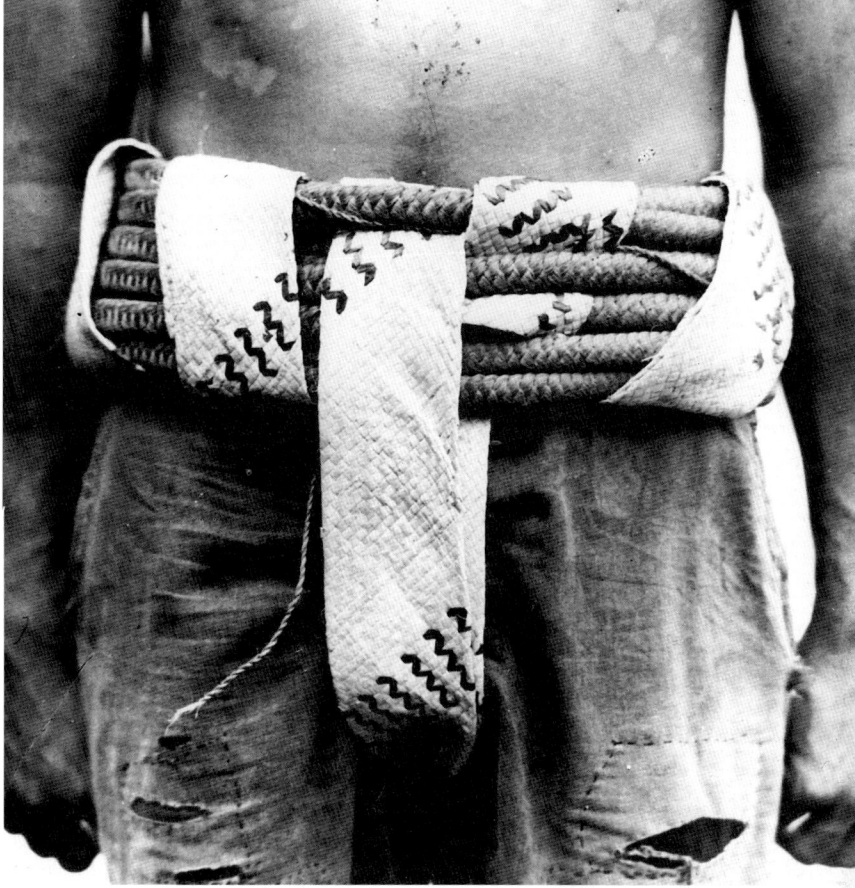

240–243

Plaiting as Protection
In many parts of the tropical world lightweight plaited armor protected hunters and warriors and those fighting their way through thorny thickets. The Micronesian corselet (Pl. 240) with its curious protection for head and neck offers the double protection of tightly plied bast cord densely interlaced. The handsome armor from Borneo (Pl. 241) is of lighter stuff covered with stout armadillo hide. Both layers are protected with a braided edging. The twilled jacket and hat worn in Muslim Madagasgar (Pl. 242) provides modesty and a bulwark against brambles. The elaborate plaited belt (Pl. 243) marks an otherwise threadbare Solomon Islander as belonging to the warrior class. The girdle of smooth round braid supports a narrow loincloth of palm fiber. Note the pattern imbricated across the interlacing.

photos: Musée de l'Homme, Paris

Density

The effects of density summarize many advantages cited for other properties. Closely packed elements give durability by resisting abrasion and "catching" of loose ends. While expansion/contraction may be limited by density, the tensile and bursting strengths are increased.

Perhaps no aspect of plaiting is so remarkably diverse as density—far greater than the norm for woven cloths. Bobbin laces vie with spiderwebs for sheerness. The openness of plaited hammocks ensures their continued popularity, just as the cool comfort of webbed and caned seating is widely appreciated. For the bamboo plaited matting of South and East Asia, those with three or more sets of elements are worked so openly that they are practical for caging small animals or making measured sieves.

In contrast, dense interlacings can inhibit the wind or secure precious substances. The "envelope" sleeping bag (p. 219) and the food cover (p. 113) protect against insects. When densely worked in 2/2 or 3/3 twills, flexible materials take on a rigidity suitable for trays and boxes.

Fans and fencing often combine densities. To achieve rigidity, fans are often twill plaited near the base while the outer reaches are worked with a spaced 1/1 interlacing. In much of the tropical world bamboo fences have densely plaited twills at the lower portion to keep out small predators and contain fowl. Wide openings in the upper segment allow breezes and partial vision.

We are trained from childhood to admire fabrics that are very fine, with a great many yarns per inch; yet "fine" the quantitative and "fine" the qualitative become confused in our subconscious. There is a universal appeal in openwork possessing both body and substance—in short, work that has integrity. Five major conditions produce openwork.

1) rigid elements
Interlacing stiff materials creates a spring action—a constant pressure that tends to prevent slippage and allows an open structure with body and substance. When combined with the features listed below, extremes are possible.

2) order of interlacing
Every weaver and basket maker knows that a 1/1 order of interlacing will produce the most secure mesh with the smallest number of elements. Alternating this with areas of more open interlacing will scarcely weaken the body. Omitted elements, the equivalent of skip denting in weaving, is another method of achieving openness.

3) holes and slits
These devices, common to crochet and eyelet embroidery, can also be found in bobbin lace. Although the equivalent of slit tapestry is rare in plaited structures, fabrics of partially joined braids are not unusual. Twining, twined plaiting, leno, and gauze weaves are the common techniques for securing widely spaced elements. A four-element braid serves this purpose in the fish trap on page 126. Secure knots permit the wide spacing of netting.

Defying convention, the rectangular base of this peanut carrier rises into two tubes instead of a single cylinder. Its balanced form serves as spout and handle. The moderately dense 2/2 interlacing allows sufficient ventilation to prevent spoilage; added braids reinforce the top and base and attach the handle.

244 |
nut carrier
2SOE, 2/2 oblique
rattan peel
6″ × 6″ × 2″
The Philippines

245 |

The oblique plaiting of this backpack will, when filled with yucca leaves and laced closed, snuggly conform to its load and the bearer. Pieroa Indians in the wilds of Venezuela make them from palm fiber with a tie of *mahajve* bark.

Applications

246

246–249

As varied as the climates and the stylistic demands of different cultures are the shoes designed to accommodate them. Hundreds of eight-thousand-year-old sandals with interlaced soles were found in a dry cave in Mexico, and Neolithic examples with braided soles have been discovered in Europe.

The Mesa Verde (A.D. 700) sandal (Pl. 246) is similar to the earliest finds. While much more refined and better preserved, the New Kingdom Egyptian version (Pl. 249) shares the obliquely plaited sole and arched strap to accommodate the foot.

Plaited with thick strips of birch bark, the shoes in Plate 248 are lighter and warmer than wooden ones and can flex to accommodate movement. The Swedes wear them with thick woolen socks. The Japanese snow boot (Pl. 247) goes over thickly padded *tabi*s. Its lower sole provides additional insulation and is replaceable.

Egyption sandal: courtesy British Museum

247

232 Interlacing

248

249

234 Interlacing

250–251

A number of wide-brimmed hats were shown in the last chapter. These Muslim hats are somewhat different. Designed to support a turban, the Afghan one in Plate 250 is made of spiraling, overlapped braids of grain straw. The top portion is couched with a geometry of the same straw. The black pill boxes from southern Celebes are so finely plaited that they resemble woven horsehair. Note the 4SOE band at left, the fine patterning, right.

4) cross bracing

This principle, intrinsic to 3, 4, or 6SOE, makes possible very open meshes. Strength can be magnified if rigid elements and/or a supporting frame are used.

5) frame tensioning

When interlacings are plaited directly on a frame, in the manner of a tennis racquet, the surface is firm despite the spacing. "Take up" resulting from the interlacing tightens each element. Mats, attached to a frame after completion, possess nearly the same tautness and protection. An inversion of this concept is the open interlacing around pots and bottles that forms a cushioning reinforcement.

Layering of interlacings provides another type of density. While the intrinsic fragility of most plant fibers would seem to negate their use as shields, lightweight density is useful in combination with sturdier materials. Fragments discovered in the ruins of ancient Mesopotamia indicate their warriors carried shields of braided fibers covered with skins. Plaited leather over shaped bark frames serves the same purpose in Africa.

Layering can also provide insulation. The double-thickness of the Guinean house shown on page 244 protects its inhabitants against both rain and temperature changes. In the same manner, Chinese "coolie" hats with broad leaves sandwiched between two layers of 3SOE interlacing form an ever-ready umbrella or parasol.

Knots and Netting

Just as knots and nets are often difficult to relate to other interlacings, the same is true of their characteristic properties. Because there are no parallel or opposing SOEs for reinforcement, the tensile strength of the cord itself is as important as the security of the knot. Flexible strands are another prerequisite: while knots are solid and unchanging, these strands must accept the required loops and bends. Since pulling only tightens knots, there is no expansion/contraction.

More than other fabrics, nets fold, twist, and elongate with great flexibility—without changing their basic structure. Although the regular grid pattern comes askew when pulled, the basic knot structure remains a constant. Wavelike undulations of submerged fishnets help mask them from the expected catch.

When Form Does Not Follow Function

Practicality or use determines most technical choices made by artisans. Embellishment provides a secondary, aesthetic choice.

However, caprice and imagination surface during a craftsman's relaxed moments; chance allows innovations, new forms, untried uses for old structures. Those few artists who can afford the luxury of unfettered creativity are bringing forth an unprecedented number of pure interlacings, with no designated applications.

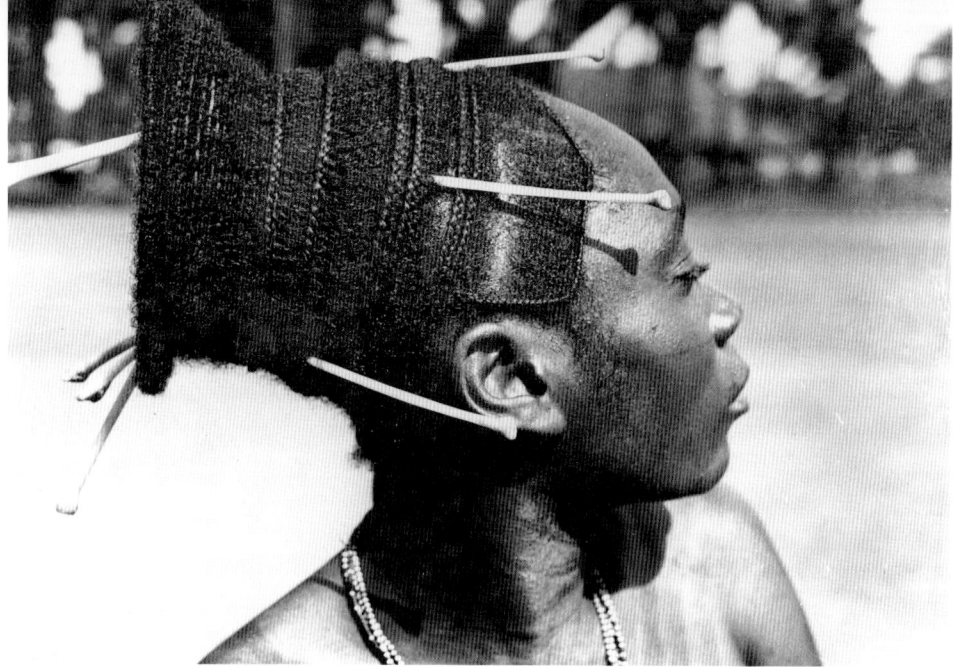

252 |
Makere woman, Zaire
collection: Musee de l'Homme, Paris
photo: Goldstein

253 |
Tibet photo: Newark Museum, New Jersey

236 Interlacing

254 |
Woman with Braid, 1886
Sir Edward Burne-Jones, England
Courtesy of Cooper-Hewitt Museum, New York
photo: Eeva-Inkeri

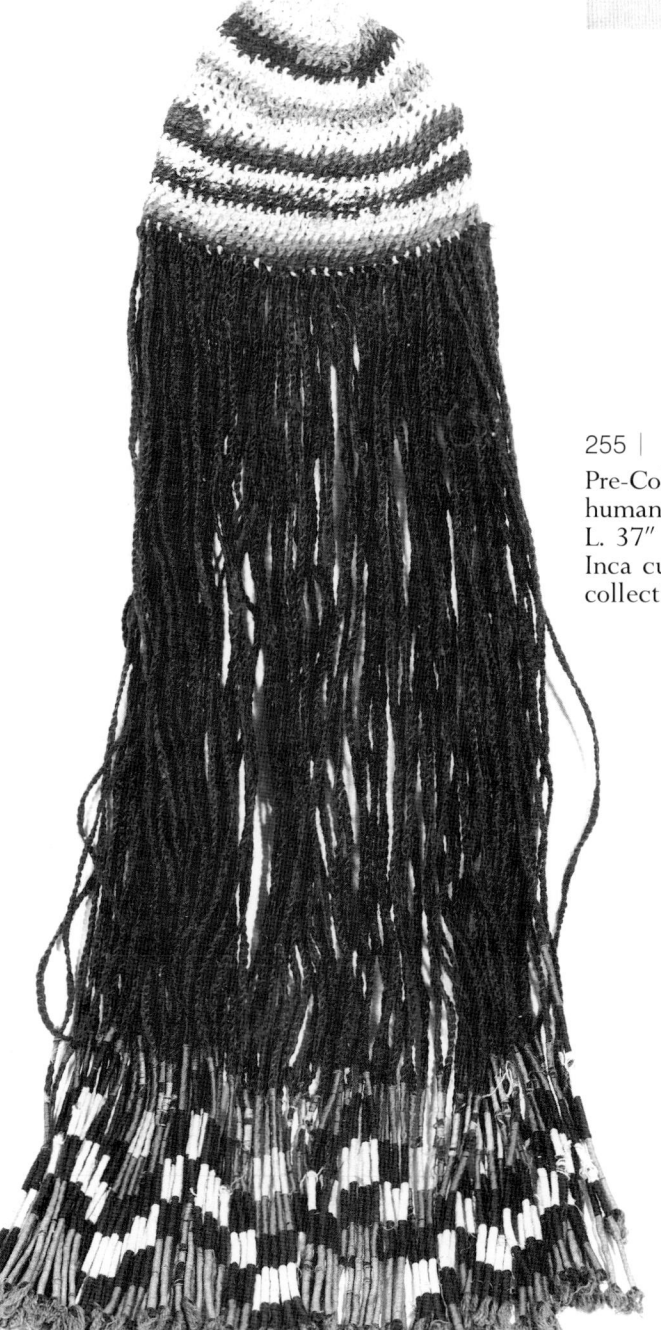

255 |
Pre-Columbian burial cap
human hair braids, knotted wool cap, wool wrapping
L. 37"
Inca culture, Peru
collection: Brooklyn Museum

252–255. Hair braids are as ancient as they are diversified. For those first millennia without scissors or razors, both men and women braided hair to keep it untangled and out of their eyes. Styles of headdress soon differentiated one people from another and become signs of status and rank.

Although this Tibetan woman's clothes are tattered, her braided hair would be envied in any culture (Pl. 253). The braiding sequence is contrary to all braided finishes either worked from large to small or worked without graduation, as in the ancient Peruvian burial wig in Plate 255.

An African headdress is often so elaborate that it must be kept for long periods and requires head rests for sleeping. The braids of the one in Plate 252 are curiously similar to Victorian braids of Plate 254.

Applications 237

In most (but not all) tubular braids interlaced over a core, the core elements are passive. Because the core elements of this brush became the active verticals of the interlacing, both the "bristles" and the handle are more secure. In the reverse twill of the interlaced handle, the center section changes to a more pronounced (and more comfortable) horizontal face.

256 |
brush
2SOE + core, 4/2 and 6/2, H-V
bast
14″ × 2″
provenance unknown

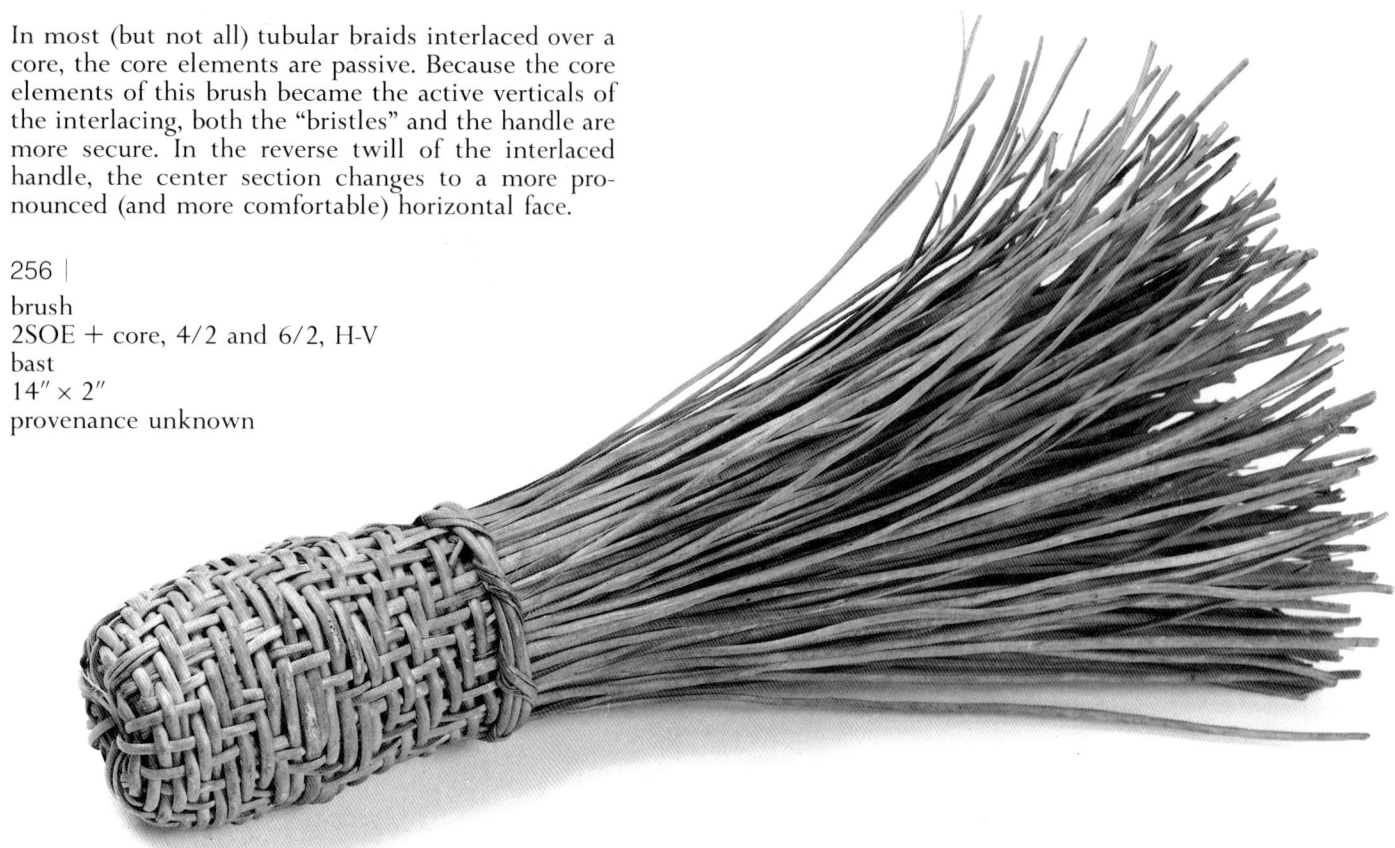

257 |
Two combs are similar to the brush in Plate 256 in that the horizontal-vertical interlacing of the handle helps to secure and spread the unfettered, working verticals. The larger comb is rather straightforward in its "holding" pattern; the smaller one is more sophisticated and, with a secondary set of verticals, more complex.

comb (right)
2SOE, 3/1, etc. H-V
wood, bast
6¼″ × 1¾″
Solomon Islands, early 20th century
collection: Newark Museum, New Jersey

comb (left)
2SOE, 2/2 H-V
wood, bast
7¼″ × 2¾″
Zaire, early 20th century
collection: Newark Museum, New Jersey

258-259 |

Braiding multiplies the length and strength of fibers, producing stout cords from fragile grasses or silken strands. The braid on an adz (Pl. 258) binds the blade to the haft and provides a trustworthy gripping surface. The maker was aware of its handsome pattern.

The adz in Plate 259, from Papua New Guinea, is strictly ceremonial. The shape is unwieldy, and the stone blade not sufficiently secured for real use. The plaited pattern, on the other hand, is ambitious in its accentuation of the compound curves through a combination of diamond twills and color effects.

photo (above): Musée de l'Homme, Paris
photo: Glenbow Museum, Calgary

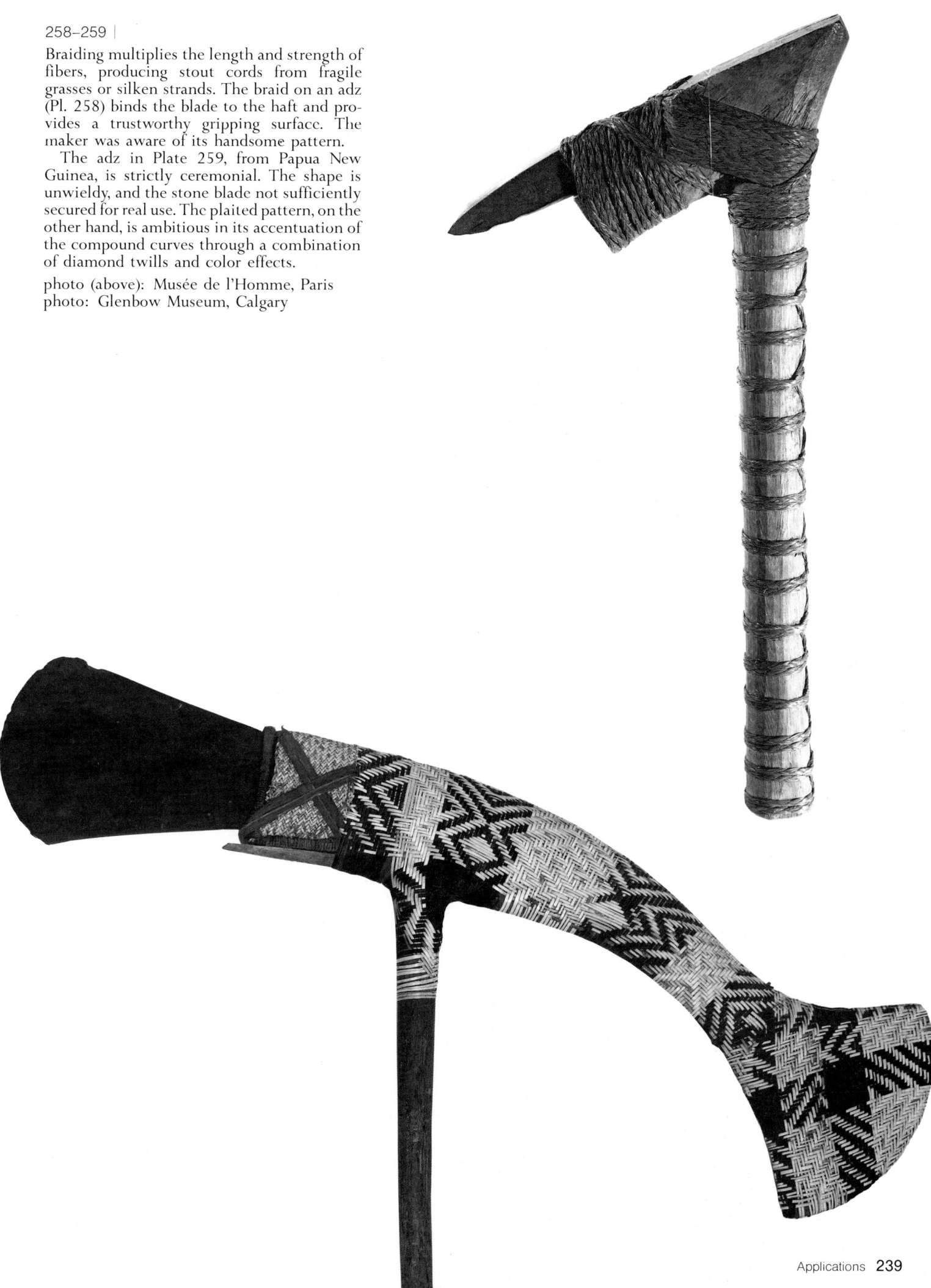

Applications 239

The footed fish baskets of Thailand are the stronger for an unusual twill construction. Horizontals interlace 3/3; verticals are alternately 2/1 and 1/2. Although sizes range from one foot to one yard high, the volumetric form, the funnel insert, and bamboo feet are common to all.

260
basket
2SOE, H-V
bamboo
14″ × 14″
Thailand, 1975

261–262 |
Because fishing baskets throughout the world have evolved from experience and economy, they have much in common; their materials must endure considerable periods of submersion in water. The cluster of wicker baskets in Plate 261 are lobster cages from Ireland's Atlantic coast. Fish traps for the warm waters of the Congo are shown with other baskets to hold the catch in Plate 262.

photo: Musée de l'Homme, Paris

263–264

To keep animals in or out, plaited fences, hurdles, coops, cages, and weirs have been in use for millennia. The wattle fence photographed in a Polish village (Pl. 264) is of Neolithic origin. The Yugoslav tower for drying wheat is shown with a gate of braided bast fiber (Pl. 263).

photos: Poland, M. de Fontanes, Musée de l'Homme, Paris
        Yugoslavia, Musée de l'Homme, Paris

Applications

265 |

Roof thatching (opposite above) is held in place by a layer of hexagonal interlacing. Like Chinese coolie hats, the multiple layers shed water. They also contain the fumes within these fermentation vats in northern Vietnam. The plaited mats provide shade to control temperature.

photo: Claeys, Musée de l'Homme, Paris

266 |

A portable hut (opposite below) being unrolled in Guinea shows the juxtaposition of an obliquely interlaced lining with a horizontal and vertical outer wall, providing a double thick insulation.

photo: Dr. Pales, Musée de l'Homme, Paris

Models such as this one duplicate large buildings (*mbure*) erected on high mounds in the Fiji Islands to serve as men's meeting places and centers for religious rites. Constructed of the same sennit braids used for the buildings themselves, the models house sacred objects for safekeeping in the *mbure*.

267 |
temple (model)
braiding
1SOE, 1/1 oblique
coir, wood, shells
H. 32½"
Fiji Islands, early 19th century
collection: Israel Museum, Jerusalem

Applications 245

268–269 |
Near Pagan, Burmese villagers prefabricate fifteen-foot-long panels for house walls. The twilled plaiting combines inside and outside bamboo peel. As the inside peel blackens with mildew, a rich geometry appears.
photo: Randall Darwall

270 |
Since ancient times, sturdy, lightweight wicker has been used for carriages and chariots. Its use for lighter-than-air craft persists in the modern age.

271 |
A grand version of plaited matting covers the walls of a Melanesian court house (Aola, Solomon Islands). Echoing the strict symmetry of the architecture, the bold color effect patterning lends dignity to simple materials.

photo: Musée de l'Homme, Paris

Applications 247

9

Motif and symbol: the philosophical resonance

Beyond the pragmatic and mundane, interlacing is an omnipresent symbol, recurring through time and place. The source can be traced to a profound level of the psyche: a psychologist might call it intuitive or archetypal, an anthropologist, esoteric or occult. Involved with rites of passage, legal transactions, and religious ceremonials, plaited objects often become the incarnation and power of the ritual itself. Equally striking are the interlaced symbols carved in wood and stone, etched in metal, inscribed on vellum, and embroidered or printed on textiles. Viking, Celtic, and Islamic artists explored the intricacies of such design motifs to their outermost limits. Today, even some nontextile corporations have chosen interlaced motifs for their trademarks.

Interlacing is, of course, as quintessentially human as the gesture of crossed arms implying authority or a defensive posture. Interlacing the ten fingers of two hands is somehow reassuring; so is the hand clasp. The Romans carried the importance of intermeshing even further in their belief that the psyche resides in the solar plexus, or plaited center. Emanating from a point just below the sternum, this strong, controlling interlaced network was perceived to flow to all parts of the body.

Ceremonial Interlacings

Although many ritual objects are interlaced, some are incidental to the ceremony, simply familiar objects assigned to special roles. In her studies of status and rank in Samoa, Margaret Mead pointed out that such objects as the best bark cloth and the best mat are associated with people of high rank. In the same way, the humble mat, a necessity of the peasant, took on a symbolic aspect as the seat of Mayan and Aztec rulers. In the drawing from Codex Mendoza (Fig. 1), Montezuma II is shown seated in his palace with mats visible in every window.

When everyday objects take on exhalted uses, ornamentation often becomes more intricate—just as function ebbs. The implement on page 239, encased in an elaborate twill, would never see duty as a weapon. Similarly, Fiji dance clubs had

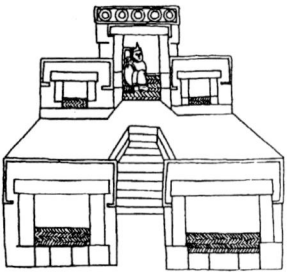

Fig. 1

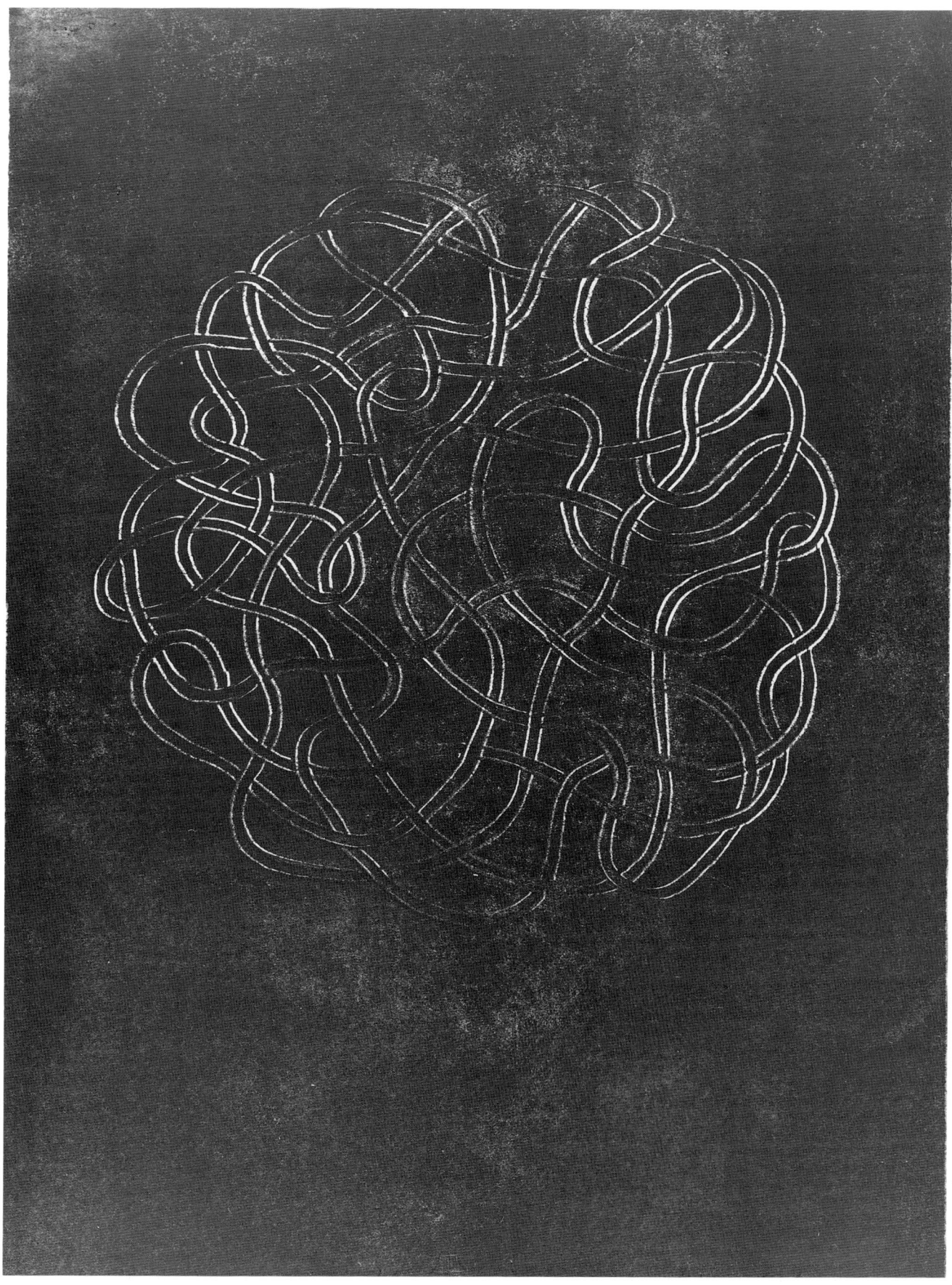

When the consummate 20th century weaver Anni Albers turned to printmaking, she produced a portfolio of lithographs titled *Line Involvements*. Freed from the horizontal-vertical constraint of the loom, she was able to trace loose strands in chaos evolving to the point of ordered interlacing.

272

VI, 1964
Anni Albers, U.S.A. (born, Germany)
lithograph; ed. 20
19¾" × 14¾"
collection: Brooklyn Museum,
  Dick S. Ramsay Fund

Motif, Symbol

273 |
mask
braiding
1SOE, 1/1 oblique
bast, wood, pigments, tusks
New Hebrides
collection: Musée de l'Homme, Paris

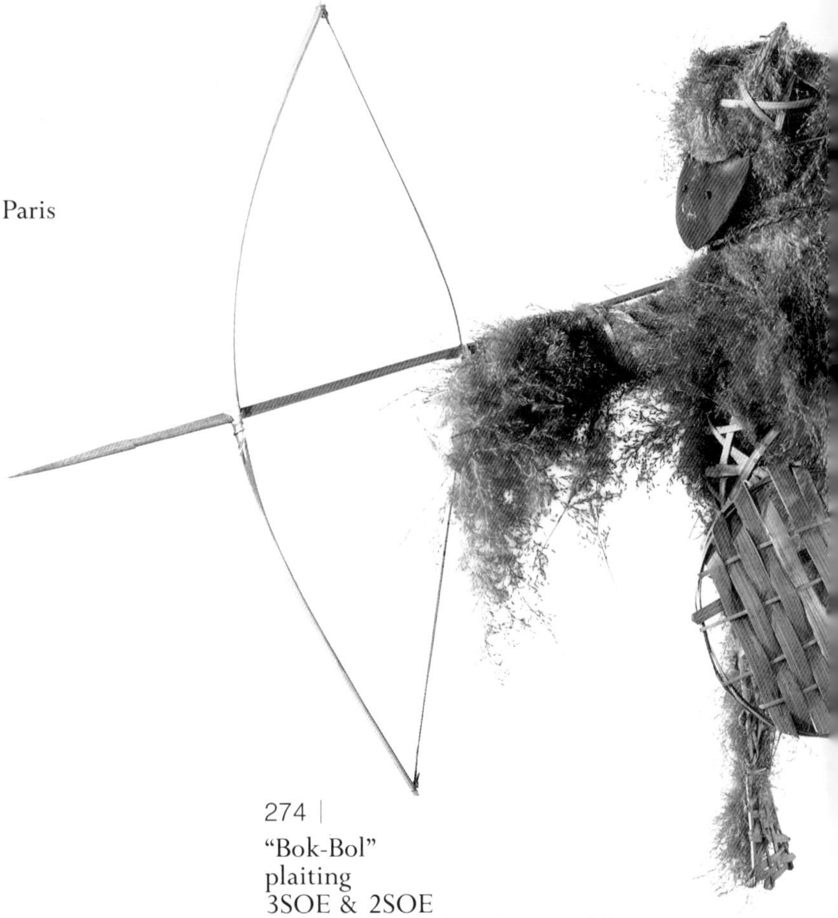

274 |
"Bok-Bol"
plaiting
3SOE & 2SOE
bamboo, palm fronds, grass blossoms
(south) Vietnam
collection: Musée de l'Homme, Paris

275 |
boar *tumban*
plaiting, braiding
2SOE, 2/2 H-V (braided edges; snout
 and ears braided with supplementary SOE)
bast, mineral pigments, feathers
64" × 25"
Tambanan village, Papua New Guinea
collection: Glenbow Museum, Calgary

250 Interlacing

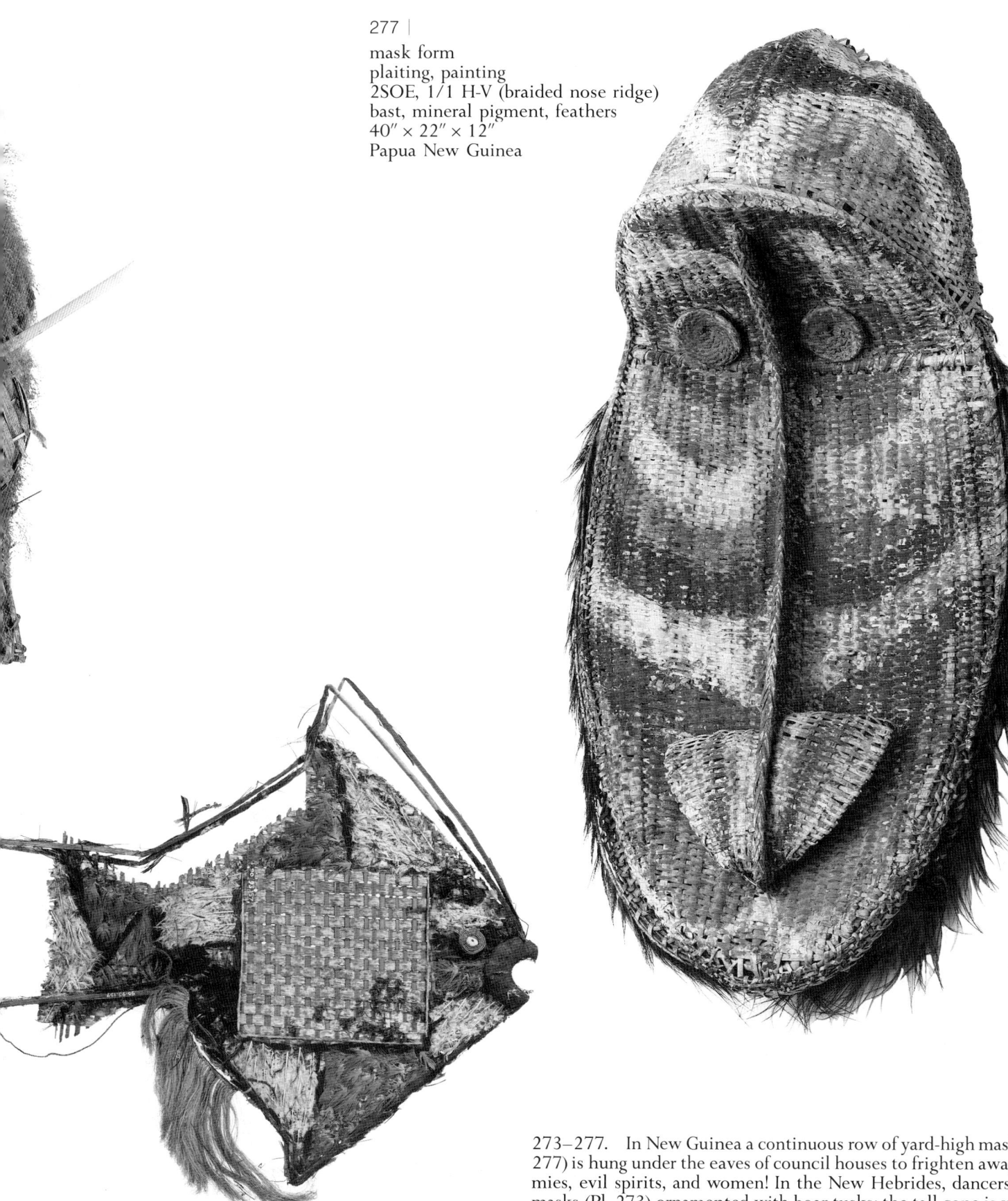

277 |
mask form
plaiting, painting
2SOE, 1/1 H-V (braided nose ridge)
bast, mineral pigment, feathers
40″ × 22″ × 12″
Papua New Guinea

276 |
ritual object
2SOE, 1/1 H-V
bast, feathers
Guiana
collection: Musée de l'Homme, Paris
photo: D. Pousand

273–277. In New Guinea a continuous row of yard-high masks (Pl. 277) is hung under the eaves of council houses to frighten away enemies, evil spirits, and women! In the New Hebrides, dancers wear masks (Pl. 273) ornamented with boar tusks; the tall cone is wound with braided bast fiber. The wild boar figure (Pl. 275) is plaited with tree fibers, painted with chalk and ochre, and decorated with cassowary feathers. It is a body cover worn in a dance preceeding boar hunts. The small archer in Plate 274, placed on top of supporting poles, protects against evil spirits for a sick person in Vietnam. His body is hexagonally interlaced, while the shield has the wholesome virtue of 1/1 interlacing. The fantasy bird form from Guiana (Pl. 276) looks decorative. It is not. Candidates for male initiation are exposed to biting ants or wasps affixed to the interstices.

Motif, Symbol 251

beautifully plaited handles. In Guiana, the plaited mats filled with biting ants, used to test the courage of boys during initiation ceremonies, are highly decorative (p. 251). Even an Easter basket, now trimmed in vivid colors and bows, probably owes its origin to pagan offerings of eggs as seasonal symbols of rebirth—presented, typically, in an egg basket.

The immovable nature of knots has often transposed them from the workday world to intellectual and spiritual realms. In early China great events were noted with large knots, minor occurences with small ones. During the sixth century B.C., Lao-zu, deploring innovation and change, called upon his followers to return to the "spirit of former times when people used knotted cords for records." Hawaiian tax collectors kept complete inventories of property on knotted cords; pueblo dwellers used them for calendars. Scholars believe that the intricate, decimally knotted *quipus* of the Incas even recorded eclipses, comets, and solar years, as well as planting and harvest times.

Many knots are believed to transmit good and evil powers great distances from their magical object. Either layman or shaman can prepare them and cast the spell—in silence or accompanied by special incantations. In China knot tying is traditionally avoided at the time of birth or death because it might impede the arrival and departure of the soul; yet, there is a Chinese good luck knot symbolizing longevity. The four corners of Jewish prayer shawls have series of knots of numerological import, which add up to the number equivalents of the first two letters of the name of God plus the 613 commandments in the Torah. In the Middle Ages, knots were often used for illiterate people to "sign" legal contracts. This practice may explain why a number of noble families incorporated knots in their crests—as well as the origin of the phrase "tying the knot."

In *Basic Textile Techniques*, Kristen Bühler said that meshes of nets or string constructions are frequently used in magic rites to contain such intangibles as ghosts, demons, or diseases. She adds that in Queensland, a net fastened to the aching part of the body relieves pain, while in Borneo the sick may be wrapped in nets as a cure. Tena Indians of Alaska used netting over doorways to entangle evil spirits; eighteenth-century Scandinavians followed the same practice. This concept of nets as mental or moral snares is widespread.

The ceremonial change from braids to loosened hair marked a transition from maidenhood to marriage in numerous societies. In many Jewish households the sabbath dinner is accompanied by braided bread and braided candles. Among the Kwakiutl Indians of British Columbia, a tubular plaited head ring symbolized the Fire and Death Bringer, attesting that the wearer had the powers of a shaman.

Unique and Arcane Objects

A second category of interlaced ritual accessories were designed specifically for esoteric roles, without foundation in the everyday world. In Malaysia a "spirit perch" of crossed sticks on a central pole is crowned with a circular zigzag fold braid of bast fibers to provide shade for resting spirits. In

Lia Cook's "pressed weave" hangings are unusual in their industrial rayon yarns that are loom woven, meticulously finished to flatten their round elements, then overpainted with plaited images.

278

Two Point Four, 1980 (detail)
Lia Cook, U.S.A.
woven, overpainted
2SOE, "fancy twill," H-V
rayon
5' × 4'
collection: Carol and Henry Sinton
courtesy: Louise Allrich Gallery, San Francisco

279

In the Middle Ages interlaced motifs appeared on capitals and columns of both Christian and Islamic buildings. Carved in gray marble, this pair of columns faces the Mosque of Oman on the great square of old Jerusalem.

Nowhere is plaited imagery so ubiquitous as in Africa. While it is a common motif in the Arab cultures of North Africa, the Copts of Egypt employed both braided and woven images as dominant motifs, especially for textiles. Such images are also common south of the Sahara. Most frequently they are carved on such wooden objects as head rests and drinking vessels. For the extraordinary "grass velvets" of Zaire, interlaced motifs are worked in cut and loop pile.

280

skirt panel
woven with supplementary weft
2SOE + 1SOE, 1/1 H-V
raffia
59" + 22"
Kuba people, Zaire, early 20th century

Mariyo Yagi of Kyoto has interlaced a classic rope splice to represent the fusion of *yin* and *yang*.

281

T-85, 1985
Mariyo Yagi, Japan
splicing
2SOE, 1/1 oblique
hemp, black granite
84" × 45" × 8"

282–283. The baskets of Ed Rossbach and John McQueen are modern classics, sought not as decorative art but as expressions of a rare harmonious order.

282 |
two forms, 1983
Ed Rossbach, U.S.A.
2SOE, 1/1 oblique
ash splints, mulberry paper, paint
22″ × 9″; 19″ × 7″

283 |
Tower, 1983
John McQueen, U.S.A.
multi-SOE, various interlacings
wood splints
3′ × 11″ × 11″

Motif, Symbol **257**

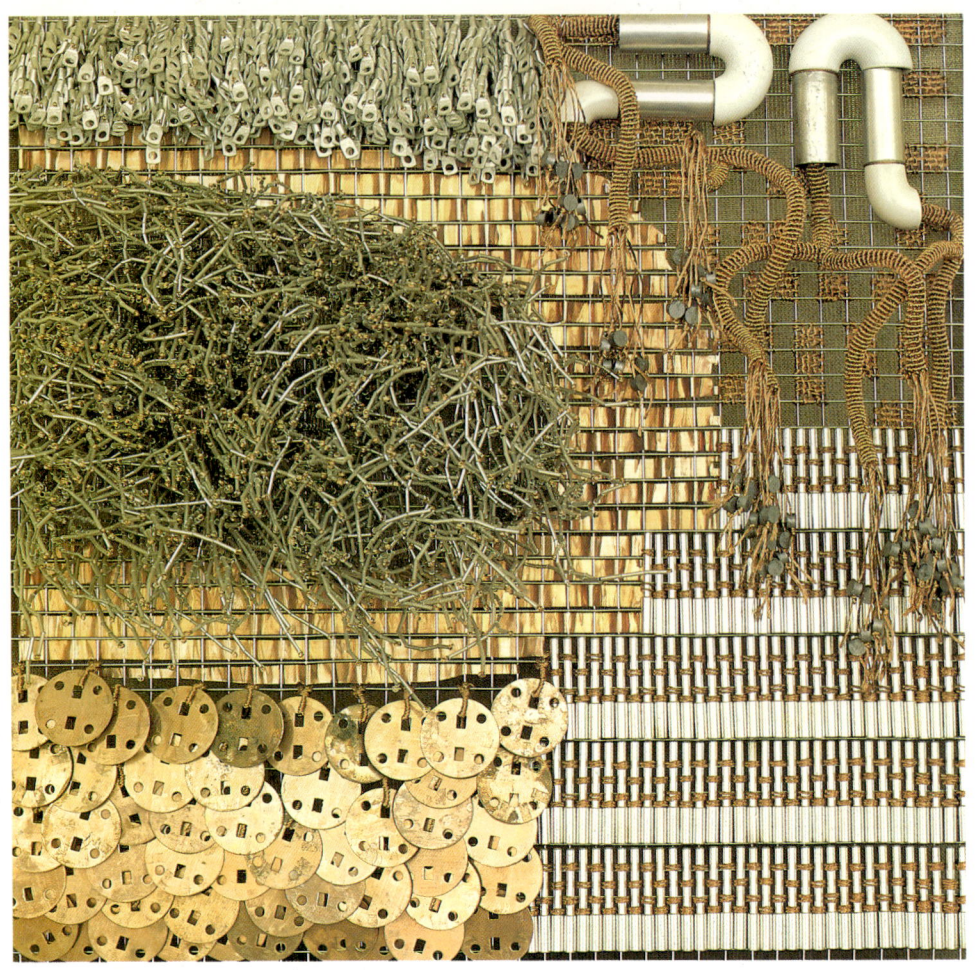

Working over a steel mesh, Liselotte Siegfried has interlaced a variety of communications materials for a seven-part commission outside the Power and Light Co., Zurich. One is shown—without its glass case.

284 |
The Promenade, 1983
Liselotte Siegfried, Switzerland
24″ × 24″ × 2″
photo: Atelier Koenig

285 |
plaited environment, c. 1978
 (detail)
1SOE, 1/1 oblique
paper

285–286. Plaited environmental works are rare, but two from California are shown here. The first, by U.C.L.A. students working with Jarmila Machova under James Bassler, is a myriad of gleaming white stalactites. Nance O'Banion's, with the presence of a ballet set, is similar to her much larger series.

286

Temporary Obstacles, 1983
Nance O'Banion, U.S.A.
plaiting, tying
bamboo, cord, paint
6' × 3' × 2'

287–288. Although Kari Lønning's baskets are typically twined, the vertical elements of her double-walled series are joined with a broad, interlaced horizontal plane. Dona Look's basket in Plate 288 is a simple statement of classic perfection, so much more valuable for its rarity today.

287
Form 4, in Rattan, 1984
Kari Lønning, U.S.A.
twining, plaiting
2SOE, 1/1 radial
rattan
11″ × 17″

288
basket, 1984
Dona Look, U.S.A.
plaiting, stitching
2SOE, 1/1 oblique
birch bark, grass, waxed linen
9″ × 8″ × 8″

289 |
The wide bamboo bands of a modern Japanese basket are interlaced to achieve a richly architectonic pattern. The structure is secured with supplementary lacing elements, and an appropriate rim is attached by a top braid.

Guiana, the trick braid illustrated on page 144 distracted the bush spirit from his mischief. The blessings of the Nile have been evoked by a plaited sheaf of wheat hung in Egyptian doorways. Palm Sunday in Mexico is still celebrated with decoratively braided palm leaves.

For the Bira tribal initiation ceremony in the Congo, shamans wear braided armbands with long, cascading raffia strands. In movement these undulate like the wings of a mythical bird to frighten the young men. For the Blackfoot people of the Great Plains, a pipe with a braid suspended from its stem is a symbol of power.

Carl G. Jung has written that when a chief or shaman puts on a mask for a ritual ceremony, he is not merely disguised as a beast or demon, he *is* that beast or demon—and so shares a "psychic identity." Crucial to theatrical and seasonal ceremonies in innumerable cultures, masks transform the wearers into what Jung calls an archetypal image. The emotions they evoke are so strong that the masks themselves are objects of veneration.

The Iroquois mid-winter ceremony of the three sisters—corn, beans, and squash—features members of the Corn Husk Society wearing masks of concentric braids to impersonate the spirits who inhabit the reverse side of the earth. Miniatures of these masks are carried to avoid bad dreams. When they place a taboo on a garden, Papuan dancers wear massive plaited headdresses in the form of a cone topped with a grimacing face.

The Mystery of Interlaced Signs

Certain interlaced symbols occur in such widely diversified cultures that it is difficult to attest to their underlying meaning. Even when field anthropologists are told that a sign represents a specific god or supernatural force, they have difficulty comprehending the implications within the alien context of their own life experiences. If there are no living representatives of a culture to observe or question, interpretations may be simply guesswork.

Most of these signs came into being in preliterate societies when storytellers and shamans used them to illustrate abstract concepts. Signs could be drawn in the sand or embodied in crafted works. Once imbued in memory, the meaning would remain.

Archetypal truths underlie the commonality of such signs. Symbols involving cojoining and descendancy indicate where members stand in relation to a family, clan, or larger group. Two elements passing over and under each other imply the confrontation of opposing forces such as positive and negative, good and evil, or mankind against the unknown. This juncture also parallels the Oriental search for harmony between the *yin* and *yang* counterforces, which, in dynamic balance, maintain order in the world. These themes are paralleled in many of the world's religious systems.

Nine interlaced motifs are noted here for their surprisingly widespread recurrences.

Two interlaced ovals can be found as a design motif of the

Fig. 2

Fig. 3

Fig. 4

Fig. 5

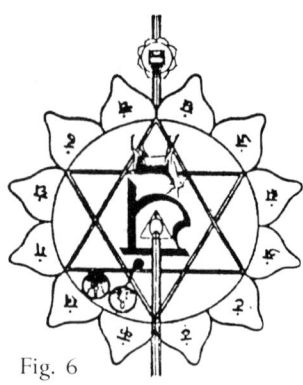
Fig. 6

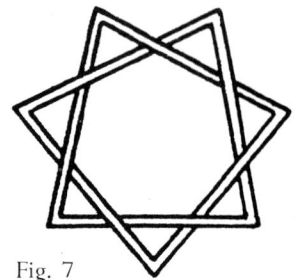
Fig. 7

Bushongo of Zaire (Fig. 2). Dr. Franz Boas says they represent the back and head of a python. The Yoruba of Nigeria, the Mayans, and the South Appalachian Cherokees (Fig. 3) use the same sign. Mutual Benefit Life Insurance Company has taken the compact version of this sign as a trademark (Fig. 4).

With six points derived from two interlaced triangles of the Seal of Solomon (Fig. 5), the Star of David is the symbol of Judaism. For Hindus it symbolizes the heart chakra (Fig. 6), while the unending interlace of a seven-pointed star is considered mystic (Fig. 7). The arcane signs of Freemasonry and alchemy include similar five- and nine-pointed stars.

290–292 |

Although there is no way to illustrate the breadth of interlacing as symbol and ornament, three examples are shown here. The earliest (Pl. 290) an illumination from the Berthold Missal, Germany (about A.D. 1200), speaks of an all-embracing faith. Interlacing, the dominant motif in Africa south of the Sahara, is carved on an East African headrest (Pl. 291). The terra cotta tiles in Plate 292 (overleaf) are from Louis Sullivan's Guaranty Building in Buffalo, New York.

collection: (Berthold Missal), Morgan Library, New York
photo: (tiles) Patricia Layman Bazelow, courtesy of Canon Design, Inc.

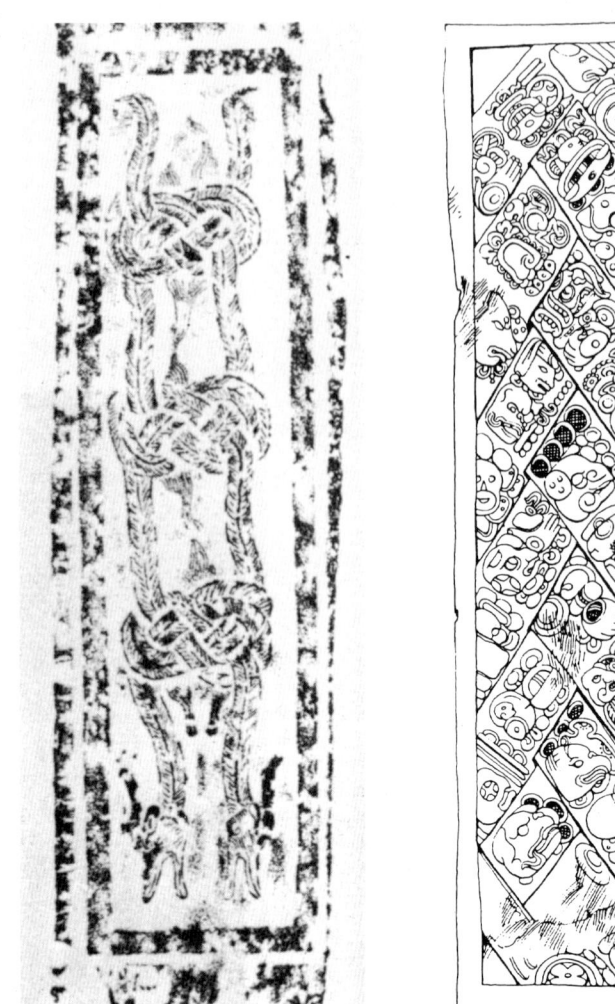
Fig. 8

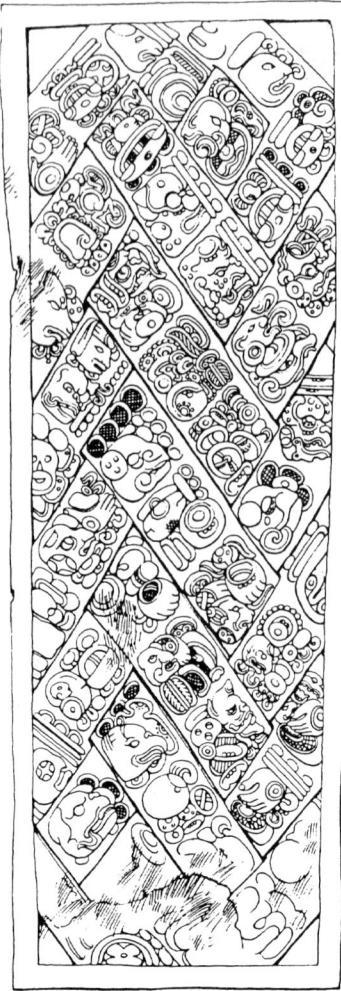
Fig. 9

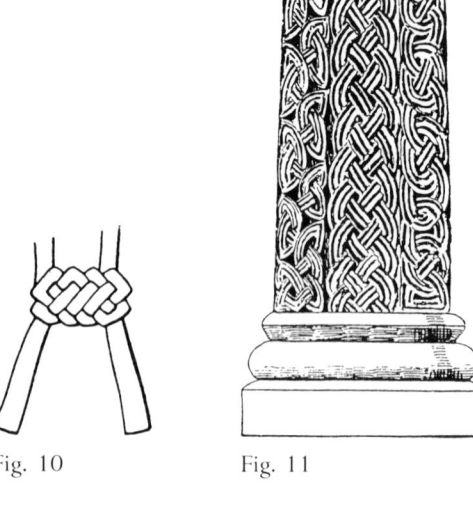
Fig. 10   Fig. 11

Fig. 12

The range of carrick bend motifs extends from the stone carvings of a Lui-Song dynasty tomb (A.D. 424) in Shandong, China (Fig. 8), to a flat stamp from Texcoco, Mexico (Fig. 10).

Braids as design motifs occur in Coptic textiles and Italian Romanesque architectural ornament (Fig. 11) as well as African carvings and fabrics. The double cross of eleventh-century Greek orthodoxy was braided. As symbols of high authority, braids were engraved on Mayan stone steles. Hieroglyphs on the famous stela at Copan (Fig. 9) must be read in the order of the plaiting.

Most intriguing are the labyrinthine interlacings of Celtic and Islamic art. Leonardo da Vinci did a series of these patterns (Fig. 12), likening them to searches for the lost unity of mankind.

When a single element circles back to become one with its origin—uniting the antipods in a ceaseless arabesque—it takes on the mystique of the Eternal, the Infinite. Earthly problems are held in abeyance as the eye tries to follow the circuitous interlacing.

Fig. 13

Fig. 14

Fig. 15

Fig. 16

Fig. 17

Fig. 18

Fig. 19

Fig. 20

The combination of a circle within a square (or the reverse) connected by an interlaced cross configuration was said by Carl Jung to lead our thoughts in the direction of the "divine sun." Another view, that this symbol represents the vegetal cycle paralleling life and rebirth, is manifested in a traditional "knot" garden for herbals. Originating with the myth of Osiris, it is also held to symbolize the unconscious, the repressed, the forgotten—in other words, inner complexes too complicated to unknot. It recurs as an architectural motif in medieval cathedrals (Fig. 13) and as heraldry of the twelfth-century constable of Chester, perhaps derived from a Nordic sign to exorcise evil spirits (Fig. 14).

The Chinese good luck knot (Fig. 16) is known as the knot of fate in Tibetan rugs (Fig. 15); for the Japanese it is the treasure knot (Fig. 17), a symbol of longevity.

Representing the fusion of man and God, interlaced crosses are symbols of both Greek and Roman Catholicism (Fig. 18). The Celts elaborated the theme for their carved stone crosses (Fig. 19), while the Borough of Bury turned the symbol into a textile motif, accompanied by two shuttles and a woolly lamb (Fig. 20).

The implications: a postlogue

Still unwritten, a major history will one day document the transition of plaiting to weaving. Detection will be laborious—the thread of evidence is slight. It is also doubtful whether anyone can ever ascertain that the oldest known evidence of weaving is indeed the earliest. As analytical methods increase in sophistication and as additional examples are discovered, well-documented comparisons from one site or region to another will aid in piecing together the great jigsaw puzzle.

Certainly looms were invented by numerous peoples during their Neolithic and Bronze Age phases of development. An aspect of this was the gradual transition from hides to spun animal and vegetable fibers, making possible plaited fabrics, and finally woven or knit cloths.

In historical perspective, weaving supplanted plaiting because it was quicker to produce and more consistent. At some sacrifice: products of the loom were, by nature, flat and limited to horizontal-vertical structures. Since increasing or decreasing cloth width on a loom was impractical, cutting and sewing became vital. Early woven fabrics, most often used for blankets and garments, required little shaping or sewing. The poncho is a typical example, so are the toga, sari, sarong, and the many Japanese kimono shapes. For these, garment design was primarily the weaver's responsibility, borders and finishes were integrated, and stitching was minimal. Pleating, gathering, shirring, and smocking were means to shape fabrics without cutting or altering their rectangular shapes. As fabric production was mechanized in both Europe and Asia from the fourteenth century onward, cut and sewn garments became more common—particularly for the upper classes.

Today, when cloth production is swift and efficent but labor for sewing in ever-shorter supply, monolithic fabric structures such as knit stockings and gloves may point to the future. Knit as a complete unit, then shaped and sized over a heated form, the nylon stocking is the most automated garment. And the most democratic—maid and mistress wear the same. A large part of this turnabout is the uniquely appropriate use of thermoplastic fiber, which can be shaped with heat and, thus, retain a specific contour for the life of the garment.

Plaited forms have the same potential. Their lack of industrial development can be attributed to the preponderance of woven textiles in Europe—long before the Industrial Revolution. Because techniques for carding, yarn spinning, finishing, and fulling had improved from the late Middle Ages, the transition from hand weaving to power looms was a relatively easy one. Braids in the fancy forms of passementerie were expanded for machine production in the nineteenth century. Few other plaited innovations have appeared since.

Today, the state of the arts of automation and computerization make dimensional plaited forms practicable. All that is lacking is the machines to make them. Shaped tubular weaving and tubular braids are equally feasible, as is the further industrialization of bobbin laces and frame-braided garments. If machine plaiting in the round seems remote, there is much to commend it. The life-size plaited figure on page 16 demonstrates that any form is possible. Oblique interlacing of garments would conform to body movement with the same facility as bias-cut textiles. Use of stretch and thermoplastic yarns could also accommodate shaping.

Undoubtedly, research laboratories of the great mills and fiber producers will play a large part in bringing about such major changes. Since the big companies have the most to gain, such innovations could well start with them. Meanwhile, craftspeople with poetic and prophetic prototypes will probably be the forerunners. Changes instituted by postindustrial craftspeople meld the traditional and electronic worlds. Japan's Jun'ichi Arai, a master of both the Jacquard loom and the computer, is already power-weaving simple garments complete without sewing.

In the field of education, interlacing presents an infinity of structures worked in inexpensive materials with the simplest of tools. Available to students of all ages, plaiting teaches control, counting, and aids in small motor-muscle coordination. Braiding variations alone could challenge participants—at all levels of sophistication. The nineteenth-century concept of basketry as a simple skill reserved for genteel ladies, the retarded, and blind has long been outmoded. Its intricacies are currently challenging the most sophisticated craftsmen, while the straightforward classic styles established by the Shakers and the Iroquois continue to set standards worthy of imitation.

For the developing world, interlaced basketry is probably the most successful export. Preparation of materials and production of pieces provide work for hundreds of thousands on every continent. Although quality and cost vary widely, most of the work is quite satisfactory—considerably above the average "export craft." Basketry items, not easily broken in shipment, seem unaffected by the whims of season and fashion. Interestingly enough, the late twentieth century is witnessing remarkable innovations within "indigenous" plaited forms, particularly in The Philippines, Indonesia, and Thailand. In China's recent drive to get foreign exchange, basketry and wickerwork are the only crafts undergoing a creative process. Such trade is vital to the countries producing and exporting them. This is industry without smokestacks and heavy equipment, worked in villages rather than urban slums.

The developed nations importing these items are equally enriched. Plaited straws, bamboos, reeds, and willows go far toward satisfying a hunger for natural materials so lacking in modern spaces. In the mid-nineteenth century, reacting to the deprivation and ostentation of a new industrial society, John Ruskin and William Morris cautioned us not to lose sight of homely materials, their fabrication and expression of function. These tenets of the Arts and Crafts Movement, which became an aesthetic basis of twentieth-century design, are the more valuable today.

At the time these tenets were formalized, custom-designed, hand-built housing was still available. Even humble row houses for millworkers evidenced expressions of materials and joinery. Not so today. On Park Avenue or in Harlem, inner city or tract, new housing is as bland as dishwater. A sense of materials is absent; so is architectural detail. More to the point, these "shoe boxes" are all the same. The character, the individuality must move in with the contents. Among these "furnishings" there is a place for meaningful expressions of materials and simple, reassuring processes. The texture and broken color, the pattern of woven and printed fabrics, can play a role in compensating for indoor lives in cities.

The other handcrafted interlacings could contribute more. If too few Westerners now perceive the joy of living with fiber interlaced so honestly and perceptibly, that number should grow. The ambiguities of contemporary lifestyle could be offset by these examples of an essential order.

One parameter is that we sustain, through patronage, the highest level of handcraft still available in remote areas of the world. The second is that, with the knowledge at hand and the leisure available in the developed world, we create our own interlacings. The fulfilling, centering, systemic process of making them has much to commend it.

Bibliography

PREHISTORIC ORIGINS

Abramova, Z. A. "Paleolithic Art in the U.S.S.R." Translated by Catherine Page. *Arctic Anthropology* 4 (1967): 1–179. Mezin drawing on p. 22 is from p. 151.

Adovasio, J. M. "Prehistoric Textiles and Cordage from Guitarrero Cave, Peru." *American Antiquity* 38 (1973): 84–90.

———. "The Antiquity of Plaiting in the New World." Xeroxed. Pittsburgh: University of Pittsburgh, 1985.

———, McPherron, Alan, and Srejovic, D. *Textile Impressions from Divostin.* Belgrade: 1974.

Bender, Barbara. *Farming in Prehistory: from Huntergatherer to Food Producer.* New York: St. Martin's Press, 1975.

Broudy, Eric. *The Book of Looms, A History of the Handloom from Ancient Times to the Present.* New York: Van Nostrand Reinhold, 1979. The first chapter discusses the early history of interlacing.

Bühler, Kristin. "Plaiting with Stretched Thread, A First Step Towards Weaving." *Ciba Review* 63 (1948): 2306–14.

Burnham, Harold. "Catal Hüyük, the Textiles and Twined Fabrics." *Anatolian Studies* 15 (1965): 169–74.

Campbell, Bernard G. (edit.). *Humankind Emerging.* New York: Little Brown, 1976.

Cosgrove, C. B. "Caves of the Upper Gila and Hueco Areas in New Mexico and Texas." *Papers of the Peabody Museum of Archaeology and Ethnology* 24 (2): 1–181. Cambridge: Harvard University, 1947. Includes braiding diagrams.

Crowfoot, Grace M. "Textiles, Basketry and Mats." *A History of Technology,* 1. Edited by Charles Singer; E. J. Holmyard; and A. R. Hall. Oxford: The Clarendon Press, 1954.

D'Harcourt, Raoul. *Textiles of Ancient Peru and Their Techniques.* Edited by Grace G. Denny and Carolyn Osborne. Translated by Sadie Brown. Seattle: University of Washington Press, 1962. Basic text on Pre-Columbian techniques. Chapt. 10 includes plaiting and braiding.

Douglas, Frederick H. *Periods of Pueblo Culture and History.* Leaflet 11: 11–25. Denver: Denver Art Museum Department of Indian Art, 1930.

Evans, Arthur. "New Archaeological Lights on the Origins of Civilization in Europe." *Science,* 44 (Sept. 1916): 399–409.

Goodall, Vanne, ed. *The Quest for Man.* London: Phaidon, 1975.

Gribbon, John and Cherfas, Jeremy. *The Monkey Puzzle, Reshaping the Evolutionary Tree.* New York: McGraw-Hill, 1982. Points out that baskets permit the sharing that made us human, pp. 172–6.

Guernsey, S. J. and Kidder, A. V. "Basketmaker Caves of Northeastern Arizona." *Papers of the Peabody Museum* 8 (2). Cambridge: Harvard University, 1921. Indicates that early examples of interlacing in this region are rare.

Hadingham, Evan. *Secrets of the Ice Age.* New York: Walker, 1979. Plaited rope found in Lascaux cave, p. 187; possible Paleolithic bridles ill., p. 110.

Harvey, Amy E. "Archaeological Fabrics from the Lower Missouri Valley." *Irene Emery Roundtable on Museum Textiles, Archaeological Textiles,* pp. 133–8. Edited by Patricia L. Fiske. Washington, D.C.: The Textile Museum, 1974.

Hawkes, Jacquetta and Woolley, Sir Leonard. "Prehistory and the Beginnings of Civilization." *History of Mankind* 1. Great Britain: Unwin Bros., 1963. Descriptions and probable dates of earliest basketry known at time of publication.

Helbaek, Hans. "Textiles from Catal Hüyük," *Archaeology Magazine* 16 (1963): 39–46.

Holmes, William. "Prehistoric Textile Fabrics of the United States, Derived from Impressions of Pottery." *Third Annual Report of the Bureau of American Ethnology:* 393–425. Washington, D.C.: Smithsonian Institution, 1884. Application of nets or pliable mats to ceramics before firing, pp. 393–425.

Isaac, Glynn and McCown, Elizabeth, edits. *Human Origins, Louis Leakey and the East African Evidence.* Menlo Park, CA: W. A. Benjamin, 1976.

———. "The Food Sharing Behavior of Protohuman Hominids." *Scientific American* 238 (1978) pp. 90–108. Expands theory that baskets paved the way for human evolution.

Jennings, Jesse D. "Danger Cave," *Supplement to American Antiquity* 23, no. 2, part 2 (1957). The Society for American Archaeology, University of Utah Press.

———and Norbeck, Edward. *Prehistoric Man in the New World.* Chicago: University of Chicago Press, 1964. Basketry of Desert Culture in the Americas, pp. 149–176.

Kent, Kate Peck. *Prehistoric Textiles of the Southwest.* Albuquerque: University of New Mexico Press, 1983. Covers braids, sprang, and the White House Shirt. (Quotation from p. 315).

Kidder, J. Edward, with Esaka, Teruya. *Prehistoric Japanese Arts, Jōmon Pottery.* Tokyo: Kodansha International, 1968. The name of the Jōmon period is derived from characteristic pottery impressed with cords and mats.

Kuttruff, Jenna T. "Prehistoric Textiles Revealed by Potsherds." *Shuttle, Spindle and Dyepot* 11, no 3 (1980): 40.

Lancaster, Jane B. *Primate Behavior and the Emergence of Human Culture.* New York: Holt Rinehart and Winston, 1975.

Leakey, Richard E. and Lewin, Roger. *People of the Lake, Mankind and its Beginnings,* New York: Avon Books, 1978. Argument for early origins of interlacing reinforced on pp. 101, 118, 125, 127, 139.

Leakey, Richard E. *The Making of Mankind.* New York: E. P. Dutton, 1981. Studies of early hominids and contemporary gatherer-hunters.

Lee, R. B. and Devore, I., edits. *Man, the Hunter.* Chicago: Aldine Pub. Co., 1968.

Marshack, Alexander. *The Roots of Civilization. The Cognitive Beginnings of Man's First Art, Symbol and Notation.* New York: McGraw Hill, 1971. Unique analysis of prehistoric art symbols.

Mellaart, James, *Earliest Civilizations of the Far East.* New York: McGraw Hill, 1965.

———. *Catal Hüyük.* New York: McGraw Hill, 1967.

———. *The Neolithic of the Near East.* New York: Scribner's, 1975. Specifics on the beginnings of basketry and fabrics (quotation from p. 19).

Neumann, Erich. *The Great Mother, An Analysis of the Archetype.* Princeton: Princeton University Press, 1963. The Goddess of Fate section shows the archytypal feminine as a weaver and spinner, p. 227–239.

Petitpierre, A. G. "The Headgear of Primitive Peoples." *Ciba Review* 35 (1940): 1246–50. Discussion of earliest forms of plaiting.

Schuetz, Madith K. "An Analysis of the Val Verde County Cave Material." *Bulletin of the Texas Archaeological Society* 27 (1956): 129–37 and fig. 15.

Taylor, Walter W. "Some Implications of the Carbon 14 Dates from a Cave in Coahuila, Mexico." *Bulletin of the Texas Archaeological Society* 27 (1956): 215–34. Dating of 6,000 to 5,000 B.C. for large find of sandals.

Tanner, Clara. *Prehistoric Southwestern Craft Arts.* Tucson: University of Arizona Press, 1976. Archeological study of Basketmaker II, III and Pueblo impressions on shards, early examples, pp. 15–92.

Vogt, Emil. *Geflechte und Gewebe der Steinzei,* 1. Basel: Verlag E. Birkhäuser, 1937. Diagrams of basketry and textile techniques found in Swiss Neolithic cultures.

———. "Basketry and Woven Fabrics of the European Stone and Bronze Ages." *Ciba Review* 54 (1947): 1945–64.

Weltfish, Gene. "Prehistoric North American Basketry Techniques and Modern Distributions." *American Anthropologist* 32 (1930): 454–95.

———. "Problems in the Study of Ancient and Modern Basket Makers." *American Anthropologist* 34 (1932): 108–17.

———. *The Origins of Art.* New York: Bobbs Merrill, 1953. (Quotations from pp. 49 and 53.)

Zihlman, Adrienne L. "Women as Shapers of the Human Adaption." in *Woman the Gatherer,* edited by Frances Dahlberg, pp. 75–120. New Haven: Yale University Press, 1981. Research on the earliest gatherers and their tools: baskets.

CLASSIFICATION

Baumhoff, M. A. "Introduction to Basketry: A Proposed Classification by Hélène Balfet." *University of California Archaeological Survey Reports* 38, paper 47 (1957), pp. 1–21. Berkeley.

Bühler, Kristin. "Basic Textile Techniques." *Ciba Review* 63 (1948): 2295–305.

Bühler-Oppenheim, Kristen und Alfred. *Die Textiliensammlung Fritz Iklé-Huber im Museum für Völkerkunde und Schweiz.* Museum für Völkerkunde, Basel. Denkschrift der Schweiz. Naturforschenden Gesellschaft 78, Zurich: 1948. Classified analysis, in German, of fabric techniques; includes diagrams.

Dusenbury, Mary. "Braiding in Japan." In *In Celebration of the Curious Mind,* edited by Nora Rogers and Martha Stanley, pp. 80–102. Loveland, Colorado: Interweave Press, 1983. Well-defined classification of braids with good diagrams for making them.

Emery, Irene. *The Primary Structures of Fabrics, an Illustrated Calssification.* Washington, D.C.: The Textile Museum, 1966 (revised 1980). Basic comprehensive text on fabric classfication. (Quotations from pp. 56, 61, and 68).

Kliot, Jules and Kathe. "Looking at Lace." *Fiberarts* 9, no. 2 (1982) pp. 43–9. Classification of lace with enlarged photos.

Lehmann, J. *Flechtwerke Aus Dem Malayischen Archipel.* Frankfurt Am Main: Joseph Baer Co., 1912. Diagrammatic classification of basketry by mathematical formulas.

Seiler-Baldinger, Annemarie. *Systematik der Textilen Techniken.* Basel: Museum für Völkerkunde, 1973. Diagammatic classification incorporates references from many sources.

———. *Classification of Textile Techniques.* Ahmadabad, India: Calico Museum of Textiles, 1979. A translated revised version of above text.

———. "Problems of Textile Classification." In *Irene Emery Roundtable on Museum Textiles.* Washington, D.C.: The Textile Museum, 1976. (Quotations from pp. 85–6).

Weltfish, Gene. *Preliminary Classification of Prehistoric Southwestern Basketry.* Washington, D.C.: Smithsonian Institution Misc. Collections 87, no. 7 (1932). Classification based on U.S. regions with subdivisions by technique.

HOW-TO BOOKS

Abernathy, June Fulton and Tune, Suelyn Ching. *Made in Hawai'i.* Hawaii: Kolowalu Books, 1983. Braiding of ti leaf sandals and fern leis.

Anderson, Dilys. "French Canadian Arrow Sash Finger Weaving." London: *Quarterly Journal of the Association of Weavers, Spinners and Dyers* 96 (1975).

Atwater, Mary Meigs. *Byways in Handweaving.* New York: Macmillan, 1954. Plaiting chapter has instructions for *ceinture flèché,* Neolithic and Mexican double braiding.

Baizerman, Suzanne and Searle, Karen. *Finishes in the Ethnic Tradition.* St. Paul: Dos Tejedoras, 1978. Techniques for ending textiles, many applicable to plaiting.

Barker, June. *Decorative Braiding and Weaving.* Newton Centre, Mass.: Charles Branford Co., 1973. Braiding and narrow band techniques.

Barrett, S. A. *Indian Notes and Monographs, The Cayapa Indians of Ecuador,* part 2. New York: Museum of the American Indian, Heye Foundation, 1925. Diagrams for twill patterns, basketry starts and finishes. Explanations of techniques for 3SOE structures.

Belash, Constantine A. *Braiding and Knotting Techniques and Projects,* 1936. Reprint. New York: Dover Publications, 1974. Directions for working the basic types.

Bernal, Susan Scott. "Slentre Braiding." *Shuttle, Spindle and Dyepot* 9, no. 2 (1978): 63–7. Instructions for seven variations.

Berthier, Marc P. G. *The Art of Knots, A Sailor's Handbook.* New York: Doubleday, 1974. Humorous approach to seamen's knots, well illustrated.

Bigon, Mario and Regazzoni, Guido. *The Morrow Guide to Knots for Sailing, Fishing, Camping and Climbing.* New York: Quill/105, 1982. Different colored elements make directions easy to follow.

Blanchard, Mary Miles. *The Basketry Book, Twelve Lessons in Reed Weaving.* New York: Scribner's, 1937.

Brittain, Judy. *The Bantam Step-by-Step Book of Needle Craft.* Toronto: Bantam, 1979. Chapter 3 includes knotting, netting, braiding, and weaving instructions with some unusual examples.

Brotherton, Germaine. *Rush and Leafcraft.* Boston: Houghton Mifflin, 1977. Mats, belts, baskets, and ornaments made by braiding or checkerwork.

Cahlander, Adele with Zorn, Elayne and Rowe, Ann Pollard. "Sling Braids of the Andes." *Weaver's Journal,* Monograph 4. Boulder: Colorado Fiber Center, 1980. Computer-drawn diagrams.

Cason, Majorie and Cahlander, Adele. *The Art of Bolivian Highland Weaving.* New York: Watson-Guptill, 1976. Section on looped and other braiding.

Chamberlain, Marcia and Crookett, Candace. *Beyond Weaving.* New York: Watson-Guptill, 1974. Varied knotting, plaiting, and braiding techniques.

Christopher, F. J. *Basketry,* 1951. Reprint. New York: Dover Publications, 1952. Instructions for table mats, trays, and baskets worked from bast fibers.

Collingwood, Peter. *The Techniques of Sprang, Plaiting on Stretched Threads.* New York: Watson-Guptill, 1974. The authoritative book on the subject..

Coulter, Doris. "Fingerweaving Being Revived by Cherokees." *Shuttle, Spindle and Dyepot* 5, no. 3 (1974): 55–6.

Dawson, Amy. *Bobbin Lace Making for Beginners.* Poole, Dorset: Blandford Press, 1978. Explained in simple stages.

De Leon, Sherry. *The Basketry Book.* New York: Holt, Rinehart and Winston, 1978. A primer for basketry and netting techniques.

Dendel, Esther Warner. *The Basic Book of Fingerweaving.* New York: Simon & Schuster, 1974. Detailed instructions for working Osage, Chinese, Peruvian, and Mexican braids.

——. *African Fabric Crafts, Sources of African Design and Technique.* Newton Abbot: David and Charles, 1974. Units on braiding a Liberian rice bag and palm leaf plaits.

Fisch, Arline M. *Textile Techniques in Metal for Jewelers, Sculptors and Textile Artists.* New York: Van Nostrand Reinhold, 1975. Applications of braiding, 3SOE, and other plaiting to metal "threads."

Flores, Luis Alberto. *El Guasquero Trenzados Criolos.* Buenos Aires: Cesarini Hermanos, 1960. Gaucho leather knots and braiding, good diagrams.

Fry, Eric C. *The Book of Knots and Ropework, Practical and Decorative.* New York: Crown, 1977.

Fuhrmann, Brigita. *Bobbin Lace, A Contemporary Approach.* New York: Watson-Guptill, 1976. The basics plus decorative extras.

Glashauser, Suellen and Westfall, Carol. *Plaiting, Step-by-Step.* New York: Watson-Guptill, 1976. Lives up to title, also art fiber examples.

Goodloe, William H. *Cocount Palm Frond Weaving.* Rutland, Vt: Tuttle, 1972. Hats, baskets, fans, etc. worked with center rib intact.

Gordon, Joleen. *Edith Clayton's Market Basket.* Halifax, N.S., 1977. Directions for a splintwood basket.

Grant, Bruce. *How to Make Cowboy Horse Gear.* Cambridge, Md.: Cornell Maritime Press, 1956. Diagrams of successive stages.

——. *Encyclopedia of Rawhide and Leather Braiding.* Cambridge, Md.: Cornell Maritime Press, 1972. Encompasses braided and knotted leather work of American and Argentine cowhands.

Graumont, Raoul and Hensel, John. *Encyclopedia of Knots and Fancy Rope Work.* Cambridge Md.: Cornell Maritime Press, 1952. Comprehensive reference for knots and braiding, 746 plates but directions often too cryptic.

Hart, Carol and Dan. *Natural Basketry.* New York: Watson-Guptill, 1980. How to make wicker, splint, and non-interlaced baskets.

Hartung, Rolf. *Fils et Tissus, Travaux Textiles.* Paris: Dessain & Tolra, 1969. Special braids plus simple plaiting and knotting techniques.

Harvey, Virginia I. *The Techniques of Basketry.* New York: Van Nostrand Reinhold, 1978. Clear, concise explanations of basketry and other plaiting techniques, includes mad weave.

Hensel, John. *The Book of Ornamental Knots.* New York: Scribner's, 1973. Instructions for working variations on the carrick bend.

Hiroa, Te Rangi (Peter H. Buck). *Arts and Crafts of Hawaii, Section III, Plaiting.* Honolulu: Bernice P. Bishop Museum Special Publication 45, 1964. Starts and endings for plaited mats; section on patterning.

Hough, Walter. *The Hopi Indian Collection.* U.S. National Museum Proceedings 54 (1919): 235–96.

Kent, Kate Peck. "The Braiding of a Hopi Wedding Sash." *Plateau* 1940: 48–52, Published by N. Arizona Society of Science and Art, Museum of Northern Arizona. Well-detailed analysis.

Kinoshita, Masako. "Kumihimo". *Shuttle, Spindle and Dyepot* 11, no. 3 (1980): 19–21. Japanese bobbin braid technique.

Kliot, Kaethe and Jules. *Bobbin Lace, Form by the Twisting of Cords.* New York: Crown, 1973.

——. *Bobbin Lace Technique.* Berkeley: Lacis, 1975. Leaflet on technique.

——. *Kumi Himo, Techniques of Japanese Plaiting.* Berkeley: Some Place Publications, 1979. Introduction to methods with traditional diagrams.

Kliot, Jules. *Sprang, Language and Techniques.* Berkeley: Some Place Publications, 1979. Helpful booklet.

Lambeth, M. *Discovering Corn Dollies.* Aylesbury, U.K.: Shire Publications, 1974. Fold braid instructions and historical background.

LaPlantz, Shereen. *Plaited Basketry: The Woven Form.* Bayside, CA: Press de LaPlantz, 1982. Varied types, also imbrication; photos of ethnic examples.

———. *The Mad Weave Book.* Bayside, CA: Press de LaPlantz, 1984. Lucid explanation of this complicated structure.

Leeming, Joseph. *Fun with String.* New York: Dover Publications, 1974. Includes braids.

Macfarlan, Allan and Paulette. *Knotcraft, The Practical and Entertaining Art of Tying Knots,* 1967. Reprint. New York: Dover Publications, 1983.

Mason, Otis T. "Basketwork of the North American Aborigines." *Report of the U.S. National Museum,* part 3 (1884): 291–306.

———. "Aboriginal American Basketry: Studies in a Textile Art without Machinery." *Report of the U.S. National Museum* (1902): 171–548. Analysis of major basketry techniques.

———. "Vocabulary of Malaysian Basketwork: A Study of the W.L. Abbott Collections." *Proceedings of the U.S. National Museum* 35 (1908): 1–51. Basketry terms and technology.

Osornio, Mario A. Lopez. *Trenzas Gauchas.* Buenos Aires: Libreria Y Editorial "El Ateneo," 1943. Range of practical braids is broad. Diagrams understandable without Spanish explanations.

Perry, L. Day. *Seat Weaving.* Peoria: Charles A. Bennett, 1940. Chair caning with up to 6S0E.

Robinson, Sharon. *Braiding Rugs.* Santa Rosa, CA: Thresh Publications, 1976. Preparing, plaiting, and stitching elements of braided rugs.

Rosenbaum, Helen. *The Braid Book.* New York: Wallaby Books, 1979. Guide to braiding hairdos.

Shaw, George Russel. *Knots, Useful and Ornamental.* New York: Collier Books, 1979.

Southard, Doris. "Bobbin Lace, just twist, cross, and throw." *Shuttle, Spindle and Dyepot* 5 no. 3 (1974): 77–8.

Speiser, Noémi. *The Manual of Braiding.* Basel: Published by the author, 1983. Comprehensive survey; instructions difficult to follow.

Stephens, Cleo M. *Willow Spokes and Wickerwork.* Harrisburg: Stackpole Books, 1975. Plaiting willow and bark.

Tacker, Sylvia. "Verkkonauhaa." *Shuttle, Spindle and Dyepot* 9 no. 4 (1980): 12–14. Finnish sprang braids.

Tod, Osma Gallinger. *Earth Basketry.* New York: Crown, 1972. Helpful for basketry starts and endings.

——— and Benson, Oscar H. *Weaving with Reeds and Fibers,* 1948. Reprint. New York: Dover Publications, 1975.

Turnbaugh, Sarah Peabody. "The Ring Basket of the Anasazi." *Shuttle, Spindle and Dyepot* 9 no. 1 (1977): 101–2.

Turner, Alta R. *Finger Weaving: Indian Braiding.* New York: Sterling, 1973. Clear, succinct reference.

Waller, Irene. *Knots and Netting.* New York: Taplinger, 1977. Instructions and artists' applications of decorative netting.

Wollenberg, Jackie. "Braiding with Bobbins." *Shuttle, Spindle and Dyepot* 7 no. 1 (1975): 90–1.

Wright, Dorothy. *The Complete Book of Baskets and Basketry.* New York: Scribner's, 1977. Directions with historical and ethnic examples.

GENERAL

Adovasio, J.M., *Basketry Technology, A Guide to Identification and Analysis.* Chicago: Aldine Publishing Co., 1977. Manual for analyzing archaeological examples; criteria could be valuable for recording contemporary work.

Albers, Anni. *On Weaving.* Middletown, CT.: Wesleyan University Press, 1965. Section on ancient looms; color effects diagrams apply to plaiting.

———. *On Designing.* Middletown, CT. Wesleyan University Press, 1961. One artist's illuminating thoughts on technique.

Anquetil, Jacques. *La Vannerie.* Paris: Dessain et Tolra/Chêne, 1979. History, applications, and techniques with diagrams and color photos.

Barbeau, Marius. *Assomption Sash.* Ottawa: National Museums of Canada, Bulletin 93, Anthropological series no. 24 (1972). History, directions, and photos of old examples.

Barrow, Terence. *The Art of Tahiti.* London: Thames and Hudson, 1979. Includes unusual braid applications.

Bath, Virginia Churchill. *Lace.* Chicago: Henry Regnery Co., 1974. International examples and short history.

Birrell, Verla. *The Textile Arts.* New York: Schocken Books, 1973. Overview of all fabrics; pinpoints braid and lace techniques.

Bobart, H.H. *Basketwork through the Ages.* London: Humphrey Milford, 1936. Historic overview with quotes from ancient sources.

Brandford, Joanne Segal. "From the Tree Where the Bark Grows." *North American Basket Treasures from the Peabody Museum.* Cambridge: New England Foundation for the Arts, 1984. Exhibit catalogue demonstrating the diversity of native American basketry production.

Brigham, William T. *Mat and Basket Weaving of the Ancient Hawaiians.* Honolulu: Memoirs of the Bernice Pauahi Bishop Museum 2 no. 1 (1906). Collection of interlacing extends from fans to weapons.

Chen, Hsia-sheng. *The Art of Chinese Knotting.* New York: China Institute of America, 1981. Exhibit catalogue of intricate historical knotting.

Conn, Richard. *Native American Art in the Denver Art Museum.* Denver Art Museum, 1979. Reference for many interlacings.

Constantine, Mildred and Larsen, Jack Lenor. *Beyond Craft: The Art Fabric.* New York: Van Nostrand Reinhold, 1973. Numerous examples of contemporary interlacings.

———. *The Art Fabric: Mainstream.* New York: Van Nostrand Reinhold, 1981. Includes plaited Art Fabric.

Cooper-Hewitt Museum catalogue. *Hair.* Washington, D.C.: Smithsonian Institution, 1980. The lore and the styles.

Corbin, Patricia. *All About Wicker.* New York: E.P. Dutton, 1978. Indicates the broad possibilities of this medium.

Crowfoot, Grace M. "Handicrafts in Palestine, 1. Plaiting and Fingerweaving." *Palestine Exploration Quarterly* (1943): 75–88.

Dockstader, Frederick J. *Indian Art of the Americas.* New York: Museum of the American Indian, Heye Foundation, 1973. Photos of Assomption sashes, Cherokee basketry, rugs and other artifacts.

Douglass, W.A. *Braiding and Braiding Machinery.* Eindhoven, The Netherlands: Centrex Publishing Co., 1964. Technology of mechanized braiding.

Fishel, Walter G. "Maori Textile Techniques." *Ciba Review* 84 (1951): 3034–54.

Fox, Judy Kellar. "Plaited Silk: Myrna Wacknov." *Shuttle, Spindle and Dyepot* 16, no. 2 (1985): 44–5.

Hayward, Helena, ed. *World Furniture.* Middlesex, U.K.: Hamlyn, 1965. Ancient caning examples.

Hald, Margrethe. *Olddanske Tekstiler.* Copenhagen: 1950. Survey of sprang with English summary.

Horiuchi, Toshiko. *From a Line.* Kyoto: Senshoku to Seikatsu Sha, 1986. Extensive examination of fabric structures; drawings are a tour-de-force.

James, George Wharton. *Indian Basketry,* 1909. Reprint. New York: Dover Publications, 1972. Information gathered from turn of the century basketmakers.

Jensen, Elizabeth Jane. "Wickerwork Basket Weaving in Four-strand Designs." *Shuttle, Spindle and Dyepot* 13, no. 4 (1982): 20–6.

Kavasch, E. Barrie. "Indian Basketmaker of the Bayou." *Garden* 6, no. 6 (1982): 12–6. New York Botanical Garden. Traditional work.

Kent, Kate Peck. *Pueblo Indian Textiles: A Living Tradition.* Sante Fe: School of American Research Press, 1983. Frame braided Hopi wedding belt.

Kite, Pat. "The Tree Circus." *Garden* 4 no. 6 (1980): 13–8. New York Botanical Garden. Fantastic interlaced trees.

Larsen, Jack Lenor with Bühler, Alfred and Solyom, Bronwen and Garrett. *The Dyer's Art: Ikat, Batik, Plangi.* New York: Van Nostrand Reinhold, 1976.

Larsen, Jack Lenor and Weeks, Jeanne. *Fabrics for Interiors, A Guide for Architects, Designers and Consumers.* New York: Van Nostrand Reinhold, 1975. Woven and nonwoven fabrics; glossary of terms.

Lepperhoff, Bernard. *Die Flechterei.* Leipzig: M. Janecke, 1914. Photos and diagrammatic explanations of braiding machinery.

Lewis, Fulvia. *Lace.* Firenzi: Edizioni Remo Sandron, 1980. Splendid enlargements.

Lübke, Anton. "Bamboo." *Ciba Review* no. 3 (1969): 21–39. Preparation and use in several cultures.

Lynford, Carrie A. *Iroquois Crafts.* Washington, D.C.: United States Bureau of Indian Affairs, 1945. Corn husk mask, wampum, 3SOE sifter, and snowshoes.

Man-made Fiber and Textile Dictionary. New York: Celanese Corp., 1981. Handy reference for technical terms.

Malarcher, Patricia. "What Makes a Basket a Baket." *Fiberarts*, 11, no. 1 (1984): 34–41. Contemporary basket makers' nontraditional work.

Meilach, Dona Z., and Menagh, Dee. *Basketry Today with Materials from Nature.* New York: Crown, 1979.

Miles, Charles and Bovis, Pierre. *American Indian and Eskimo Basketry, A Key to Identification.* Sante Fe: Pierre Bovis, 1969.

Moore, N. Hudson. *The Lace Book.* New York: Tudor, 1937. History with anecdotes.

Palliser, Bury. *History of Lace.* London: Sampson Low, Marston & Co., 1910. Romance of lace as well as history.

Park, Betty. "John McQueen, The Basket Redefined." *American Craft* 39, no. 5 (1979).

Pfannschmidt, Ernst-Erik. *Twentieth-Century Lace.* New York: Scribner's, 1975. Traditional and contemporary work.

Picton, John and Mack, John. *African Textiles, Looms, Weaving and Design.* London: British Museum Publications, 1979.

Prendergrast, Mick. *Feathers and Fibre, A Survey of Traditional and Contemporary Maori Craft.* New York: Penguin, 1984. Color effects used in this region.

Ronald, Paul. *The Basketmakers' Company.* London: The Worshipful Company of Basketmakers, 1978. A guild history with sidelights on techniques.

Rossbach, Ed. *Baskets as Textile Art.* New York: Van Nostrand Reinhold, 1973. Widespread survey of materials, forms and techniques.

———. *The New Basketry.* New York: Van Nostrand Reinhold, 1976. Includes plaiting and related structures.

———. "Thinking about Historical Baskets." *Fiber Arts* 11, no. 2 (1984) 32–3. Today's experimental basketry.

Roth, Walter E. "An Introductory Study of the Arts, Crafts and Customs of the Guiana Indians." *38th Annual Report of the Bureau of American Ethnology,* Smithsonian Institution (1916–1917): 92–121 and 282–411. Braids, basketry, and sprang.

———. "Additional Studies of the Arts, Crafts, and Customs of the Guiana Indians." *Bureau of American Ethnology, Bulletin 91,* Smithsonian Institution (1929).

Schuette, Marie. "Technique and Origin of Lace." *Ciba Review* 73 (1949): 2685–98.

Sprigg, June. *By Shaker Hands.* New York: Knopf, 1979. Fine drawings of plaited chair seats and baskets.

Stephenson, Sue H. *Basketry of the Appalachian Mountains.* New York: Van Nostrand Reinhold, 1977. Classic baskets.

Steward, Julian H., edit. *Handbook of South American Indians,* Bulletin 143, Smithsonian Institution (1949).

Teleki, Gloria Roth. *The Baskets of Rural America.* New York: E.P. Dutton, 1975. Historical survey.

———. *Collecting Traditional American Basketry.* New York: E.P. Dutton, 1979. Background information.

Thesiger, Wilfred. *The Last Nomad.* New York: E.P. Dutton, 1980. Plaited architecture in remote areas of Iraq.

Thorpe, Azalea Stuart and Larsen, Jack Lenor. *Elements of Weaving.* New York: Doubleday, 1978. Introduction to techniques.

Thompson, Frances. *Antique Baskets and Basketry, A Collector's Guide.* New York: A.S. Barnes, 1977. Survey of world basketry; tips for collectors.

Waller, Irene. *Textile Sculptures.* New York: Taplinger, 1977. Includes plaited work of major fiber artists.

Watt, James C.Y. *The Sumptuous Basket, Chinese Lacquer with Basketry Panels.* New York: China Institute of America, 1985. Impressive, primarily 17th century pieces.

Whitford, Andrew Hunter. *North American Indian Arts.* New York: Golden Press, 1973. Concise explanations of tribal basketry, weaving, and braiding.

Yadin, Yigael. "The Finds from the Bar-Kokhba Period in the Cave of Letters." Jerusalem: *Judean Desert Studies,* 1963. Analysis of 2nd century baskets.

SYMBOLISM

Adachi, Fumie, trans. *Japanese Design Motifs, Japanese Crests.* Compiled by the Matsuya Piece-Goods Store, 1913. Reprint. New York: Dover Publications, 1972.

Albers, Anni et al. *The Woven and Graphic Art of Anni Albers.* Washington, D.C.: Smithsonian Institution Press, 1985. A master weaver's textiles and her graphics of "line involvements."

Bain, George. *Celtic Art, The Methods of Construction*, 1951. Reprint. New York; Dover Publications, 1973.

Belknap, William Jr. "20th Century Indians Preserve Customs of the Cliff Dwellers." *National Geographic* Feb. 1964: 196–211. Taboo of Mesa Verde plaited ring supports.

Boas, Franz. *Primitive Art*, 1927. Reprint. New York: Dover Publications, 1955. Bushongo designs.

———. "The Social Organization and Secret Societies of the Kwakiutl Indians." *U.S. National Museum Annual Report*, 1895: 311–738. Magical implications of certain interlaced forms.

Boutell's Heraldry. London: Frederick Warne, 1950, revised 1978.

Brandt, Philip. "Tibetan Carpets." *Echo of Things Chinese* 3, no. 11 (1973): 30–39.

Brown, Peter. *The Book of Kells*. New York: Thames and Hudson, 1981. Celtic interlace as a design motif.

Bühler, Alfred. "The Essentials of Handicrafts and the Craft of Weaving Among Primitive Peoples." *Ciba Review* 30 (1940): 1057–88. Religious rites in craftwork.

Bühler, Kristen. "Demons of Illness Caught in Nets," also "Plaiting Games and Magic Knots." *Ciba Review* 63 (1948): 2317–20.

Chevalier, Jean. *Dictionnaire des Symboles*. Paris: Robert Laffont, 1969.

Cirker, Hayward and Blanche. Monograms and Alphabetic Devices. New York: Dover Publications, 1970. Interlaced monograms.

Cooper, J.C. *An Illustrated Encyclopaedia of Traditional Symbols*. London: Thames and Hudson, 1978.

Day, Cyrus L. "Knots and Knot Lore, A Study in Primitive Beliefs and Superstitions." *Western Folklore* 9 (1950). California Folklore Soc., University of California Press.

———. *Quipus and Witches' Knots, The Role of the Knot in Primitive and Ancient Societies*. Lawrence: University of Kansas Press, 1967.

Enciso, Jorge. *Design Motifs of Ancient Mexico*, 1947. Reprint. New York: Dover Publications, 1953.

Fairbairn, James. *Fairbairn's Crests of the Families of Great Britain and Ireland*. London: Thomas C. Jack, 1860.

Gerspach, M. *Coptic Textile Designs*, 1890. Reprint. New York: Dover Publications, 1975.

Gillon, Edmund V., Jr. *Geometric Design and Ornament*, 1930. Reprint. New York: Dover Publications, 1969.

Goff, Beatrice Laura. *Symbols of Prehistoric Mesopotamia*. New Haven: Yale University Press, 1963. Ninevite 5 ware ceramics incised interlace patterns.

Holmes, W.H. "Aboriginal Pottery of the Eastern U.S." *20th Annual Report of the Bureau of American Ethnology* (1898–9): 70–80. Stamp designs and textiles for ceramic patterning.

Hornung, Clarence P. *Handbook of Designs and Devices*, 1932. Reprint. New York: Dover Publications, 1946.

Jones, Owen. *The Grammar of Ornament, Illustrated Examples from Various Styles of Ornament*. London: Bernard Quaritch, 1868.

Jung, Carl G. *Man and His Symbols*. London: Aldus Books, 1964.

Koch, Rudolf. *The Book of Signs*, 1930. Reprint. Dover Publications, 1955.

Kurth, Willi. *The Complete Woodcuts of Albrecht Dürer*, 1927. Reprint. New York: Dover Publications, 1963.

Lehner, Ernst. *Symbols, Signs and Signets*, 1950. Reprint. New York: Dover Publications, 1969.

Lumholtz, Carl. "Symbolism of the Huichol Indians." *Anthropology* 2, Memoirs of the American Museum of Natural History, 3 (1900).

Nappen, Barbara. "In the Web of Superstition, Myths and Folktales about Nets." *Fiber Arts* 9, no. 2 (1982): 30–1.

Robicsek, Francis. *A Study in Maya Art and History: The Mat Symbol*. New York: The Museum of the American Indian, Heye Foundation (1975). Plaiting as symbol for high authority.

Siegal, Richard; Strasfeld, Michael and Sharon. *The First Jewish Catalogue*. Philadelphia, Jewish Publication Society of America, 1973.

Smeets, Rene. *Signs, Symbols and Ornaments*. New York: Van Nostrand Reinhold, 1982.

Speltz, Alexander. *The Styles of Ornament*, 1906. Reprint. New York: Dover Publications, 1959.

Wade, David. *Geometric Patterns and Borders*. New York: Van Nostrand Reinhold, 1982.

Williams, Geoffrey. *African Designs from Traditional Sources*. New York: Dover Publications, 1971.

Glossary–Index

Adovasio, J.M., 24, 26–27
active elements, 40, 88. Elements that interwork with other active elements or around static (passive) elements.
Albers, Anni, 249
Ashby, Mary, 180
asymmetrical balance, 48. *See* symmetrical balance.
asymmetrical braiding, 80–81, 152–53

Bacharach, David Paul, 195
balance, 45, 48, 203. The count of one SOE in relation to the count of another. *See also* symmetrical balance.
Baldwin, Ben, 227
Barnes, Dorothy Gill, 62, 111, 191
Basket Maker epochs, 24, 188
bast, 44. Cellulosic fibers extracted from leaves, stems, bark, and husks of various plants.
Bentham, Leonard, 67
Blumenthal, Betsy, 190
bobbin lace, 41, 92–95, 165. One SOE wound on bobbins and interworked from a common starting line or lines.
braiding (1SOE), 41, 81–91, 114–155, 236–37; joined, 135–43; machine, 155; slit leather, 144–45, 164, 208; three-dimensional, 86–89. Oblique interlacing of one SOE sharing a common starting point and worked with loose ends. *See also* asymmetrical, core, fold, frame, neolithic, repp, slentre, wraparound, and tubular braiding.
brocading. Patterning worked with supplementary elements.
Bryant, Lois, 2, 4

caning, 110–13, 227
carrick bend and knot, 40, 65, 68, 69, 74, 76–79, 264
Carlson, Ken, 208
Chapnick, Karen, 130–31, 136
checker or checkerwork. In basketry, a balanced 1/1 interlacing.

Chinese braid, 64, 82–83
classification of braiding, 119; of interlacing, 65–113; chart, 66; other authors', 30–36
coiling, 38, 154. Basketry technique that involves the stitching of a passive spiraling element by an active element.
Collingwood, Peter, 30, 91
color effect(s), 45, 202–15. Pattern produced by sequencing of two or more colored elements.
complex fabric structure(s), 41; 1E and 2E, 71, 74, 78; 1SOE, 84–85, 88–89; 2SOE, 98–103; 3SOE, 109–10. Any fabric structure plus a supplementary element, elements, or set(s) of elements. If the supplementary element(s) are removed, the basic fabric structure remains complete.
compound fabric structure(s), 41; 1E, 76; 1SOE 84–85, 88–89, 135; 2SOE, 100, 104–05, 111, 244–45; 3SOE, 109–10. Any fabric structure interlaced with two or more layers. Commonly, the layers are identical in material and interlacing.
core braid, 124–25. Tubular braid with a supplementary central element. A few rare core braids are compound, with the inner and outer braids exchanging elements.
Cook, Lia, 253
count of elements, 43. The fineness or coarseness of interlacings as measured by the number of elements in a linear or area unit such as an inch or centimeter.
Crain, Joyce, 197

damask, 51. Fabric structure characterized by alternating areas of opposing floats on one face. These are face reverse patterns.
de Amaral, Olga, 57
density, 45, 47, 152, 230. The degree of openness or compactness with which elements are interworked.
direction of elements, 39, 69. The orientation of worked elements in relationship to an edge.
d'Harcourt, Raoul, 32–33
Ditzel, Jorgen and Nana, 227
double weave, 105. Compound structure in which elements of one SOE interlace with elements of another SOE and vice versa.
Du Grenier, Robert, 195

element (E), 38. A strand with the potential for being interworked to form a fabric structure. Yarn is a continuous element, horsehair is a discontinuous element.
Elliot, Lillian, 198
Emery, Irene, 32–34, 39, 50, 75, 99
endings (for interlacings), 174–81

fabric, 38. Generic term for all pliable planar structures worked with elements, plus intermeshed fiber structures such as felt, paper, leather, and bark cloth.
fabric structure, 38. The system by which fibers or linear elements are enmeshed or interworked.
face, 50. One side of a fabric structure.
face reverse pattern, 50–51, 54–55, 161. Floats of opposing SOEs dominate in alternating areas of one face (for example, damasks).
face reverse structure, 50–51. Floats of one SOE dominate on one face while floats of another SOE dominate on the reverse face (for example, denim twill).
fiber(s), 44, 192. Substance with a high length to breadth ratio, flexibility, cohesiveness, and uniformity. Animal fibers may be external in origin (fur, hair, wool) or they may be internal (sinew). Plant fibers come from leaves or stems (linen, ramie), and seed hairs

(cotton, kapoc). Asbestos is a mineral fiber.
filament(s), 43, 192. A continuous strand secreted by animals (silk) or manmade (nylon).
Fisch, Arline, 14, 30, 117, 193
flexibility, 44. The degree to which an element can bend and turn. Thus influences the character of the finished work.
float, 50, 53. Passage of one element over two or more elements.
fold braids, 86–87, 116–17, 119–20, 129, 132–33, 140, 190. 1SOE structures worked with flat elements that accept a fold. Typically, the angle of interlacing is H-V.
four sets of elements structure(s) (4SOE), 110–12
Fox, Sheila, 132
frame braiding, 42, 90–91, 127, 147–49, 164. This structure, also known as interlaced sprang, consists of 1SOE, which is stretched on a frame and obliquely interlaced in such a manner that both ends of the web are simultaneously duplicated.
Fuchs, Douglas, 128

gatherer-hunters, 18, 24
Golder, Stuart, 193
Greedy, Allan, 61
Greek key motif, 22–23
Grossen, Francoise, 125
grouping or grouped element, 44–45, 72–73. One element made up of two, three, or more strands

Harvey, Virginia, 30, 136
horizontal-vertical (H-V) interlacing, 40, 76, 86, 96–98. Structures in which one or more sets of elements interlace at approximately 90 degrees to the selvage.
Houdouin, Guy, 9, 209

imbrication, 102–03. Overlapping supplementary elements, which may completely cover the interlacing SOEs, used to produce patterning.
interlacing, 10–11, 38, 42; origins, 17–29; symbols, 248–65. Fabric structure that is interworked so that each element passes over and under elements that cross its path—without other engagements such as twisting or linking.
interlinking, 38, 41. Repeated interconnecting of an element to itself or to an element of an SOE by passing under and back over the same element.
intermeshing. Fabric structures composed of fibers that have become entangled through the use of heat, steam, or pressure.
interworking, 38. All fabric structures created with linear elements—including, of course, interlacing. Intermeshed fabrics such as felting and paper are not in this category.

Jamart, Susan, 60, 213
Janeiro, Jan, 148
Japanese knot and bend, 69, 76–78
Jung, Roland, 103

Kacillas, JoAnne, 189
Kaufman, Glen, 190
Kent, Kate Peck, 115, 152, 154
knot(s), 235; classification, 65–79. A 1E or 2E structure in which an element circles back to interwork with itself (and/or another element).
Krejci, Luba, 94–95
Krout, Jonathan, 63
kumihimo, 114, 119. Japanese braiding technique worked with a stool and bobbins.

La Plantz, Shereen, 105, 107, 136, 180
Leakey, Richard, 18, 19
Lønning, Kari, 260
Look, Dona, 260
loom, 42, 43. Mechanism used to weave textiles. It is composed of heddles and a reed. Vertical elements form the "warp," and horizontal elements pass back and forth to form the "weft."
looping, 38. Fabrics that are formed by interconnected loops. They are usually worked with one continuous element (for example, knitting and crochet).
Lyman, Susan, 200

MacCallum, Barbara, 196
mad weave, 60, 105, 190
Marciante, Louis, 201
Martin, Lisa, 200–01
materials of interlacing, 182–201
McQueen, John, 186–87, 199, 209, 257
mesh, 38, 188, 192. A woven, plaited, knit, or knotted fabric with more or less evenly spaced wide openings.
Miyajima, Isamu, 106
modifiers, structural, 45, 220–35; materials as, 43–45, 182–188. Characteristics that influence interlaced structures. Material modifiers are such things as size, form, and color. Structural modifiers condition the interworking through such variables as density and balance.
multidirectional interlacing, 7, 40. Structures in which the elements move in circular or irregular directions rather than either H-V or oblique directions.

neolithic braiding, 82, 83, 85, 171
Nicholson, Anne McKenzie, 139
Nio, Kenji, 116
nonelements, 74, 78, 98–99. Supplementary elements that are not interlaced (for example, beads, feathers, or a core).

O'Banion, Nance, 200, 259
oblique interlacing, 39. Structures that are plaited on the diagonal in relation to the outer edge.
one set of elements structure(s) (1SOE), 39; classification, 81–95. Fabrics in which all strands interwork in the same manner (for example, braids).
order of interlacing, 41, 50–56, 154, 230; chart, 56. Numerical sequence in which elements pass over and under other elements. Over one, under one is expressed as 1/1; over two, under two is 2/2, etc.
Owen, Rod, 134

paired elements, 45
passive elements, 40. Static elements that are interworked by active elements.
patterned elements, 209
Peleg, Rina, 15
pitch, 39, 45–47. Angle at which elements or SOEs cross in oblique interlacing. "Steep" indicates a more vertical angle; "shallow," a more horizontal one.
plaiting, 41. Fabrics interlaced with one or more SOE. This includes interlacings that are oblique, H-V, spiral, multidirectional, or combinations of these.
plied elements, 44. Two or more strands twisted together to form a single element.
Pliny the Elder, 216
Pollack, Mark, 132–33, 209, 212
processing of an element, 192

radial interlacing, 40, 96–98, 168. A spiral course taken by an element or elements passing over and under radiating spokes.
Rehsteiner, Lisa, 125
repp braids, 127, 134, 151. 1SOE structures whose strands are alternately grouped and then interlaced as separate elements to produce a relief pattern.
resilience, 44, 222. The relative "stretch and return" of an element, determined by the inherent nature of the material and by such processing as twisting or plying.
Reynolds, Sage, 12
Riemerschmid, Richard, 37
Rocchia, Peter, 223
Rossbach, Ed, 186, 188, 256–257

Sandoval, Arturo, 188, 196, 209
satin, 50, 296. Structure characterized by long, staggered floats.
Sauer, Richard, 64
Seiler-Baldinger, Annemarie, 34–36
Sekijima, Hisako, 7
selvage, 69, 93, 174. The edge of the fabric structure. The term combines the words "self" and "edge."
set of elements (SOE), 39. All the elements of an interlaced structure that interwork in the same manner and direction.
Siegfried, Liselotte, 94, 258
single element structure(s) (1E), 39; classification, 68–76. Structure in which one strand circles about to interwork with itself. The Turk's head and the carrick are classified as single element interlacings.
six sets of elements structure(s) (6SOE), 214–15; classification, 110–13

slentre braids, 145–46. 1SOE structures worked with elements that loop around the fingers. They are interlaced by moving elements successively from finger to finger and hand to hand.

Smith, Sherri, 13, 64, 85, 105, 209

solidity, 44. The softness or hardness of an element.

specific density, 44. Weight in relation to linear measure, i.e., how many yards per pound or meters per kilogram. Wire and mineral filaments have high specific densities; straws and bulked yarns have low specific densities.

Speiser, Noémi, 89, 115, 119, 146, 152

spiral interlacing, 40. Structure in which interworking progresses in a circular direction rather than back and forth from edge to edge (for example, Turk's head and tubular braids).

splicing, 93, 255. The joining of two ends of cordage by interlacing. An end may loop back to interlace into the same cord, producing an eye splice.

spokes, 40, 97, 168. Elements that radiate out from the center of spiral interlacing.

sprang, interlaced. *See* frame braiding.

starting points, 162–73

supplementary elements, 41, 74–75, 84–85; sets of elements, 41, 100–03, 108, 109

symmetrical balance, 45. Two or more SOEs with an equal number and size of elements.

symmetrical braiding, 80–81

take-up, 45. The degree of foreshortening caused by the undulation of elements during interworking. Take-up is affected by solidity, flexibility, and size of elements, or by the tension under which elements or SOE are pulled or weighted.

temporary baskets, 19, 20, 160, 168. Containers that are created as they are needed, utilizing any available material.

tensile strength, 220

tension, 45, 152. The relative tautness with which elements are worked throughout a structure. All of one SOE may be relaxed or all tightly drawn. Occasionally, some elements within a set are taut, others not.

textile(s), 42. An H-V structure, formed on a loom.

Thivas, Cecilia, 102

three sets of elements structure(s) (3SOE), 172–73; classification, 104–10

tie-down(s). Occasional exchange of elements in compound structures.

Trentham, Gary, 154

tubular braiding, 40, 86–87, 122–126, 164, 175. Oblique 1SOE interlacing that follows a circular path.

Turk's head knot, 40, 68, 74

twill(s), 50, 52–53, 59, 166–67, 202–03, 247. Series of staggered floats that create diagonal lines of patterning.

twining, 38, 41. Structure interworked by twisting two elements as they pass over and under an opposing SOE.

twist, 44, 152. The torsion of an element or plied elements; this adds both strength and length. Two or more hues may be plied for color variation. Flat elements may be twisted to produce an ornamental effect.

two sets of elements structure(s) (2SOE), classification, 96–105

Van Blaaderen, Maria, 30–31

Van Derpool, Karen, 189

van Epen, Marÿke, 47

vertical-oblique interlacing, 98–99

Wakisaka, Haru, 61

warp, 40, 42. The SOE positioned vertically on a loom.

wattle. Fencing that has been interlaced or twined with flexible plant fibers and rigid posts. Also used in architecture for walls.

weft, 40, 42. The SOE interlaced horizontally across the warp.

Weltfish, Gene, 22, 23

wickerwork, 99, 223, 224, 227. Interlaced willow basketry and furniture.

wraparound braids, 64, 125, 146, 152

Yagi, Mariyo, 254

Acknowledgments

The author wishes to express appreciation for advice and assistance provided by the following:

Dr. J.M. Adovasio, University of Pittsburgh, Pennsylvania

The late Junius B. Bird, the American Museum of Natural History, New York

Richard G. Conn, Denver Art Museum, Denver, Colorado

Dr. Kate Peck Kent, School of American Research, Santa Fe, New Mexico

Anne P. Rowe, The Textile Museum, Washington, D.C.

Paul Sampson, National Geographic Society, Washington, D.C.

Milton Sonday, Cooper Hewitt Museum, New York

Dorothy Tricerico, Fashion Institute of Technology, New York

Alta Turner, New York

Virginia Harvey

The following appreciation for reading and correcting the early drafts and advising the author:

   Ed Rossbach
   Win Anderson
   Randall Darwall
   Mark C. Pollack
   Mildred Constantine
   Bernard Kester

and my thanks to the staffs of the research libraries of:

   The American Museum of Natural History, New York

   Cooper Hewitt Museum, New York

   The Metropolitan Museum of Art

   The New York Public Library

定価9,500円
in Japan

289142